Preface

Writing this introduction to the philosophy of religion has fulfilled an ambition for us both. For a start, it is not every day that one is able to write a book with one's sibling! Moreover, we have both taught philosophy of religion over a period of some seven years, and have come up against similar problems. The subject-matter of philosophy of religion should be exciting and stimulating, concerned as it is with issues such as the existence of God, the problem of evil and suffering, miracles, immortality, etc.; yet all too often students complain that the literature produced by practitioners of the subject is both difficult and tedious. Perhaps this is because introductions to the subject are often aimed at those already working in this field, rather than at the genuine novice. By way of contrast, we have assumed no such prior engagement. Introductions to the philosophy of religion can baffle and bore; in writing this book we hope to do neither.

Our aim has been to provide sixth-formers and undergraduates with a book that introduces the principal ideas forming the core of any course in the philosophy of religion in an accessible way. At the same time, in the later chapters we have also introduced some of the contemporary debates and developments in the discipline; they should be of particular interest to those already engaged in the subject. In so doing we have used not only the writings of philosophers and theologians habitually drawn upon by philosophers of religion, but also examples drawn from feminist writing and from literature. Religion should be seen as providing colour to life; as such, we have sought to produce an introduction which stimulates and excites, encouraging the reader to pursue some of the ideas that are outlined and the sources that are used. One way in which we hope to achieve this end is through the use of box exercises. These are designed to help students monitor their own understanding of the subject, whilst aiding the development of their own thinking about the issues under consideration. We are building upon Wittgenstein's comment that 'anything your reader can do for himself, let him!'

The structure of the book is as follows: in chapter one we seek to define the philosophy of religion. Introductory texts tend to ignore the problematic nature of religion and plunge straight into the main focus for the philosophy of religion (i.e. accounts of God, miracle, evil, etc.). This is an unsatisfactory omission, and in this chapter we offer a consideration of different definitions of religion, and some opening reflections on what it means to pursue the philosophy of religion.

Chapter two turns our attention to what often proves to be the heart of philosophical discussions of religion: the arguments for the existence of God, and the attributes that are ascribed to this God. Our aim in this chapter has been to introduce students to the God of theism. Chapter three picks up on these ideas by considering some of the challenges that have been levelled against theism. Thus, the problem that evil poses for the God of theism is considered, and the problem of theistic language addressed. Theism presupposes that only a supernatural being (God) can account for the nature of this world and the practice of religion. In considering alternative *natural* histories of religion, this presupposition is challenged, for, as such thinkers as Hume, Tylor and Feuerbach argue, a supernatural explanation is not required to explain adequately the presence of religion in this world.

Chapter four is the pivotal chapter of the book. While earlier chapters have largely been concerned with exploring the traditional approach to the philosophy of religion – that is, theism – chapter four offers some alternative approaches to the subject, which include the effect that Wittgenstein's writings have had upon some practitioners of the discipline, and the critique made

The Philosophy of Religion
A Critical Introduction

Beverley Clack and Brian R. Clack

Polity Press

First published in 1998 by Polity Press
in association with Blackwell Publishers Ltd.

Editorial office:
Polity Press
65 Bridge Street
Cambridge CB2 1UR, UK

Marketing and production:
Blackwell Publishers Ltd
108 Cowley Road
Oxford OX4 1JF, UK

Published in the USA by
Blackwell Publishers Inc.
Commerce Place
350 Main Street
Malden, MA 02148, USA

601456

ISBN 0-7456-1737-9
ISBN 0-7456-1738-7 (pbk)

A CIP catalogue record for this book is available from the British Library
and has been applied for from the Library of Congress.

Typeset in 11 on 13 pt Sabon
by Ace Filmsetting Ltd, Frome, Somerset
Printed in Great Britain by T J International, Padstow, Cornwall

This book is printed on acid-free paper.

100198073

Contents

by feminists of the theist's approach. Chapter five explores the tension between these alternative approaches and the traditional approach of theists by considering two key topics within the philosophy of religion (miracle and immortality), thereby offering the student the opportunity to assess the efficacy of these different approaches. In the final chapter we focus on the problems facing any account of religious belief in a secular world. In response, we offer a possible way forward for religious belief which takes on board some of the ideas concerning the human focus of religion.

Most introductions to the philosophy of religion turn out to be, in practice, apologetic exercises by Christian philosophers. This introduction differs from such an approach, centring on the human dimension of religion and religious belief, rather than advocating a prior theological or religious commitment. If we draw disproportionately upon the Judaeo-Christian inheritance, this is not to suggest that these responses are correct; rather, it reflects the focus of the discipline as it stands. Indeed, our aim is to show that religion can be meaningful if given a human focus, and that philosophy of religion can be exciting if pursued in a creative way. We hope that our readers will agree with us.

Beverley Clack, Roehampton Institute, London
Brian R. Clack, St Clare's International College, Oxford

Acknowledgements

The authors and publishers gratefully acknowledge permission to reprint copyright material in this book as follows: Dylan Thomas: 'Do not go gentle into that good night, from *Dylan Thomas: Collected Poems 1934–1953*, edited by Walford Davies and Ralph Maud, London: J. M. Dent and Sons, 1988. Reprinted by permission of David Higham Associates, and New Directions Publishing Corporation New York.

Every attempt has been made to trace copyright holders. The authors and the publishers would like to apologize in advance for any inadvertent use of copyright material.

We would also like to thank the following for their help and support in the writing of this book: Grace Jantzen for her careful reading of the manuscript and her helpful comments; Rebecca Harkin at Polity for her guidance, encouragement and patience; Sarah Dancy for her painstaking work on the text; Philippa Donald, for discussions on the work of Iris Murdoch; the members of the Philosophy and Religion Cluster Group at Roehampton Institute, London; and the philosophy students at Roehampton Institute, St Clare's International College, Oxford, and elsewhere, in particular Gina Balsamo, Lydia Davis, Jonathan Herapath, Patrycja Kaszyńska, David Nicholson and Helen O'Sullivan. On a more personal note, we would also like to thank our parents, Alan Clack and Ann Clack, for their support and guidance; and, as always, Robert Lindsey and Celia Stringer for their unfailing love. And finally, we would like to dedicate this book to Edward Walker, an inspirational teacher, without whom none of this would have been possible.

I

Religious Belief and the Philosophy of Religion

This book is an introduction to the philosophy of religion. It aims to provide a grounding in the central questions about religion which have concerned philosophers for two and a half thousand years. These questions include such matters as whether it can be demonstrated that a god exists; whether belief in that god is compatible with the appalling amount of suffering which we see around us in the world; whether there is a life after death; whether religion can be explained away as a dream of the human mind; and so on. Before we can embark upon these questions, however, we must gain some understanding of what our subject-matter is. In other words, when we engage in the philosophy of religion, what are we philosophizing *about*?

I   What is Religion?

When thinking about religion there is always the danger of focusing only on the religion that is dominant in our own culture. We may call this the 'Parson Thwackum Fallacy', after Thwackum's remark in Fielding's *Tom Jones*: 'when I mention religion I mean the Christian religion; and not only the Christian religion, but the Protestant religion; and not only the Protestant religion, but the Church of England.'

This tendency to confuse the Christian religion with religion *per se* is not an uncommon phenomenon within the philosophy of religion. This is largely because the questions and problems typically encountered within this discipline are those drawn, if not exclusively from Christianity, at least from the theistic Judaeo-Christian tradition. Thus our concerns are predominantly with the issues raised by belief in an all-powerful, all-knowing supremely benevolent and perfect being. Indeed, such matters form the substantial part of this book. Nevertheless, it would undoubtedly be an error to think that the doctrines of theism could be let loose from the larger history of religion, and dealt with as though they had no connection with the overall development of humankind's religious consciousness. For if Christianity does entertain belief in a God such as that defined above, then this belief is the product of a long history of human thought. And this history must be taken into account when assessing the feasibility of theistic belief. Indeed, as we will see in a later chapter, many theorists hold that the truth of religion can be disproved by attention to this history.[1] A less dramatic approach, and one more suited to an opening chapter, is simply to locate Christianity within the larger context of religion. This brings us to the vexed question of the nature of religion, and thus to an area of great controversy: how to define 'religion'.[2]

How would you define 'religion'?

There have been two main ways of defining religion: the *substantive* and the *functionalist*. According to the first, religion is defined in terms of its belief content. The most famous of substantive definitions was offered by the Victorian anthropologist E. B. Tylor, who defined religion simply as the 'belief in spiritual beings'.[3] For Tylor, religion centres on a belief in the supernatural, on the belief that alongside the world of mundane things (human beings, animals, inanimate objects) there exists a realm of super-empirical beings. Specific religious doctrines and beliefs are thus attempts to define these supernatural realities: so the statement 'God is good' will, on this view, be taken as the description of a particular characteristic of a super-empirical being, just as the statement 'Mother Theresa of Calcutta was good' is the description of a particular characteristic of an empirical being.

Tylor's definition of religion may seem appealing. At the very least, if we take Christianity as our model, the description of religion as belief in supernatural beings seems appropriate. Within Christianity we find belief in God, in Jesus Christ, in the Holy Spirit, and also, for some, in angels and demons. The Christian religion is, moreover, peppered with stories of miraculous occurrences. There is the offer of a life after this earthly existence. On reflection, it seems to be thoroughly supernatural in character.

On the other hand, when we turn our attention to religions other than Christianity, we discover that Tylor's definition is somewhat misleading. Take, for example, something that we would all wish to label a 'religion': Buddhism. It is a conspicuous feature of (at least some strains of) Buddhism that the belief in gods and spirits is absent. And even where the existence of gods is contained within the world-view of the Buddhist, these beings play no crucial role within that religion. Confronted with this, the substantivist will have to deny that Buddhism counts as a religion, which would surely be a bizarre consequence of adhering to Tylor's definition. Furthermore, if we reflect upon our own religious sensibilities and our experience of different religious traditions, we are led to ask whether it is adequate to condense all of this into *one* feature, i.e. the belief in the supernatural. Religion consists of many diverse elements. There are certainly beliefs involved, but there are also other elements: codes of conduct; complex systems of rituals into which one must be initiated; a social dimension; an experiential element.[4] None of these features is included within the standard substantive approach, and hence the multi-dimensional nature of religion seems not to be respected or even recognized. Religion is certainly more than cool adherence to a rather bizarre belief or system of beliefs. We would not regard someone as religious who claimed to believe in God but who then added, 'Of course, this makes no difference to my life; I wouldn't care if God didn't exist!'

The functionalist approach is markedly different from the substantivist position. As its name indicates, a functionalist definition is one which lays stress on the functions rather than the belief content of religion. The functionalist contends that what is essential in religion is not the content of its doctrines (and certainly not belief in the supernatural), but rather the role it plays in society, the way in which religion serves to bind together the members of a community into one coherent whole. This makes a functionalist definition true to the etymology of 'religion', which may stem from the Latin *religare* ('to bind'). This emphasis on the binding qualities of religion was pioneered by Emile Durkheim,[5] but a more recent functionalist definition is to be found in the work of J. M. Yinger.[6] Yinger's claim is that what distinguishes a religion from a non-religious institution is its concern with the *ultimate*. Politics, for example, is focused on non-ultimate ends, dealing with such matters as how a nation can defend itself, feed itself, maintain law and order, ensure justice for all, and so on. These utilitarian concerns spring from non-essential facts of human life; ultimate concerns are perennial factors in the human condition which no amount of good government could solve. Such features include frustration, suffering, death, and, according to Yinger, the function of religion is to offer a way of coping with such ultimate problems. Thus he defines religion as: 'A system of beliefs and practices by means of which a group of people struggles with these ultimate problems of human life. It expresses their refusal to capitulate to death, to give up in the face of frustration, to allow hostility to tear apart their human aspirations.'[7] So when believers come together for an act of worship, or to perform a ritual, the essential element of this action is not its relation to some superhuman reality, but rather its manner of cementing a community's ties.

These differing species of definition lead us to divergent views of religious belief and practice. If we accept a substantive definition, we may be inclined to think of religion as a rather speculative enterprise, as a system of arcane and perhaps bizarre beliefs about supernatural realities. Religion is seen as something akin to philosophy: in the work of Tylor and of James Frazer[8] it is conceived in exactly this way, as a primitive (and erroneous) philosophy of nature. Acceptance of a functionalist definition, on the other hand, is likely to lead us to a radically different account of the nature of religion which emphasizes its human dimension, and its emotive rather than its speculative purpose.[9] To illustrate this, consider just one example of a ritual action: blessing the fields after sowing seeds, or reciting an incantation or spell over them. If religion is viewed as a speculative enterprise, then the ritual may be seen as an attempt to influence the growth of the crops, based on the belief that there is some supernatural entity who controls fertility and who can be appealed to and supplicated. The contrasting functionalist account will emphasize the human, affective dimension of the crop blessing. What might be detected in such an agricultural rite would be a method whereby what is held to be of value or significance in human life is reflected upon by a religious community. So an agricultural ritual in a primitive society (or a harvest festival in a Christian country) is not an attempt to appeal to or to thank a supernatural being; rather, it functions as an outlet for the ritualists' feelings towards the source of their food, and hence of their continued survival as individuals and as a community. So feelings of hope, joy and anxiety are *expressed* in such rituals.

This is not just a matter for understanding 'primitive' religions. A consideration of the Christian religion should not take it for granted that its doctrines are in the nature of descriptions of supernatural realities and events. As we will see in later chapters, it may well be that religious systems are more like frames of orientation; they may express deep-felt emotions about the human condition; or they may be systems for self-reflection and assessment, rather than theoretical explanations of this world and the human life within it.

Is religion principally concerned with explaining and understanding the nature of the universe, or does it have a more emotional basis? What features of religious belief might lead you to your conclusion?

II The Philosophy of Religion

If we take account of the different definitions of religion considered in the previous section, what implications do these have for those practising the *philosophy* of religion? In this section we will consider this question, alongside an analysis of the way in which the discipline has concerned itself with the question of God.

Philosophy of religion is a difficult discipline to define; perhaps, then, it is not surprising that the subject is often embarked upon *without* being defined by its practitioners. In his introduction to the subject Brian Davies refrains from offering any succinct definition. After admitting that 'it is difficult to say what the philosophy of religion is', he sets out the kind of topics likely to be studied under the umbrella term 'philosophy of religion'.[10] These topics centre on the different ways in which the existence of God can apparently be 'proved', the attributes (or characteristics) of God, the question of divine action (e.g. miracle), and life after death. This is interesting. We have just spent some time considering different ways of defining 'religion'. Now it seems that, despite these different definitions, philosophy of religion is to be defined according to its subject-matter – i.e. according to a *substantive* definition of religion. Moreover, the substance of religious belief is equated with belief in a divine being; religion, it seems, is to do with 'God'.

Davies is not alone in offering this kind of approach to the subject. J. C. A. Gaskin's 'outline of the philosophy of religion', *The Quest for Eternity*, argues that it deals with a concept of God that is common to all the great monotheistic faiths; that is, 'theism'.[11] According to philosophical theism, 'God' is a being whose existence can be proved by rational argument; a God whose character is as follows: all-powerful (omnipotent), all-knowing (omniscient), unchanging (immutable), incapable of suffering (impassible), eternal and perfectly good. Likewise, books that comprise of selections of readings in the subject suggest that theism is the chief concern of the philosopher of religion.[12] All this suggests that if we are to determine whether religion is meaningful or not, then we seem to be committed to an enterprise which considers whether there are good grounds for belief in God.

However, this offers a rather limited perspective on the nature and scope of religions and their practice. As we have already seen, religion includes more than belief in a supernatural God. Perhaps we would be on more fruitful ground for our definition of philosophy of religion if we were to consider the *methodology* employed by its practitioners. In setting out his argument for atheism, Robin Le Poidevin asks whether philosophy of religion is a contradiction in terms; after all, religion involves a fundamental faith commitment to a certain set of beliefs which will transform one's life, while philosophy is concerned with questioning beliefs and seeking rational justification for the beliefs that we hold. However, Le Poidevin argues that philosophy is a useful way of approaching religion, precisely because it challenges the explanations for human life offered by the religious.[13] Here is an understanding of philosophy of religion as a critical discipline, a discipline that seeks to clarify and question religious beliefs. This understanding of philosophy of religion is common to many introductions to the subject. Peter Vardy sees it as concerned with the quest for truth;[14] Michael Peterson, William Hasker, Bruce Reichenbach and David Basinger define it as the intellectual discussion of religion.[15] Baruch Brody writes that it involves the 'careful analysis of the meaning and implications of religious doctrines'.[16]

It would seem, then, that philosophers of religion have been concerned with seeking *explanations* (and possibly justifications) for the kind of things that a religious believer believes. So, rational proofs for the existence of God are offered in response to the question, 'why believe in God?'. When philosophy of religion is done in this way, its chief concern is with the rational basis for religious belief. For some, such as Davies and Richard Swinburne,[17] the aim is to provide this rational basis for religious belief. For others, such as Le Poidevin, and J. L. Mackie,[18] the aim is to show that such a basis is not possible; that religion is meaningless and without good grounds.

While we might question the wisdom of defining religion purely in terms of belief in God, the understanding of God offered by philosophical theism is also problematic. At the outset, the notion that God's existence can be proved raises difficulties for the understanding of God being offered. If God's existence can be 'proved', this would seem to suggest that God is an object amongst other objects: God can be described in terms similar to those applied to dogs, human beings, rocks. This seems to run contrary to many religious beliefs. God is often understood as totally different from human beings; if this is the case, how can I 'prove' that God exists? I know what it would be like to prove that my friend exists (I can take her pulse, listen to her heartbeat, etc.). But how could I prove that 'God' exists? Is God the same kind of entity as my friend?

Further problems arise from the different characteristics or 'attributes' ascribed by the philosophers to God. Some attributes seem to contradict others. For example, can a God who cannot experience suffering be all-knowing? In other words, can God be omniscient *and* impassible? Some attributes, particularly the notion of omnipotence (that is, that God is all-powerful) do not seem to make much sense when held against the fact of evil and suffering in this world. Moreover, who has decided which characteristics God should have?[19]

The first part of this book will focus on the arguments associated with philosophical theism. This is important, because philosophy of religion has, in the main, understood itself as dealing with explanations and justifications for the religious belief in God. As such, the substantive definition of religion will be assumed. The second part of this book questions this understanding of religion. Is religion always about belief in God? As we have seen, functionalist accounts of religion suggest a different approach to understanding and interpreting religious belief and practice. Should philosophers of religion be offering justifications for religious beliefs, or should they be describing, with clarity and care, the kind of religious beliefs that people hold? As we shall see, there may be different ways of considering the role of philosophy of religion which suggest different understandings of religion and the nature of 'God'.[20]

> What do you mean by 'God'? To what extent does your definition of this word cohere with the theistic concept outlined above?

III Developing the Concept of God

In chapter two we shall consider in some detail the theistic concept of God. Before doing so, it is important to be aware of the different strands which have contributed to the account of God offered by the philosophers. Some of the problems and contradictions surrounding the concept of God seem to arise in part because of the varied sources which go to make up the philosophers' account of the divine, and it is only by having some idea of the beliefs that have been fed into this concept that we will be able to unravel these difficulties.

Ancient Greek mythology and philosophy has been particularly influential in shaping the western concept of God. In Greek mythology, the gods and humanity were very similar. The gods took on human form and attributes: they could be just as capricious and lustful as ordinary men and women.[21] Likewise, humans could often be taken as gods. Some people were believed to combine divinity and humanity; for example, Hercules and Achilles were understood in this way, because it was believed that they had one parent who was human and one who was a god. Divinity and humanity, therefore, were not understood as radically distinct states. The Greek philosophical tradition rejected this mythological understanding. In its place, Plato proposed a dualistic account of reality: this shadowy material world was contrasted with the 'real' world of ideas.[22] His later followers were to emphasize the metaphysical nature of God; associated with the Platonic notion of 'the Good' which transcended this world, God was understood as completely separate from human beings. The idea of God that it put forward was abstract, radically distinct from humanity. Christianity, when it spread beyond Palestine to the Greek-speaking world, was profoundly influenced by these ideas of the radical distinction between God and humanity. The concern of the great theological councils of the early Church was to clarify the nature of God's being. In many ways, these events form the basis for the philosophical approach to theology and religion.[23]

At the same time as owing much to the classical Greek world, the western concept of God is also dependent upon the biblical tradition. The Jewish awareness of God included human-like characteristics: jealousy, anger and revenge were very much part of the Old Testament's account of God. Yet the complete split between God and humanity was also emphasized, and it was the gravest mistake for human beings to think themselves equal to God. The main concern of the Jewish people was to be God's people and follow God's ethical law.

Christian theology – and subsequently the philosophical approach to theology – was formed by its interaction with the Jewish and Greek world-views. It is not surprising, therefore, that there should be elements within the concept of God that do not fit together easily. How are we to understand a God who has been made flesh in the person of Christ, yet is radically distinct from human beings? Can the concrete and the abstract, the personal and the impersonal, be brought together in one united account of divinity? The philosophical movement of the late seventeenth and early eighteenth century, known as the Enlightenment, was to complicate matters further.

The main legacy of the Enlightenment was the claim that the distinctive human characteristic lay in the ability to reason. As such, all human beliefs and attitudes should be subjected to the eye of reason. Religion was not exempt from such an approach, and with it the concept of God. God became less a religious certainty with whom one had a personal relationship, and more a philosophical concept whose coherence needed to be established. This rather cool approach tended to separate the concept from its roots in a religious community. The notion of God could be considered apart from the religious systems within which its meaning had been established. And so the roots of the philosophy of religion as a discipline distinct from theology can be found. Such a step was by no means welcomed by all. The French thinker Blaise Pascal sought to distinguish the God of the believer from the God of the philosophers; as he put it, God is ' "God of Abraham, God of Isaac, God of Jacob", not of philosophers and scholars'.[24] This tension between the philosopher's construct of God, and the believer's God remains, as we shall see.[25]

These, then, are the diverse sources that contribute to the philosopher's attempt to talk of God. These roots undoubtedly go some way to explaining the difficulties that arise when philosophers attempt to offer a coherent account of the nature of that mysterious word 'God'. Whilst theism will dominate our approach to the first part of this book, we shall also consider different accounts of what 'God' might mean, and thus what religion involves. But for now our task is to engage with the philosophers' attempts to establish the existence and characteristics of God.

Suggested reading:

Brian Davies, *An Introduction to the Philosophy of Religion*, Oxford: OUP, 1993, introduction.

J. C. A. Gaskin, *The Quest for Eternity*, Harmondsworth: Penguin, 1984.

Robin Le Poidevin, *Arguing for Atheism*, London: Routledge, 1996, introduction.

J. L. Mackie, *The Miracle of Theism*, Oxford: OUP, 1982, introduction.

Michael Peterson, William Hasker, Bruce Reichenbach and David Basinger, *Reason and Religious Belief*, Oxford: OUP, 1991, ch. 1.

Peter Vardy, *The Puzzle of God*, London: Collins Flame, 1990, ch. 3.

2

Natural Theology

1 Arguments for the Existence of God

Introduction

One of the main concerns of the philosophy of religion has been to show that a rational basis for religious belief is possible. Central to the monotheistic faiths, which form the context for most western philosophy of religion, is the belief that there is a God who transcends the world in which we live. While faiths such as Christianity claim that God has been revealed to humanity through the special revelation of Jesus Christ, a different approach has also been advocated. Rather than claim that God can only be known if 'he' chooses to reveal 'himself,'[1] some philosophers and theologians have claimed that he can be discerned through the use of reason or through contemplation of the natural world. This 'natural' theology forms the context for the philosophical attempt to establish the existence of God through reasoned thought or from evidence gleaned from the world or the structures of human life.

Arguments that seek to prove that God exists fall into two distinct categories: a priori and a posteriori. An a priori argument is an argument *independent* of any evidence drawn from experience. It does not rely in any way on experience as a starting point, nor upon empirical evidence. Rather, it relies upon the analysis of an idea. So, we do not have to meet or know any spinsters in order to understand that they must be female. Such an understanding is contained in the definition of what a spinster is. An example of this kind of argument is considered in this chapter: the ontological argument is an argument which attempts to establish the existence of God by analysing the content of the word 'God'.

A priori arguments are relatively rare. The other arguments for the existence of God which are considered in this chapter are a posteriori arguments; that is, arguments that start from something we know, which itself provides the basis for the claim that God exists. So, the argument from design starts from the apparent order of the world, and argues that this cannot be the result of chance. Instead, it is claimed, there must be a creator who is responsible for this world.

The Ontological Argument (A PRIORI)

The ontological argument for the existence of God is different from other arguments for God in that it does not rely upon external material to support the idea that 'God exists'. Rather, it focuses on the distinctive quality of God's *being* (or 'ontology'). By offering a particular definition of 'God', the argument claims that, given that definition, God *must* exist. If we understand what the word 'God' means, it will be seen to be a contradiction to say that God does not exist.

Anselm and the ontological argument

The most famous version of the ontological argument was formulated by Saint Anselm (1033–1109) in his meditation called the *Proslogion*. The fact that Anselm sets out his argument in the context of a prayer has led some to query the success of this argument as a 'proof' for the existence of God. For Anselm, the existence of God is self-evident; otherwise why would he be praying to this God? Others, however, have pointed to parts of this work where Anselm suggests that such an argument could convert the non-believer.

Anselm begins his argument by offering a definition of God. God is 'that than which nothing greater can be conceived'. He then considers the fool of the Psalms who 'in his heart says that there is no God' (Psalm 14:1). Anselm argues that the fool accepts the definition of God, yet refuses to accept that God exists. So the fool has accepted that God exists as an idea in his mind, but he refuses to accept that God exists in reality. Anselm thus makes a distinction between that which exists in the mind, and that which exists both in the mind *and* in reality. An analogy between this account and the work of an artist might prove useful. When an artist conceives of a painting, that picture is in the artist's mind; when the painting is finished, it exists both in the mind of the artist and in reality (on the canvas). So the fool understands this much: that the idea of God is in his understanding, if not in the world. This leads Anselm to make the following point:

> And certainly that than which nothing greater can be thought cannot exist only in the understanding. For if it exists only in the understanding, it is possible to think of it existing also in reality, and that is greater. If that than which nothing greater can be thought exists in the understanding alone, then this thing than which nothing greater can be thought is something than which a greater can be thought. And this is clearly impossible. Therefore there can be no doubt at all that something than which a greater cannot be thought exists both in the understanding and in reality.[2]

In brief, Anselm is claiming that to accept that God exists as an idea in the mind and not to accept that God exists in reality is incoherent. If God is that than which nothing *greater* can be thought, God must exist in reality, as well as the mind. Why? Focus on that word 'greater'. Anselm asks: which is greater? That which exists in the mind alone or that which exists in reality? It must surely be that which exists in reality. Therefore if God is that than which nothing *greater* can be thought, he must exist both as an idea in our minds *and* in reality.

Gaunilo of Marmoutiers, a monk living at the same time as Anselm, was not convinced by his argument.[3] He claimed that

Here is a simplified form of Anselm's argument:

1 God is that than which nothing greater can be thought.
2 God exists, at least in the understanding, or in the mind.
3 But that which exists in the mind is not as great as that which exists both in the mind and in reality.
4 So if God exists only in the mind, he is *not* that than which nothing greater can be thought.
5 Thus, as God is that than which nothing is greater can be thought, God must exist in reality as well as in the mind.
6 Therefore God exists.

How convincing do you find Anselm's argument? How might a critic respond to his ideas?

the reasoning involved in this 'proof' of God's existence would lead to absurd conclusions if applied to other areas of life. In order to illustrate this criticism, Gaunilo sets up a parallel ontological argument for the most perfect island, an 'island than which no island greater can be thought'. We can imagine this perfect island. We can imagine the golden sands, the coral reefs, the numerous palm trees. Given Anselm's reasoning, it must be that this island exists, otherwise it would not be 'an island than which no island greater can be thought'. Gaunilo argues that this is absurd: just because we can imagine such an island does not mean that it exists. In order to establish that there is such an island we need further evidence. We cannot move from the existence of this island in the mind to its existence in reality *without* further empirical evidence.

Gaunilo's argument can itself be criticized. His idea of 'the most perfect island' is perhaps incoherent. We do not know what it would mean to talk of such an island. For me, with my phobia of sharks, it might involve the omission of these creatures; if you are fascinated by marine life, sharks might be necessary for the island to be 'perfect' for you. It has been claimed that the incoherence involved in talking of the most perfect island is not reflected in the idea of the most perfect being. This being is carefully defined – as all-knowing, all-powerful, supremely benevolent and so on – a careful definition which leaves no room for questioning the nature of this perfect being. Anselm's response to Gaunilo's argument reflects this point. Anselm argues that the ontological argument deals with a unique case (God) and as such cannot be applied to other cases. While Anselm may have felt that he had refuted Gaunilo's criticism, further challenges to his argument were to follow.

Descartes' ontological argument: existence as a perfection

Descartes' form of the ontological argument appears in his *Meditations on First Philosophy*.[4] Like Anselm, Descartes defines 'God' as 'a supremely perfect being' (i.e. he possesses all perfections). If this definition is accepted, Descartes argues, we must conclude that God exists. Why? Because, for Descartes, existence is a perfection. If God is a supremely perfect being, and if existence is a perfection, it follows that God, by definition, exists. In Descartes' words: 'Existence can no more be separated from the essence of God than the fact that the sum of its three angles is equal to two right-angles can be separated from the essence of a triangle.'[5] So just as we cannot conceive of a triangle the internal angles of which *do not* amount to 180 degrees, so we cannot conceive of God *not* existing. Existence is essential to the nature of God.

Kant's critique

Immanuel Kant put forward some of the strongest objections to the ontological argument, and his objections may mirror misgivings we might have about moving from a definition of God to 'proof' that God exists in reality. Descartes' form of the argument makes explicit a feature of the ontological argument implicit in Anselm's argument: existence is understood as a perfection. Much subsequent discussion (and criticism) of the ontological argument has focused on this idea. How is existence to be understood? Kant formulates his challenge to the ontological argument around this question.[6] Kant's central point is that both Anselm and Descartes understand 'existence' to be a predicate or attribute of a thing. This, Kant claims, is problematic. Kant asks us to focus on the notion of 'existence'. Kant wants to argue that whatever can be thought of as existing can also be thought of as *not* existing. There is no contradiction, despite Anselm's and Descartes' objections, in saying, 'God does not exist'. Descartes claimed that to say this was a contradiction in terms, similar to saying that 'bachelors are married males'. Kant's point is that this is fundamentally wrong: no statement regarding the existence of a thing (whether that thing be a person or God) can be analytically true. Statements regarding existence are synthetic statements: in other words, their truth is dependent upon external evidence. When we say something 'exists' we need something more than just a definition of what that something is. We need evidence to show that that something does, indeed, exist. For example, if I said to you 'unicorns exist', you would presumably want more from me than a potted definition of what a unicorn is – i.e. a white horse with a horn growing out of its forehead. You would want evidence. Where did I see this creature? Did I take a photograph? Did anyone see it with me? You might even want to ask for medical reports on my mental condition! In other words, you would want some kind of external information to support my claim that 'unicorns exist'. And the same goes for the claim that 'God exists'.

This leads us to the most important part of Kant's critique. Kant rejects the basic assumption upon which Descartes' argument rests: namely, the assumption that existence, like goodness or beauty, is a predicate or characteristic that something can either have or lack. In Kant's words: God doesn't need to physically exist in order to exist.

> 'Being' [or existence] is obviously not a real predicate; that is, it is not a concept of something which could be added to the concept of a thing. It is merely the positing of a thing as existing in itself. If we take the subject (God) with all its predicates (among which is omnipotence), and say 'God is', or 'There is God', we attach no new predicate to the concept of God, but only posit the subject in itself with all its predicates.[7]

This is a crucial point: existence is not a predicate, and as such it cannot be a perfection. Existence tells us something *about* an object, rather than something about *the nature of* that object. To say that something exists adds nothing to the description of an object, but rather says that there is an instance of such an object in the world. Let us further explore the function of the term 'existence'. Suppose I say to my philosophy of religion students that whoever gains the highest mark in the forthcoming exam will be given a new car. I then present the lucky student with the choice of two cars. Both are exactly the same, except that one car exists and the other does not. Given that particular choice, it is likely that the student will opt for the existing car. This example might convince us, with Descartes, that existence is indeed a perfection.

But let us take this example a stage further. Imagine that in choosing the car to present to the student, I visit a car showroom. The salesman shows me the gleaming rows of brand new cars, and asks me what sort of car I would like to purchase. 'Oh,' I reply, 'an existing car please.' Presumably the salesman would be somewhat baffled by this response. According to Descartes' reasoning, I *have* told the salesman something about the car that I would like. Kant would deny that this is the case: I have said nothing about the *kind* of car I would like (i.e. a 'family car', an 'Alfa Romeo', and so on).

Reflecting upon the example of the car given above, consider this question of existence. Do you think that it is better to exist than not to exist? If so, is the ontological argument convincing, or do we need to take other factors into consideration?

Malcolm's defence of Anselm's argument

In his famous paper 'Anselm's Ontological Arguments', Norman Malcolm agrees with Kant that existence is not a perfection or a predicate.[8] He does, on the other hand, detect in the *Proslogion* another argument which is not open to that particular criticism. The second argument concentrates on the distinctive nature of God's existence, and arises as part of Anselm's response to Gaunilo's criticisms. God's existence is understood as 'necessary';

that is, it is not dependent on anything else for its existence. An island such as that postulated by Gaunilo does not *necessarily* exist, for it is dependent on all sorts of things for its continued presence in the world. In short, its existence is 'contingent'. If it were struck by a nuclear warhead of sufficient power it would cease to exist; if the sea rose it would be submerged and its vegetation and life destroyed. Anselm goes on to argue that something that is dependent upon nothing for its existence and is not in danger of passing out of existence, something whose non-existence is logically impossible (i.e. something that is necessary), is obviously superior to ('greater than') something whose existence is *contingent* or dependent on other things. Malcolm maintains that normal existence is not a perfection, but that this necessary existence is a perfection, and hence the most perfect being must be in possession of it. Therefore, God, as defined by Anselm, necessarily exists.

At one point in his argument, Malcolm makes the following remark on Anselm's argument: 'What Anselm has proved is that the notion of contingent existence or of contingent non-existence cannot have any application to God. His existence must either be logically necessary or logically impossible.'[9] Malcolm maintains that God's existence is not logically impossible, that it does make sense to speak of a necessarily existent being. Others, such as J. N. Findlay, have rejected this notion. In contrast to Malcolm, Findlay proposes an ontological argument *against* the existence of God.[10] His argument is simple. The adequate object of religious worship must be the most perfect being. This being must be thought of as being necessarily existent as its non-existence is logically impossible. However, for the reasons supplied by Kant, the idea of a necessarily existent being is incoherent. Therefore God does not exist.

It would seem, then, that not only is the ontological argument subject to criticism, it is also open to an inversion which argues for the non-existence of God. As such, its status as a 'proof' for the existence of God seems inconclusive. A clever play on words, dependent on an analysis of concepts and definitions, it seems that the *context* of Anselm's argument in a prayer has to be taken seriously. As Anthony O'Hear comments, we can only understand the significance of the ontological argument if we see it in the religious context of Anselm's time.[11] For Anselm and his contemporaries, existence itself was a good. Life was to be celebrated and gloried in as God's great gift to humanity. By endowing God with existence, one was stressing the beauty of life. This suggests that the faithful may find the argument useful as a means to reflecting on the God in whom they already believe, but it will do little to convert the non-believer to the doctrines of theism.

The Cosmological Argument

What is commonly referred to as the cosmological argument is, in fact, a group of related arguments, all of which take a conspicuous feature of the world as we find it, and then reason back to its ultimate explanation, which turns out to be God. Of these varying cosmological arguments, the most persuasive one is also known as the 'first cause' argument. Part of the reason for the appeal of the cosmological argument can be illustrated by contrasting it with the ontological argument. A difficulty with the latter is the overwhelming feeling that it constitutes little more than an intellectual trick: we are asked to accept some rather strange premises and then are (uncomfortably) obliged to accept the conclusion that God exists. This kind of unease should not confront us when we encounter the cosmological 'proof'. Here, premises are not conjured up from nowhere. Rather, the argument starts, not from definitions, but from our general experience of the world, and, moreover, from an incontestable fact: namely, that *something exists*. The recognition of that fact is all the cosmological argument needs to get going, coupled with a desire to answer the age-old question, 'Why is there something rather than nothing?' Proponents of the cosmological argument contend that it is only by reference to God that this question can be answered.

Thomas Aquinas and the cosmological argument

The most famous version of the 'first cause' argument is to be found in the *Summa Theologiae* of Thomas Aquinas (1224–75). It constitutes the second of Aquinas's 'Five Ways', or five arguments for the existence of God. Aquinas writes:

> In the world of sensible things we find there is an order of efficient
> causes. There is no case known (neither is it, indeed, possible) in
> which a thing is found to be the efficient cause of itself; for so it
> would be prior to itself, which is impossible. Now in efficient causes
> it is not possible to go on to infinity, because in all efficient causes
> following in order, the first is the cause of the intermediate cause
> and the intermediate is the cause of the ultimate cause, whether
> the intermediate cause be several, or one only. Now to take away
> the cause is to take away the effect. Therefore, if there be no first
> cause among efficient causes, there will be no ultimate, nor any
> intermediate, cause. But if in efficient causes it is possible to go on
> to infinity, there will be no first efficient cause, neither will there
> be an ultimate effect, nor any intermediate causes; all of which is
> plainly false. Therefore it is necessary to admit a first efficient
> cause, to which everyone gives the name of God. [12]

In other words, Aquinas is saying that we can enquire about the
cause of any particular thing which exists. Imagine someone asks
you to specify the cause of your own existence. You would probably cite the existence of your parents, perhaps when they met,
and the dates on which you were conceived and subsequently
born. You might be satisfied with that as an explanation of your
existence, but it is in no way a complete explanation. Why? Because you have failed to account for why your *parents* exist. An
adequate explanation of your own existence must also explain
the existence of your parents, and, by extension, must also explain why *their* parents existed, and so on back through the centuries. The explanation for our existence will thus involve a long
chain of causes, stretching back to the beginning of time. For
Aquinas, that chain of causes implies a first, uncaused cause,
namely God. If you like, God caused the Big Bang to occur about
eighteen billion years ago. So from the fairly basic question of
why anything exists, we have arrived at a demonstration of the
existence of God.

Critiquing the first cause argument

The cosmological argument was fiercely attacked by David Hume
in his *Dialogues Concerning Natural Religion* (1779). The

Dialogues is a fabulous piece of philosophical writing, taking the form of an after-dinner conversation about religion and philosophy. Three characters predominate the discussion. Philo is a sceptic, and it has been claimed that this character most closely approximates Hume's own philosophical position. Demea is the pious believer who distrusts philosophy. Cleanthes, while also a believer, contends that it is possible to attain knowledge of God through philosophy. In Part IX of the *Dialogues*, Hume has one of his characters – Demea – put forward a form of the cosmological argument. Demea says:

> Whatever exists must have a cause or reason for its existence; it being absolutely impossible for any thing to produce itself, or be the cause of its own existence. In mounting up, therefore, from effects to causes, we must either go on in tracing an infinite succession, without any ultimate cause at all, or must at last have recourse to some ultimate cause that is *necessarily* existent.[13]

Demea contends that the idea of an infinite causal regression is unintelligible. The chain cannot simply stretch backwards: it must have some ultimate cause or some reason for its very existence. Given that this option is then closed to us, we must posit the existence of some being 'who carries the REASON of his existence in himself',[14] and this, of course, is God.

The remainder of Part IX is given over to a critique of Demea's argument. Through the character of Cleanthes, Hume advances a number of significant criticisms. The first concerns Demea's notion of a being whose existence is *necessary*. In opposition to this, Cleanthes gives voice to the objection, noted in our treatment of Anselm, that 'there is no Being . . . whose non-existence implies a contradiction'.[15] If it is the case that the notion of a necessary being is incoherent, then the cosmological argument, if it rests on such a notion, will fail.

Cleanthes' next objection extends this point in a naturalistic direction. If we must make appeal to a necessarily existent being, then why cannot we plump, not for a god, but for the material universe itself? The universe would then be the cause of its own existence. This may seem an odd idea, but any argument we offer against this notion will equally apply to the God hypothesis.

Perhaps the most important of Cleanthes' arguments focuses on a conspicuous feature of Demea's presentation of the proof. Demea has said:

> In the infinite chain or succession of causes and effects, each single effect is determined to exist by the power and efficacy of that cause which immediately preceded; but the whole eternal chain or succession, taken together, is not determined or caused by anything: And yet it is evident that it requires a cause or reason, as much as any particular object which begins to exist in time.[16]

So Demea wants to move beyond the causes of *particular things* to the cause of *the whole thing*. And this, says Cleanthes, is illegitimate: 'Did I show you the particular causes of each individual in a collection of twenty particles of matter, I should think it very unreasonable, should you afterwards ask me, what was the cause of the whole twenty. This is sufficiently explained in explaining the cause of the parts.'[17]

Hume's point is persuasive. If I have a collection of items in my briefcase, you may indeed enquire about the cause of those things. In that case, I would take a single item – for example, a book – and explain to you where it was printed and bound, and, perhaps, that it was originally a tree. Imagine that I do this with all the items in my briefcase, and that you then say: 'No, I didn't mean the cause of each individual thing in your case. I meant the cause of *all those things* taken together.' This, says Hume, is unreasonable. But if this is an unreasonable request, then so is the entire project of the cosmological argument, for it seeks, not for the causes of particular things, but for the cause of everything, or for the cause of the universe in its entirety.

A similar critique to that of Hume is launched by Bertrand Russell: 'The whole concept of cause is one we derive from our observation of particular things; I see no reason whatsoever to suppose that the total has any cause whatsoever.'[18] For Russell, the cosmological argument is far from a forceful demonstration of the existence of a deity. On the contrary, it is little more than a logical fallacy, moving erroneously from the acceptable premise that every (individual) thing has a cause to the (confused) conclusion that everything (collectively) has a cause. To use

Russell's memorable example, while it is certainly true that every person has a mother, this does not entail that the human race as such has a mother.[19]

> 'I should say that the universe is just there, and that's all.' Russell contends that the universe is simply a 'brute fact' and that it is therefore futile to look for an explanation of it. Is this a helpful attitude? Or is the existence of the universe crying out for some ultimate explanation? Does the cosmological argument provide us with just such an explanation?

Whether or not the cosmological argument works depends upon the extent to which its defenders can overcome the criticisms levelled at it by the likes of Hume and Russell, and upon whether one is puzzled by the existence of the universe and wishes to search for a satisfying answer to that puzzlement. Even if we do feel that the cosmological argument has something to offer, it is not necessarily the case that we will equate the 'first cause' with what we tend to mean by 'God'. If we consider the world, the kind of place it is, the things that happen in it, we might want to ask what *kind* of cause is needed to bring about this effect? It is far from obvious that a first cause need be equated with a God who has, say, the characteristics of goodness, love and knowledge. And this becomes far from clear if we consider the next of the arguments for God's existence, which attempts to move from the apparent order in the world to the idea that there is a designer or creator for all that is, and that designer is God.

The Argument from Design

Yes, God is good – in earth and sky,
From ocean depths and spreading wood,
Ten thousand voices seem to cry;
God made us all, and God is good.

I hear it in the rushing breeze;
The hills that have for ages stood,

The echoing sky and roaring seas,
All swell the chorus: God is good.

Yes, God is good, all nature says,
By God's own hand with speech endued;
And man in louder notes of praise,
Should sing for joy that God is good.

The sentiments behind this hymn by John Hampden Gurney (1802–62) are similar to those expressed in the argument from design. When we consider the world in which we find ourselves, when we consider the beauty of the world, we find the word 'creation' seems the most adequate word to use. It is difficult to attribute such beauty, such 'design' to mere chance. We find so much that is ordered and beautiful in this world that we want to speak about it being 'created' or 'designed'. The argument from design takes the order and apparent purpose in the world, and moves from that order and purpose to postulate a designer who is responsible for it. And that designer is God.

Paley's watch

The most famous form of the design argument is given by William Paley.[20] Paley's argument takes the form of a story. You are wandering on a heath and happen to find a stone. Unless you are a geologist, the question of how that stone got there is unlikely to interest you. But if you came across a watch, the question of how that got there *would* be of interest. You would probably pick it up. Then you would discover that it has a purpose. You might examine the carefully made parts and infer from these that the watch must have a maker. Paley takes this story and uses it as an analogy for the world. Like the watch, the world is such that we need to talk of a creator in order to explain it.

Paley uses his analogy of the watch to make several important points about the idea of 'creation'. Firstly, he argues that it would not weaken our inference that the watch was the product of design if we had not seen a watch before, and did not know that a watch was the product of human beings. Secondly, even if the watch went wrong or was seldom exactly right, we would still postulate the existence of a watchmaker. We don't need to show the watch to be perfect in order to move to the belief that it was created. Having said that, we might have cause to question the *character* of the creator if it is not perfect.[21] Thirdly, Paley argues that even if parts of the watch were missing, that would not undermine the claim that the watch was created. Finally, he argues that the watch is insufficient to explain its existence; only an external creator can serve to explain its presence.

Moving from the watch to the world, Paley argues that the world is just as complex a mechanism as a watch. Observe the rotation of the planets or the orderly procession of the seasons. Look at the functions of our own bodies: as has been claimed in an advertisement for private health insurance, our brain is more powerful than the most powerful computer. Thus, for Paley, the universe resembles some contrived mechanism (such as a watch) and must similarly be accounted for by reference to some intelligent or purposive agency. This analogy between the world and a machine has not gone unchallenged, as we shall see when we turn to Hume's critique.

Swinburne's orderly universe

In his book *The Existence of God*, Richard Swinburne presents a version of the design argument which he calls a 'teleological argument from the temporal order of the world'.[22] Swinburne believes that the order we see around us is a remarkable fact about the world. In particular, he thinks it most striking that the world runs according to regular laws. As he puts it: 'The universe might so naturally have been chaotic, but it is not – it is very orderly.'[23] Swinburne argues that some explanation is required for the striking orderliness of the universe. We can either explain this order in scientific terms, i.e. as a result of scientific laws, or we can seek an explanation which grounds this order in the free, conscious choices of a person (God). Swinburne denies the sufficiency of the scientific explanation; after all, we are seeking an explanation for the laws that science postulates. Instead, he looks to the second solution, and contends that God is the explanation for the orderliness of the universe.

Critiquing the design argument

Numerous arguments have been directed against the design argument, most of which are voiced by David Hume in his *Dialogues Concerning Natural Religion*. In the *Dialogues*, the character of Cleanthes is presented as an advocate for the design argument. He moves from the order in the world to postulate an intelligent mind which created it. Much of the *Dialogues* is taken up with a heated debate on the validity or otherwise of this idea. The criticisms of this notion are put forward by the character of Philo.

At the outset, Hume levels a general criticism at the argument from design. The argument presupposes that the world is analogous with a machine. But is this an appropriate analogy? In many ways, it seems more accurate to describe the world as a living thing: 'The world plainly resembles more an animal or a vegetable than it does a watch or a knitting-loom.'[24] This comment is particularly relevant when we consider modern accounts of the nature of the world put forward by environmentalists like James Lovelock.[25] According to Lovelock's 'Gaia' hypothesis, the world is best paralleled with a living organism, where each part contributes to the whole. This would suggest that the design argument begs the question: if the world is like a machine, then the claim that there is a designer would seem to make sense. But if the world is more like a vegetable, then the idea of a 'designer' seems inappropriate.

Hume himself accounts for the presence of order and human life by means of the Epicurean hypothesis. The universe consists of a finite number of particles in random motion. In unlimited time these go through every possible combination. This will sometimes produce order, sometimes disorder; sometimes it will produce conditions whereby life is possible, at other times it will not. The presence of human life in the universe is nothing special, but simply the product of a chance arrangement of matter. In other words, Hume substitutes *chance* for *purpose*.[26]

This criticism seems to prefigure the claims of evolutionary theory, which further undermines the argument for design. Darwin suggests a different account of the apparently designed bodies of animals. Through his account of the 'struggle for survival', Darwin claims that the process of evolution leads toward more complex and well-adapted forms of life. Organisms adapt to their environment and become increasingly attuned to their particular niche. This might look like design, but it is not; it is in fact a perfectly natural process which does not require a designer. Viewed in this way, the design argument has been rendered redundant by science.

Below are two poems with very different understandings of the connection between nature and God:

> Tyger! Tyger! burning bright
> In the forests of the night.
> What immortal hand or eye
> Could frame thy fearful symmetry?
>
> When the stars threw down their spears,
> And water'd heaven with their tears,
> Did he smile his work to see?
> Did he who made the Lamb make thee?
>   (William Blake)
>
>   . . . I have felt
> A presence that disturbs me with the joy
> Of elevated thoughts; a sense sublime
> Of something far more deeply interfused,
> Whose dwelling is the light of setting suns,
> And the round ocean and the living air,
> And the blue sky, and in the mind of man:
> A motion and a spirit, that impels
> All thinking things, all objects of all thought,
> And rolls through all things.
>   (William Wordsworth)

Compare and contrast these accounts of nature. Can we move from the facts of this world to a comprehensive definition of the nature of God?

Perhaps the strongest assault on the design argument comes from the use that Hume makes (through Philo) of the fact of evil.

Cleanthes claims that it is possible to infer things about God from the facts of this world. Philo claims that this approach is mistaken. Consider this world which theists claim to have been created by God. What *kind* of God would create a world like this?[27]

Cleanthes is not the only person to make the 'mistake' of moving from a particular account of the world to God. Nature poets like Wordsworth and religious believers like Paley give an account based upon only *one* aspect of the natural world. They have considered the order and beauty of the world, and have moved from this aspect to claim that this is evidence for the creation of the world by a benevolent God. But the order and beauty we see in the world is only one part of the story; we also see ugliness, cruelty and suffering.[28] Cleanthes and his 'friends' have claimed that beauty and order in the world leads us to belief in a benevolent God who created such beauty. But if we begin from the 'facts' of evil, what *kind* of God is implied? The image of God drawn from the facts of creation is hardly that of the loving, merciful, heavenly father of believers. Indeed, if we work from the facts of a nature that is 'red in tooth and claw'[29] we seem to arrive at a rather unsavoury picture of what God might be like.

Hume, through Philo, makes exactly this point. By all means, he says, look at the world and work from the facts of this world to an understanding of what God might be like. But if you are going to pursue this method, you must be willing to look at the disorder and chaos as well as the order and beauty. In a famous passage from the *Dialogues*, Hume puts these words in the mouth of Philo:

> Look round this universe. What an immense profusion of beings, animated and organised, sensible and active! You admire this prodigious variety and fecundity. But inspect a little more narrowly these living existences, the only beings worth regarding. How hostile and destructive to each other! How insufficient all of them for their own happiness! How contemptible or odious to the spectator! The whole presents nothing but the idea of a blind nature, impregnated by a great vivifying principle, and pouring forth from her lap, without discernment or parental care, her maimed and abortive children. [30]

This graphically illustrates the problem of working from the 'facts' of the world to a concept of God. Beauty and order suggest an acceptable, benign image of a God who is benevolent and caring; evil and suffering suggest an unpleasant, disinterested, possibly even wicked deity. If the picture of God offered by the design argument is that of a cosmic workman, we must consider all aspects of his handiwork. A friend of mine employed an electrician who was more often to be found in the pub than working on her house. When he eventually 'finished' the work, she had to get another workman in to finish the job properly! He was not a good workman; why should we infer that the creator of this world is any better, if we take into account the poor workmanship (for example the San Andreas Fault), as well as the cruelty, suffering and evil found in this world?

This is an important point for Hume. He argues that 'when we infer any particular cause for an effect we must proportion the one to the other, and can never be allowed to ascribe any qualities, but what is exactly sufficient to produce the effect'.[31] In order to understand what Hume is getting at, imagine that you can see one side of a set of scales. You can observe that ten ounces is outweighed by something on the other side. As such, you have good evidence that the unseen object weighs more than ten ounces. However, you cannot infer from this that it weighs one hundred ounces or is infinitely heavy. Thus there may well be evidence of design in the world, but all we can conclude from this is that the world is the work of a design-producing being. What we cannot say is that the designer of the world is God: or at least the benevolent God of Christianity. As Hume puts it:

> Allowing, therefore, the gods to be the authors of the existence or order of the universe; it follows, that they possess that precise degree of power, intelligence, and benevolence, which appears in their workmanship; but nothing farther can be proved, except we call in the assistance of exaggeration and flattery to supply the defects of argument and reasoning.[32]

Some have argued that Hume has conclusively destroyed the force of the argument from design.[33] Brian Davies is less than convinced.[34] He feels that the design argument is a reasonable response to the facts of the world. After all, the world displays a high degree of order; it appears to have been ordered intelligently, and therefore it does seem reasonable to postulate an external cause responsible for that order.

Strangely, in view of the harshness of Hume's words about the dangers of inferring from things in this world to God, Philo does in one place accept that the beauty of the world may make us pause to consider the nature of that world. In his words:

> In many views of the universe, and of its parts, particularly the latter, the beauty and fitness of final causes strike us with such irresistible force, that all objections appear (what I believe they really are) mere cavils and sophisms; nor can we imagine how it was ever possible for us to repose any weight on them.[35]

Commentators are divided as to the significance of these words. Were they Hume's attempt to placate the ruling bodies of the Church? If so, they failed miserably, the *Dialogues* only being published after Hume's death. Or do they hint at a different way of viewing the argument from design? Hume, through Philo, appears to be saying that when we look at the world, we are often moved by the beauty contained within it. What Hume does *not* say is that the beauty of the world constitutes evidence for an existent God. Rather, his words seem to suggest that religious belief is based not upon evidence, but is a way of seeing the world.

The Argument from Religious Experience

> If there is a God, one might well expect him not merely to concern himself with the progress of the human race by bringing about the occurrence of things prayed for, providing men to do worthwhile things ... but also perhaps to show himself to and speak to at any rate some of the men whom he has made and who are capable of talking about God and worshipping him.[36]

If the argument from design is to a certain extent based upon a particular appreciation of the physical world, the argument from religious experience suggests that we can find good grounds for belief in God if we look to the kind of experiences which some people claim to have had of the divine. These personal and highly intimate experiences are thus used to argue for the existence of God. In this section we shall consider the nature of arguments of this sort by focusing on three specific areas: firstly, what constitutes a religious experience? secondly, to what extent can these experiences be understood as constituting *evidence* for an existent God? and thirdly, what are the problems associated with basing belief in God upon personal religious experience?

Defining religious experience

In his classic work *The Varieties of Religious Experience*, William James isolates the central features of a paradigm religious experience. James writes that 'personal religious experience has its roots and center in mystical states of consciousness',[37] and then proceeds to elaborate four elements of a mystical experience. The first of these elements is *ineffability*, meaning that the experience cannot be expressed in words: language is inadequate fully to impart its nature and significance to one who has not experienced it. Secondly, the experience has a *noetic quality*. The experience is not just remarkable or pleasant, for it also contains a degree of knowledge: mystical experiences are 'states of insight into depths of truth unplumbed by the discursive intellect'.[38] Though ineffability and noetic quality are the predominant features of any mystical experience, James lists two other conditions which are usually present. These are *transiency* (the experience is not long-lasting) and *passivity*. This last feature highlights the fact that such experiences, although often facilitated by personal concentration and discipline (say, yoga), involve the subject losing his or her own will, and being 'overtaken' by an experience which is, so to speak, forced upon them.

Often, such experiences may be occasioned by reflection on the natural world. One may then become aware of the unity of all things, and may even sense a spirit of nature. Recall Wordsworth rhapsodizing about the beauty of the Wye Valley, how this led him to detect 'a motion and a spirit, that impels/All thinking things, and all objects of all thought, /And rolls through

all things.'[39] Here, this delightful perception of nature leads towards a more profound, pantheistic intuition of a spirit coursing
through the world. In other kinds of religious experience, a person's encounter with the divine arises not when contemplation
of the world gives way to religious perceptions, but when all
such normal perception is interrupted and ruptured. Indeed, there
is a whole range of experiences which can be described as 'religious'. Swinburne offers the following categories:[40]

1   Experiences which the subject describes in terms of God or
    the supernatural, based on perception of an ordinary non-
    religious object. So, for example, I might witness a rather
    beautiful, but perfectly ordinary, sunset, and suddenly 'see' it
    in terms of God's creation. Someone else could experience
    the same phenomenon and, while moved, would not talk of
    the experience as 'religious'.
2   Experiences which are 'out of the ordinary', and public.
    So, the disciples 'witnessed' the reappearance of Christ af-
    ter his death. However, as with the previous example, 'a
    sceptic might have had the same visual sensations (described
    comparatively) and yet have not had the religious experi-
    ence'.[41]
3   Experiences which involve sensations private to the individual.
    I might have a dream that an angel tells me to follow a par-
    ticular course of action, which, on waking, I pursue. In many
    ways, the dream experience mirrors ordinary experience; in
    other words, the angel can be described in terms of a woman
    wearing white clothes.
4   The fourth example goes beyond the previous one. Here, the
    subject has a religious experience which cannot be described
    by using normal everyday language. Swinburne notes the ex-
    ample of mystics, who 'find it difficult if not impossible to
    describe their religious experiences, and yet feel that there is
    something to be described if only they had the words to do
    the describing'.[42]
5   The final category occurs independently of perceived sensa-
    tions. So, 'a man may be convinced that God is telling him to
    do so-and-so (e.g. follow such-and-such a vocation) and yet
    there are no auditory or other sensations occurring.'[43]

In categorizing religious experiences in this way, Swinburne highlights two key issues. Firstly, the experience may be in response to some public event, or it may arise in a purely private way. Secondly, it may involve sensations (sight, sound, etc.) which can be clearly spoken of, or it may transcend human language and concepts. Yet despite these differences, the crucial factor is the individual and their interpretation of these phenomena. This leads us to our second section: in what sense can such individual experiences be taken as providing evidence for the belief in an existent God?

Religious experience and verification

C. B. Martin at the outset of his critique of the argument from religious experience highlights a crucial issue which needs to be addressed: can we move from the claim 'I have had direct experience of God' to the claim 'God exists'?[44] The first claim interprets certain psychological/individual experiences; the second makes an existential claim that there is a God responsible for such experiences. As Martin suggests, it seems that we need to accumulate further evidence to make this jump from personal experience to a reasoned conclusion concerning the possible existence of God. Without such checking procedures the statement 'I have had a direct experience of God' is simply equivalent to 'I *seem to* have had a direct experience of God', which is merely a psychological statement. In general, when people do make bizarre claims such that they have seen, for example, ghosts, UFOs or fairies, their 'experiences' may not be enough to convince us of the existence of ghosts, UFOs, etc. We are more likely to believe that they have been hallucinating, particularly if there are no additional, more rational grounds for believing that what they claim to have experienced has actually occurred.

It has been argued that one way in which the veracity of such claims could be tested is through consideration of the effect that such experiences have on the lives of the individuals concerned.[45] Martin challenges such an idea. While even an atheist might accept that the individual has changed since their 'experience', this in no way establishes the claim that the cause of the experience is a transcendent, existent God.[46] We are back to Martin's initial point: we cannot simply move from the experience to claims that there is a God *responsible* for such experiences. Indeed, such experiences may tell us more about the psychology of the individual than the reality of God.

Richard Swinburne has challenged such a critique. In considering the reports of religious experiences, he suggests that the observer adopt two interrelated principles. Firstly, the 'Principle of Credulity', which seeks to refute the claim that we should be sceptical of our own experience, no matter how strange:

> Generally, contrary to the original philosophical claim, I suggest that it is a principle of rationality that (in the absence of special considerations) if it seems (epistemically) to a subject that x is present, then probably x is present; what one seems to perceive is probably so. How things seem to be is good grounds for a belief about how things are. From this it would follow that, *in the absence of special considerations*, all religious experiences ought to be taken by their subjects as genuine, and hence as substantial grounds for belief in the existence of their apparent object.[47]

In other words, I am generally justified in believing what I perceive with my senses. As such, if I have any 'experience of God' then I should accept this as genuine, and not a delusion or an hallucination. Swinburne's second principle, the 'Principle of Testimony', builds upon the first. We should accept what a person says, unless there are good grounds not to, i.e. if the person is a compulsive liar. In advocating these two principles, Swinburne argues that we should accept the veridical status of religious experiences. However, as we have seen, this is far from an obvious conclusion to draw. As such, we need to consider the problems facing the argument from religious experience in more depth.

Problems with the argument from religious experience

Swinburne suggests that we should accept the credibility of the witnesses unless we have reason to doubt them. These mitigating factors include the capacity of humans to lie, the possible

It may well be that religious experiences are parasitic upon previous religious training. In which case, experience cannot operate as a proof for the existence of some divine reality, for the experience is in fact dependent upon those prior beliefs.

Alvarez de Paz and other mystics have emphasized the importance of practising austerities, conquering the flesh, and mortifying the body.
Of course, this training of the body is not sufficient. The mind must be trained as well. To have a vision of the Holy Virgin one must be acquainted with the basic facts of 'Christ's birth and life and death.' To have the highest mystical apprehension of the Trinity, as did St Teresa, one must have some elementary theological training. (C. B. Martin, '"Seeing" God', in W. L. Rowe and W. J. Wainwright, *Philosophy of Religion: Selected Readings*, Orlando: Harcourt Brace Jovanovich, 1989, p. 350)

What kind of response might you make to C. B. Martin's claim? Why might experiences which lead to a change of life challenge this interpretation?

use of hallucinogenic drugs, and psychological predispositions and states. Perhaps the last feature poses the most difficulties for an argument based on religious experience. To what extent can we ever be certain that a report of a particular experience is not simply telling us something about an individual and their 'inner life' rather than about the nature and workings of an external supernatural God? Ultimately, all religious experiences are highly individualistic. Can we base universal claims about an existent God upon such highly personal and individualistic experiences?

Even if we can resolve this problem, a further problem arises if we accept the veridical status of such experiences. As Antony Flew points out: 'The varieties of religious experience include not only those which their subjects are inclined to interpret as visions of the Blessed Virgin or senses of the guiding presence of

Jesus Christ, but also others more outlandish presenting themselves as manifestations of Quetzalcoatl or Osiris, or Dionysus or Shiva.'[48] If all religious experiences led to the same conclusions about ultimate reality, perhaps they would constitute evidence for a transcendent God. As it is, they seem to tell us more about the distinctive and disparate nature of humanity's religious expression.

Conclusion

The argument from religious experience starts promisingly, based as it is in an apparent experience of the transcendent divine. As we have seen, however, significant problems arise when one attempts to move from such subjective experiences to making claims for an objective reality responsible for such experiences. While Swinburne makes some powerful claims for accepting the veridical status of such experiences, it seems that further evidence is required for accepting the existence of an external God. Such experiences may give personal satisfaction, but it is far from clear that they can be used as the basis for an objective 'proof' of the existence of God.

Conclusion: Assessing the Arguments

How successful are these attempts to establish the existence of God? As we have seen, criticisms have been raised of all the major arguments, which significantly undermine the idea that a 'proof' for the existence of God might be possible. We might, then, want to question the status of these arguments. What are their proponents hoping to achieve? It is difficult to imagine an 'unbeliever' being converted to belief in God by reflection on these arguments. Likewise, it would seem unlikely that a believer would fall into doubt if confronted by the kind of criticisms made by Kant and Hume. So to call such arguments 'proofs' seems a misnomer. Something else seems to be happening when philosophers employ such arguments.

If the detail of these arguments can be challenged, the picture of God which they present has also been challenged. All the arguments suppose a God who is an agent, an all-powerful creator

In *Culture and Value* (Oxford: Blackwell, 1980), Ludwig
Wittgenstein addresses the question of the status of the arguments
for the existence of God:

> If someone who believes in God looks round and asks 'Where
> does everything I see come from?', 'Where does all this come
> from?', he is not craving for a (causal) explanation; and his
> question gets its point from being the expression of a certain
> craving. He is, namely, expressing an attitude to all explana-
> tions. – But how is this manifested in his life? (1980, 85e)

What do you think the arguments for the existence of God achieve
in practice? Are they *explanations* for the world, or are they *expressions* of certain prior religious commitments made by those
offering them?

responsible for all that is. The theologian Paul Tillich rejects such
a view, arguing that 'it is as atheistic to affirm the existence of
God as it is to deny it'.[49] For Tillich, the idea that God is an
existent being is ridiculous. The notion of existence implies the
possibility of non-existence, and Tillich rejects the idea of necessary existence on the grounds that this concept is incoherent. Yet
despite such misgivings, it is this notion of an existent God, not
dissimilar to ourselves, which forms the basis of the theistic concept of God. And if philosophers believe that it is possible to
establish at least the logical possibility of the existence of God,
there is also an assumption amongst philosophers of religion that
the characteristics of that God can be established and explored.
It is to these attributes that we must now turn.

II   The Divine Attributes

Introduction

So far, we have considered the different attempts of some philosophers to establish the existence of God. The attempt to define

God as an existent being rests upon certain presuppositions and assumptions about the way in which the word 'God' is used. For the theist, 'God' is the name given to a supreme being. Just as the name 'B. Clack' is a label for an existent being – me! – so the word God should be understood as the name of an existent being.

Now, if we can use reason to establish the existence of God, some philosophers of religion have also believed that it is possible to use reason to establish the characteristics – or attributes – of this supreme being. Richard Swinburne offers a succinct definition of God which goes some way to encapsulating the nature of the philosophers' God. According to Swinburne, God is 'something like a "person without a body (i.e. a spirit) who is eternal, free, able to do anything, knows everything, is perfectly good, is the proper object of human worship and obedience, the creator and sustainer of the universe"'.[50] This is the classic description of the God of the philosophers: a God who is a supernatural being, a being with particular characteristics. This God is omnipotent, omniscient, omnipresent, omnibenevolent. In other words, God has the qualities of power, knowledge and love to the fullest extent possible. At the same time, this God is immutable (unchanging), impassible (unable to suffer) and perfect.

In this section, we will focus on three of these divine attributes – omnipotence, omniscience and immutability. In so doing, it will be possible to analyse the internal coherence of these concepts, whilst also considering the extent to which these concepts may contradict each other. At a later stage we will address the question of whether these attributes are desirable characteristics for God, and why they might have been attributed to God in the first place.[51]

Omnipotence

It is a commonplace amongst religious believers that God is referred to as all-powerful, or *omnipotent*, and there is certainly a biblical foundation for such a view. Jesus, for example, having said that it was easier for a camel to pass through the eye of a needle than for a rich man to enter the kingdom of God, qualifies his remark by adding: 'With God everything is possible.' Jesus's words point us towards one possible definition of omnipotence: *God can do absolutely anything he wants to do.* This will, of course, seem to encapsulate perfectly the notion of omnipotence, and yet it is a definition of that attribute which most philosophers and theologians have rejected. And they have rejected it because it entails that, alongside all the desired features of omnipotence (for example, that God can change the weather at will, can create a universe out of nothing, and so on), God would have to be able to perform what is *logically impossible*. Something which is logically impossible cannot even be conceived, let alone performed. Omnipotence would here involve the ability to draw a figure which was, at one and the same time, both a square and a circle. It would involve the ability to make an object which was, at one and the same time, entirely red and entirely blue. And God would be able to bring about certain logically impossible events: say that it was both raining and not raining, or that Tony Blair was at one and the same time both Prime Minister of Great Britain and not Prime Minister of Great Britain. Were God able to do these things, he would certainly appear to be very powerful indeed, and yet such things certainly could never be performed by a being with even unlimited power. Why? Because we just do not know what sense it makes even to talk about a square circle, so there certainly could never be such a figure. So this definition of omnipotence must be rejected, for it would immediately entail that omnipotence was an impossible characteristic, and hence that no omnipotent being could exist. This would deal a perhaps lethal blow to belief in the God of the monotheistic faiths, so theologians formulated a different notion of omnipotence.

This new definition excluded the logically impossible from the list of things God was said to be able to perform. Omnipotence can thus be defined as *the ability to perform whatever is logically possible*. This seems far more reasonable. But we are still left with a number of difficulties which have become the centre of philosophical controversy. If God is omnipotent, then he should be able to do whatever is logically possible. Playing soccer is logically possible, as are committing suicide and performing acts of sadism. But no Christian believer, for example, would want to say that God could do any of these things. It is certainly implausible to imagine God playing soccer (notwithstanding what some people might claim about Pele!). More urgently, the idea of

God either committing suicide or sadistic acts seems to go against the theistic claim that his existence is necessary (i.e. that he cannot cease to exist) and his benevolence perfect. Yet if God cannot commit suicide or be sadistic, then he is surely not omnipotent.

Attempts have been made to resolve these difficulties, and in these attempts we see a further refinement of the doctrine of omnipotence. Take the question of God's ability to be sadistic. In theological literature this problem is generally condensed into the question, 'Can God sin?' We want, of course, to say that God cannot sin – because he is morally perfect – but this leaves us with the conclusion that he cannot therefore be omnipotent. Witness Aquinas: 'Sin is an act of some kind. But God cannot sin . . . Therefore he is not omnipotent.'[52] Aquinas's solution to this problem is to focus on the notion of sin. He contends that to sin is to fail to act perfectly, and a failure to act perfectly would be the exact opposite of omnipotence. Hence, God's inability to sin is a *consequence* of his omnipotence and not a *limitation* of it.

There are problems with Aquinas's account. Principally, as Nelson Pike has argued,[53] there is no conceptual difficulty in the idea of a diabolical omnipotent being (that is, an all-powerful God who consistently acts in a wicked manner). Instead of Aquinas's defence, Pike offers an argument which centres on the distinction between divine omnipotence and the *exercise* of divine omnipotence. Pike states that 'God' is not the name of a being, but is, rather, a *title* held by an individual deity. The individual who holds the title 'God' has necessarily to act in a perfectly good way. Pike claims that 'the term "God" has been so specified that the individual who is God *cannot* sin and be God'.[54] Although the individual (for example, Yahweh) may have the power necessary to bring about morally reprehensible states of affairs, as holder of the title 'God' he must not and does not exercise that power. The case is perhaps parallel to the restrictions placed on the philosopher-rulers of Plato's ideal republic, who are prohibited from possessing wealth. It is, of course, logically possible for them to have property and money, but in their role as rulers, they are denied that luxury. Likewise, God is able to be sadistic, immoral and sinful, and yet he chooses not to be. Pike's solution does no damage to the concept of omnipotence, and God becomes, perhaps, even more worthy of praise, since he refrains from actions he could easily perform, and which might even give him pleasure.

A similar solution awaits the question of God's ability to commit suicide. God could take his own life if he wished, but, being perfect, he does not feel the despair, pain and anguish that lead tormented souls to flee this hollow vale. In each case, it is said that God can do things that are logically possible *so long as they do not contravene essential elements of the divine nature*, such as moral perfection. And this, indeed, is the ultimate resting point of the doctrine of omnipotence. This final formulation defines God's omnipotence thus: *God can do everything that it is logically possible for him to do*. Even given this less troublesome definition, it still faces a number of challenges, principal among which is what has become known as the paradox of the stone: can God create a stone that is too heavy for him to lift? If you answer this question negatively, it entails that God is not omnipotent because there is some (logically possible) thing that he cannot do (that is, he cannot create this stone). Yet if you provide an affirmative answer to the question, God is still deprived of his omnipotence, because there is still some (logically possible) task that he cannot perform (that is, he cannot lift the stone).

How informative is the notion of omnipotence that says that God can do everything that is logically possible for him to do? Given the nature of a slug, there are only a number of things that it is logically possible for a slug to do (for example, eat cabbages, sit under rocks, and so on). If a particular slug can do all those things, does it follow that the slug is omnipotent?

The purpose of the paradox of the stone is to illustrate that the doctrine of omnipotence is incoherent, and that there cannot therefore be an omnipotent God. In fact, the paradox can be successfully countered. George Mavrodes correctly states that, on the assumption that God is omnipotent, the phrase 'a stone too heavy for God to lift' becomes self-contradictory. For it becomes 'a stone which cannot be lifted by Him whose power is sufficient for lifting anything'.[55] In such a manner, the paradox is dissolved.

So we have seen that attempts to show omnipotence to be incoherent fail. It seems that the concept is, at least, intelligible. However, as we shall see in chapter three, it may be possible to critique this concept differently by focusing on the problem that evil poses for belief in an all-powerful God.

Omniscience

As we have seen, much of the difficulty surrounding omnipotence is concerned with providing a satisfactory definition of the concept. This is a problem which does not arise when examining the notion of God's omniscience (or all-knowing nature). Omniscience may be simply defined in the following way: *For all p, if p, then God knows that p*. This means that God knows everything that is true; or, what amounts to the same thing, that he knows the totality of true propositions. (This is the point of the 'if p' clause: God knows that $2 + 2 = 4$, but he does not know that $2 + 2 = 5$.) Omniscience entails that God knows the truths of mathematics and of logic. He also knows all empirical truths, such as how the laws of nature operate, exactly how many leaves there are on every tree in the world at any given time, exactly how many fleas there are in the world at any given time, and so on.

God's knowledge of such things is not especially problematic,[56] though there are, as we will see, implications for the doctrine of immutability. Where difficulties principally arise is in the claim that God has knowledge of future events. This is otherwise known as the problem of *divine foreknowledge*. Put simply, the problem is this. If God knows everything, then he knows everything that has happened in the past, everything that is happening now, and everything that *will happen in the future*. The problem with this is that it appears to rule out human freedom. Consider the following argument:

God foreknows all my acts.
What he foreknows must come to pass.
Therefore, if my acts must come to pass, then they cannot be free.

Think about what you are going to do tomorrow night. You may weigh up certain alternatives: perhaps you will go to the pub, or a restaurant, or perhaps you will stay at home and watch television. The point is that you believe that you will exercise your freedom and choose what you want. But if God infallibly knows that tomorrow night you will go to the pub, then you really have no choice in the matter: your freedom is a delusion. Human freedom is patently a gift to be cherished, so, in the face of this threat, we may be tempted to dispense with the doctrine of omniscience. But, once again, this problem can be dispelled.

The most satisfactory solution to this problem is offered by Richard Swinburne.[57] He denies that God does know what will happen in the future. This certainly protects human freedom, and, contrary to appearances, it does not limit divine omniscience. The reason for this is that Swinburne shows that it is logically impossible for future contingent events to be known. Swinburne writes: 'An omniscient person knows of every true proposition that it is true. But if propositions about the future actions of agents are neither true nor false until the agents do the actions, then to be omniscient a person will not have to know them.'[58] Swinburne's point is important. We tend to think that any statement must be either true or false. Certainly, this is true of many statements. 'I went to The Lamb and Flag last night' is either true or false. But it is neither true nor false *until* the event has (or has not) occurred. To paraphrase the argument, then:

To be omniscient, a being must know all true propositions.
Propositions about future events are neither true nor false.
Therefore, an omniscient being cannot (and need not) know what will happen in the future, and the actions of human beings are thus genuinely free.

As with the doctrine of omnipotence, then, there do not seem to be any pressing reasons why we should dispense with the idea of omniscience. The notion of an omnipotent, omniscient being is not obviously incoherent. However, problems may arise when this concept is placed alongside other theistic beliefs about the nature of God; specifically, the concept of immutability.

Immutability

To describe God as immutable is to argue for a God who is changeless. It may not initially seem clear as to why a notion of God as changeless might be important. However, closer consideration of certain features of human life might reveal why for some philosophers and theologians this has been the case. As human beings, we tend to fear change. We are all in the process of change; we are all moving closer to old age, death and decay. Our fear of change leads us to desire at least one being who is not subject to the same forces of change. We want a God who is changeless. So in the words of a well-known hymn, 'Change and decay in all about I see, O Thou who changest not abide with me.' For the Greek philosophers, the idea of a perfect God necessitated a God who could not change. There is a certain logic to this: if God is understood as perfect, any change in the perfect God could only be for the worse. Thus the perfect God could not be understood to change.

The idea of a changeless God has not gone unchallenged. If God cannot change, the connection between ourselves and God seems open to question. In the Christian tradition, this connection between God and humanity is expressed in the idea that human beings are 'made in the image of God'. But a changeless God would seem to have more in common with rocks than with human beings. Process theologians have thus argued that God is not immutable. Rather, God is dynamic, working in the world, risking chance and change.[59]

The idea of an immutable God does not sit comfortably with the idea of an omniscient God. To what extent can God be all-knowing if God cannot change? Much of our experience as human beings arises through the changing nature of our lives. If God cannot change, he would apparently be unable to share those experiences. Likewise, immutability has been connected with impassibility (the claim that God does not have emotions, and specifically that God cannot suffer).[60] There is a certain logic to this development. For the Greeks, suffering was viewed as an extreme example of the consequences of change. And again, if God is to be perfect, then God cannot suffer. But if a changeless God cannot suffer, to what extent is that God all-knowing? Would God *know* what it is to experience pain and suffering? It would seem from this brief discussion of a perhaps neglected aspect of the divine nature that there is a certain tension between the idea of a changeless God, and the idea of an omniscient God.

Conclusion

In considering these three attributes we have seen some of the problems that arise when philosophers attempt to define the nature of God. Logical problems might be raised: this was particularly the case when we considered the concept of omnipotence. However, there is little evidence that either the concept of omnipotence or the concept of omniscience are internally incoherent. More pressing is the definite tension between different attributes assigned to the theist's God; this is particularly the case when the attributes of immutability and omniscience are held alongside each other. More importantly, perhaps, problems may arise concerning the picture that such attributes paint of God. So, we might ask whether we could have a relationship with an immutable, impassible God. And as we shall see in the next chapter, we might want to challenge the notion of an allpowerful God when we consider the facts of evil and suffering.

In this chapter, then, we have focused on the key issues which have concerned philosophers engaging with the question of religious belief. We are perhaps beginning to see some problems with this theistic approach. The arguments for the existence of God are open to challenge; arguably, there are tensions within the theistic account of the nature of God. In the next chapter we shall consider in more depth some of the challenges made to the God of the philosophers.

Suggested reading:

I   Arguments for the Existence of God

C. D. Broad, 'The Appeal to Religious Experience', in W. L. Rowe and W. J. Wainwright, *Philosophy of Religion: Selected Readings*, Orlando: Harcourt Brace Jovanovich, 1989, pp. 353–62.

Baruch Brody (ed.), *Readings in the Philosophy of Religion*, New Jersey: Prentice-Hall, 1974, selections on the ontological, cosmological and teleological arguments.

Stephen R. L. Clark, *The Mysteries of Religion*, Oxford: Blackwell, 1986, ch. 7.

Caroline Franks David, *The Evidential Force of Religious Experience*, Oxford: Clarendon Press, 1989.

Brian Davies, *An Introduction to the Philosophy of Religion*, 2nd edition, Oxford: OUP, 1993, chs 4, 5 and 6.

H. H. Farmer, *Revelation and Religion*, London: Nisbet, 1954.

J. C. A. Gaskin, *The Quest for Eternity*, Harmondsworth: Penguin, 1984, ch. 3 (ii) and (iii).

R. W. Hepburn, 'From World to God', in Basil Mitchell (ed.), *The Philosophy of Religion*, Oxford: OUP, 1971, pp. 168–78.

John Hick (ed.), *The Existence of God*, London: Collier Macmillan, 1964, sections on the ontological, cosmological and teleological arguments.

David Hume (1779), *Dialogues Concerning Natural Religion*, edited by N. Kemp Smith, Indianapolis: Bobbs-Merrill, 1947.

William James (1902), *The Varieties of Religious Experience*, London: Fontana, 1960.

Immanuel Kant (1787), *Critique of Pure Reason*, tr. N. Kemp Smith, Basingstoke: Macmillan, 1950.

Hans Küng, *Does God Exist?*, London: Fount, 1980, pp. 627–64.

J. L. Mackie, *The Miracle of Theism*, Oxford: Clarendon Press, 1982, chs 3 and 5.

C. B. Martin, 'A Religious Way of Knowing' in Baruch Brody (ed.), *Readings in the Philosophy of Religion*, New Jersey: Prentice-Hall, 1974, pp. 516–29.

C. B. Martin, ' "Seeing" God', in W. L. Rowe and W. J. Wainwright, *Philosophy of Religion: Selected Readings*, Orlando: Harcourt Brace Jovanovich, 1989, pp. 335–53.

Anthony O'Hear, *Experience, Explanation and Faith*, London: RKP, 1984, chs 2 and 4.3.

Rudolf Otto, *The Idea of the Holy*, Harmondsworth: Penguin, 1959.

D. Z. Phillips, *Religion Without Explanation*, Oxford: Blackwell, 1976, ch. 2.

D. Z. Phillips, 'The Friends of Cleanthes', *Modern Theology*, vol. 1, no. 2, 1985, pp. 91–104.

Robin Le Poidevin, *Arguing for Atheism*, London: Routledge, 1996, part I.

W. L. Rowe and W. J. Wainwright (ed.), *Philosophy of Religion: Selected Readings*, Orlando: Harcourt Brace Jovanovich, 1989, pp. 96–175.

Richard Swinburne, *The Existence of God*, Oxford: Clarendon Press, 1979.

Peter Vardy, *The Puzzle of God*, London: Collins Flame, 1990, chs 8, 9 and 10.

Lubor Velecky, *Aquinas' Five Arguments in the Summa Theologiae 1a 2,3,* Kampen: Kok Pharos, 1994.

Keith Yandell, *The Epistemology of Religious Experience*, Cambridge: Cambridge University Press, 1993.

II   The Divine Attributes

Baruch Brody (ed.), *Readings in the Philosophy of Religion*, section on 'Divine Attributes', pp. 331–427.

Stephen R. L. Clark, *The Mysteries of Religion*, Oxford: Blackwell, 1986, chs 4 and 12.

Brian Davies, *An Introduction to the Philosophy of Religion*, 2nd edition, Oxford: OUP, 1993, ch. 8.

Antony Flew, 'Divine Omnipotence and Human Freedom', in A. Flew and A. MacIntyre (eds), *New Essays in Philosophical Theology*, London: SCM, 1955.

Anthony Kenny, *The God of the Philosophers*, Oxford: OUP, 1979.

Michael Peterson, William Hasker, Bruce Reichenbach and David Basinger, *Reason and Religious Belief*, Oxford: OUP, 1991, ch. 4.

W. L. Rowe and W. J. Wainwright, *Philosophy of Religion: Selected Readings*, Orlando: Harcourt Brace Jovanovich, 1989, section I.

Graham Shaw, *God in Our Hands*, London: SCM, 1987, part I.

Richard Swinburne, *The Coherence of Theism*, Oxford: Clarendon Press, 1977, chs 9, 10 and 12.

Peter Vardy, *The Puzzle of God*, London: Collins Flame, 1990, chs 12 and 13.

3

Challenges to Theism

I Evil

Introduction

In the weeks preceding the writing of this chapter, the following events took place. Nine-year-old Jade Matthews was found battered to death on a railway line (a thirteen-year-old boy has since been charged with this crime). A man with a machete attacked children and teachers at a primary school in Wolverhampton. An American airliner bound for Paris blew up, killing all on board. Siamese twins joined at the chest died. Such a random review of events creates a powerful challenge to the God of theism: in the face of events such as these, is it possible to talk of an all-powerful, loving, creator God?

Within the philosophy of religion, a particular discipline has been developed to address this question. Theodicy is the attempt to justify the theist's God in the face of such human experiences.[1] Theodicists offer solutions to the question of how evil and the good God of theism can be co-existent. To a greater or lesser extent, these solutions suggest a purpose behind the presence of evil. While evil may seem meaningless from a human perspective, if we could see things from God's perspective we would understand the greater purpose which lies behind the reality of evil. In this chapter, different theodicies will be presented and considered. Such approaches have not been without their critics. D. Z. Phillips and Dorothee Soelle are two thinkers who have challenged the propriety of this intellectual approach to the reality of evil and human suffering. In considering their views, alternative approaches to theodical explanations for evil will also be considered.

Defining Evil

At the outset, it is important to define what we mean by 'evil'. The way in which we define this will, in part, depend upon our respective outlooks. If we are adherents to Christianity, we may see evil as 'turning away from God's will'. If we are not, we may be more concerned with using this word to label the horrific actions of some human beings. For a more general definition, it may be helpful to isolate two forms of evil: moral and natural. Moral evil is the evil brought about by human beings, and includes phenomena such as war, torture, physical violence, poverty, injustice and political oppression. Natural evil includes all those things that cause suffering but which are not brought about by human agents – for instance, disease, famine, earthquakes, hurricanes, death.

It is important to note that the way in which the problem of evil has been approached by philosophers of religion has tended to focus on the problem evil poses for belief in a good and all-powerful God. Human suffering is addressed within all religious traditions (witness the Buddhist conception of *samsara*, or the sustained meditation on suffering in the Upanishads), but while evil in some traditions is the very starting point for the religion, within theism evil challenges the very plausibility of its particular view of the universe. The theological problem of evil arises when we attempt to square the nature and existence of God with the fact that there are instances of suffering – suffering being the consequence of evil. As we shall see, the God of the philosophers, given the attributes we considered in the previous chapter, faces a particular challenge from the reality of evil. If we consider the following five propositions, we are faced with an inconsistency:

1   God exists.
2   God is perfectly good.

3   God is omnipotent.
4   God is omniscient.
5   There are instances of evil in the world.

The problem is this: if God is omniscient, God must *know* that there are instances of evil in the world; if God is omnipotent, then God *must* be able to prevent these instances from occurring; if God is perfectly good, then God must *want* to prevent occurrences of evil. But there *are* instances of evil in the world, so God must either not exist, or does not have the character traditionally ascribed by theists.

This, in essence, is the question that Hume takes from Epicurus and poses in Part X of his *Dialogues Concerning Natural Religion*: 'Is God willing to prevent evil, but not able? then he is impotent. Is he able, but not willing? then he is malevolent. Is he both able and willing? whence then is evil?'[2] One way to solve the problem is to deny one of the five propositions cited above. For example, we could deny (5), that there is evil in the world. To do this, however, seems to contradict many human experiences, and seems out of step with reality. Alternatively, we could deny one of the other propositions. If we deny (4), a God who is not omniscient may not *know* that human beings suffer; in which case this God would not feel the need to prevent suffering. Yet in itself this is problematic, for it suggests a God who is stupid and senile, and thus compromises our view of what it is for God to be God. We could deny (3): if God is not omnipotent, then God cannot eradicate evil. This is a particularly popular approach amongst a number of theologians.[3] For theologians who wish to talk of a 'suffering God', the notion that God is the all-powerful controller of events makes him callous and cruel, and alienates him from the reality of human suffering. Likewise, process theologians limit the extent of God's power by maintaining that he is subject to the basic laws of the universe. Denying omnipotence escapes the problem of evil, but suggests a radically different understanding of God which may be unsatisfactory to some.

Alternatively, we could deny (2). This would safeguard God's omniscience and omnipotence, but at the expense of denying that God is benevolent.[4] While this position would seem to protect what some would see as the very qualities which make God

'God', this position is also problematic. If God is not benevolent, we are left with the notion of a <u>malevolent</u> God who takes pleasure from human suffering; or else a God who <u>simply does not care</u> whether humans suffer or not. For the atheist, the answer is obvious: deny (1). If there is no God, there is no problem of evil. In an atheistic universe, <u>suffering is a brute fact</u>, our life an absurdity.

> Albert Camus in his novel *The Plague* gives powerful expression to the sense that human life is absurd. A devastating plague afflicts the town of Oran, highlighting the absurdity of the human condition:
>
>> One of the most striking consequences of the closing of the gates was, in fact, this sudden deprivation befalling people who were completely unprepared for it. Mothers and children, lovers, husbands and wives, who had a few days previously taken it for granted that their parting would be a short one, who had kissed each other good-bye on the platform and exchanged a few trivial remarks, sure as they were of seeing each other again after a few days or, at most, a few weeks, duped by our blind human faith in the near future and little if at all diverted from their normal interests by this leave-taking – all these people found themselves, without the least warning, hopelessly cut off, prevented from seeing each other again, or even communicating with each other. (*The Plague*, trans. Stuart Gilbert, Harmondsworth: Penguin, 1948, p. 57)
>
> Is evil and suffering less problematic for the atheist than for the theist?

Theodicists are unwilling to accept the claim that evil establishes the non-existence of God. In most cases, they are also unwilling to rescind the qualities ascribed to God by philosophical theism. Their aim is to answer the problem of evil whilst maintaining the idea of a transcendent God. In the following section, some of these 'solutions' will be considered.

Major Theodicies

Augustinian theodicy

Theodicy as a philosophical discipline dates from the Enlightenment, and specifically from the writings of G. W. Leibniz who coined the term.[5] Thus, to call Augustine's writings on evil 'theodicy' is not entirely accurate: writing in the fourth/fifth centuries, he clearly predates theodicy proper. However, Augustine's writings on evil have been particularly influential, and as such must be considered in any discussion of theodicy.

Augustine's definition of evil has proved highly significant. He rejects the idea that there is one principle for good (God) and one principle for evil (the devil); such a dualistic distinction of these powers threatens the sovereignty of God. This might seem to suggest that God is the fount of all things – even evil. Augustine, however, wants to deny that this is the case. Instead he argues that it is wrong to think of evil as an active principle; evil should be understood as non-being. It is a lack of goodness. Evil is literally *no-thing*; it is a privation, a non-entity, the 'name for nothing but the want of good'.[6]

While Augustine appears to have solved the problem of maintaining God's sovereignty and God's goodness, the question of accounting for the presence of evil in the first place remains. Augustine – not surprisingly for a Christian – turns to the biblical account of the Fall of humanity given in Genesis as the source of all evil.[7] Evil enters into the creation because human beings deliberately turn away from the good which is God. All evil – both moral and natural – is thus the result of human sin.

There is an almost beautiful simplicity about Augustine's views which in itself masks some of the problems with his account of the origin and nature of evil. Firstly, if God created a perfect universe, how could evil have arisen? The idea of a perfect universe going wrong is self-contradictory. Secondly, for modern people the account of the Fall seems out of step with the ideas of natural scientists. Far from falling from the perfect state of Eden, there is good evidence for believing that human beings developed from primitive life forms; if you like, humans are heading towards perfection, not away from it.

Irenaean theodicy and the free will defence

Some ideas from the writings of Irenaeus (CE c.130–c.202) concerning evil have been popularized by John Hick. Irenaeus offers an account of evil which is significantly different from that offered by Augustine. According to Irenaeus, there are two stages of human creation. All human beings are created in the 'image of God'. However, this does not mean that they are perfect; rather they are immature creatures capable of spiritual and moral growth. The second stage necessitates the free actions of those human beings. Through their own free actions they can be transformed into the children of God; that is, they can become 'the likeness of God'.[8]

In both the Augustinian and Irenaean 'theodicies' much emphasis is placed upon the notion of human free will. According to Augustine, human freedom results in the Fall. According to Irenaeus, human freedom is necessary if human beings are to become the kind of creatures God intends them to be. 'The free will defence' thus attempts to remove the 'blame' from God for evil by focusing on the 'willful' turning away from good to evil by free human agents.

Some theodicists have gone further: if human freedom is to be a reality, evil is a necessary part of the moral universe, for it presents us with real choices about how we are to live. Just as we can freely choose to do good, so we can use our freedom to do evil. Richard Swinburne's theodicy provides a good illustration of this kind of approach.[9] According to Swinburne, evil is necessary for the creation of 'greater goods'. These greater goods are defined in two complementary ways. The main emphasis lies with the will of God. God wants human beings to know and love him freely. In order for this to happen, we have to be confronted with the choice between good (God) and evil (that which is not God). Human freedom lies in the ability to choose between God and that which is not God. Freedom is the crucial issue here. For Swinburne, there has to be a real risk involved if human beings are to learn to act responsibly: if God simply created human beings who were free but incapable of evil actions there would be no real responsibility. If evil did not result from wrong choices, then human life would be akin to a video game. If I crash a 'car' whilst playing a video game, no one is injured; there is no cost to my mistake. Swinburne argues that in order for us to become mature and responsible adults we have to be in a position to see the results of wrong action.

Connected to this point is Swinburne's account of the relationship between evil and virtue. According to Swinburne, evil and suffering give human beings the opportunity to perform at their best. A world without evils would be a world without forgiveness, compassion, bravery and self-sacrifice. In order for there to be such virtues there have to be evils which prompt people to behave in altruistic ways. In Swinburne's words: 'Evils give men the opportunity to perform those acts which show men at their best.'[10] Thus evil becomes necessary for the exercise of goodness. If human beings are to develop as persons, they must come into contact with evil and act against it. It is by acting against evil that goodness is generated. Whilst Swinburne's argument is clear enough, it is not altogether convincing. His argument rests upon the understanding that evil is 'necessary' for good. Without evil, there would be no goodness. Evil, as the spur to goodness, seems to become a good itself. Such a conclusion is based upon a misunderstanding of the connection between suffering and goodness. Swinburne appears to be arguing that good can come out of human suffering. In a way he is right: often people will look back on the difficult times in their lives as their 'formative' years. However, some kinds of suffering defy such categorization. It is difficult to see what good came out of Auschwitz. Any good that comes out of such extreme suffering should not be understood as causally connected to the evil which preceded it. A causal connection would suggest that in order for there to be good, there had first to be suffering. Perhaps we would be better advised to think of the good which comes out of such situations as a by-product of the initial experience – not something that arose *because of* the suffering, but something that arose *despite* the suffering.

A further development to the kind of theodicy advanced by

Swinburne is found in John Hick's writing. While broadly reiter-
ating Swinburne's position, Hick develops this idea. Like
Swinburne, Hick argues that human beings move through suffering and moral struggle toward perfection: 'The kind of goodness
which . . . God desires in His creatures, could not in fact be created except through a long process of creaturely experiences in
response to challenges and disciplines of various kinds.'[11] The world
is thus a place of 'soul-making', an arena where we have the opportunity to become the 'children of God'. However, unlike
Swinburne Hick accepts that the outcome of suffering is not al-

---

Anton Chekhov in his play *Uncle Vanya* offers a poetic account
of the possible effect of holding to a higher harmony theodicy.
Here, after the play has revealed the disappointments and hardship of her life, Sonya consoles herself with a picture of a life
beyond the grave where the wrongs of her life will be righted,
and her sufferings forgotten in the midst of heavenly bliss:

> We shall live out our lives, Uncle Vanya. We shall live out
> the long, long succession of days and endless evenings; we
> shall patiently bear the trials we're sent; we shall labour
> for others without respite; and when our time comes we
> shall die with resignation; and there, beyond the grave, we
> shall say that we have suffered and wept, that it went hard
> with us; and God shall be moved to pity . . . We shall hear
> the angels; we shall see the sky all dressed in diamonds;
> we shall see all the world's evil and all our sufferings
> drown in the mercy that will fill the earth; and our life will
> become as quiet and gentle and sweet as a caress. (A.
> Chekhov, *Uncle Vanya*, trans. M. Frayn, London: Methuen,
> 1987, pp. 58–9)

A theodicy which focuses on a future world seems to stress patience in the face of adversity. Why might this not be an appropriate response to the fact of evil?

ways predictable. The kind of experiences people meet in life may be soul-*breaking*, rather than soul-making. How, then, can the idea of God as creator of the system and this kind of suffering be justified? Hick argues that if the work of creation is to be completed the process of soul-making must continue beyond the grave in a realm where the person is 'subjected to processes of healing and repair which bring it into a state of health and activity'.[12] In such a higher harmony, we will grow and develop; moreover, we will understand the meaning of the suffering endured in this world.

This form of 'higher harmony' theodicy is not without its critics. According to such a view, the presence of evil *in this world* is justified by the righting of wrongs and the erasing of suffering *in a future world* . If this is the case, the meaning of *this* world is to be questioned. If evil is to be righted in the future, why fight against present evils in the here and now? Such a view might lead to inaction in this life and apathy towards the sufferings of others. Jürgen Moltmann develops this idea in his work *The Crucified God*. In rejecting the classical understanding of a God who cannot suffer, Moltmann argues that the emphasis on divine *apatheia* contributes to human apathy in the face of suffering.[13] If God does not share human sufferings, human apathy seems to find its basis in a God distanced from the sufferings of others. Likewise, if all ends in the glory of the Kingdom of God, there seems to be little reason to combat suffering in this world. This kind of approach is built upon by Kenneth Surin, who argues that we should make a distinction between 'theoretical' theodicies, such as those offered by Swinburne and Hick, and 'practical' theodicies which focus on action, offered by a thinker like Moltmann.[14] We have to ask ourselves which kind of approach is more likely to combat human evil and ease human suffering. Might a particular type of theology motivate us to action, while another renders us passive?

Process theodicy and the concept of God

If Surin's description of practical theodicy suggests a different approach to the question of evil, process theologians have offered a different *account* of evil, based on a significantly different understanding of God than that offered by philosophical theism.

Based upon the ideas of A. N. Whitehead, process theology defines God as 'bi-polar'; in other words, God is both abstract and concrete, personal and impersonal. Indeed, God depends upon the personal experiences of humans to create the concrete side of his nature. Thus evil is not sent or determined by God, but arises from the free choices of human beings. This necessitates a redefinition of divine power: God is not a coercive deity but the 'divine lure'. God 'persuades' humanity to co-operate with his good designs for the creation, but the outcome of creation depends upon the extent to which humans decide to help God. Rather than see God as 'outside' the universe, directing the action, God is understood as part of this 'process' of creation.[15]

It is in this way that the process theologian claims to have found a way around the problem of evil. As God's power has been redefined, the responsibility for evil is shifted from God. According to David Griffin, such an approach 'dissolves the problem of evil by denying the doctrine of omnipotence fundamental to it'.[16] God cannot simply 'prevent' evils occuring. Rather, 'God acts in the world . . . by seeking to persuade individuals to actualize the best possibilities that are *real* possibilities for them'.[17] Divine persuasion takes time: 'Insofar as God can move these individuals to change their ways, it must be over a very long period of time. (This is why evolutionary change occurred so gradually until relatively recently on our earth.)'[18] So what does God do when humans experience the reality of evil? For the process theologian, God is 'the fellow sufferer who understands'.[19] God should not be understood as sending suffering, but as sharing human suffering.

Glad to be me? Individualism and the problem of evil

The connection between the apparently abstract considerations of philosophers of religion and the values of the society in which they write can be illustrated by a recent trend in theodical writing. According to William Hasker and Robert Merrihew Adams, the problem of evil can be solved by answering the following question honestly: On the whole, am I glad that I exist?[20] If the answer to this question is 'yes', I have to recognize the factors that led to my birth. My existence is dependent upon a whole sequence of events that preceded it. Included within this sequence of events are occasions and happenings that would not be readily attributed to my private history. These events include instances of apparent evil and suffering. The whole set of contingent experiences and events is required in order for me to be 'me'. To take one example: my life is dependent upon my parents meeting, falling in love, marrying and conceiving me. In turn, their lives were dependent upon their parents meeting, and so on. The choice of partner is also determined by other events; for example, the devastation of the First World War killed millions of young men. If that conflict had not occurred, it is quite possible that my grandparents would have met and married different people, meaning that my mother would not have been born, and neither would I! According to Hasker and Adams, if I accept with gladness the mere fact that I exist, I have to recognize that my existence is dependent on factors of this kind. Good events and 'evil' events are necessary for my existence. Evil becomes something which must be accepted.

This is a particularly seductive argument. How many of us would answer Hasker and Adams's question negatively? Yet the egocentrism of this argument seems peculiarly western. The individual is of paramount importance; more than that, *I* am of paramount importance. On closer inspection, this argument seems to heighten the difficulty raised by evil. Can an event such as Auschwitz be justified by my existence? This seems a peculiar way to address the issue of evil and raises a significant question concerning all theodicies. In attempting to justify all evils, to show evil to be purposive, theodicists appear to neglect Augustine's insight concerning the *nature* of evil. For Augustine, evil is *no-thing*; it is *nonsensical*. Attempting to make meaningful something which by definition is meaningless distorts the issue. Taking seriously this conclusion has led to increased criticism of the discipline of theodicy. How adequate is the theodical approach to evil and suffering?

Critiquing Theodicy

In his book *The Evils of Theodicy*, Terrence Tilley argues that far from 'solving' the problem of evil, theodicists, by the very language that they use when considering the problem, exacerbate the effects of evil. In the face of human suffering it is not enough to formulate abstract arguments. Indeed, he cites his own experience as a hospital orderly:

> I was called to the newborn nursery late one night and told to take to the morgue a baby who had lost her fight for life. She fitted comfortably on my left arm like any newborn – placing her on a guerney would have been a silly waste of time. Her receiving blanket covered her face. I expected the elevator to travel non-stop to the basement. But much to my horror, the car stopped and a man and a woman walked in. The door closed. They looked at my starched white uniform, my silent bundle, my frozen face. As we rode down, the man said very simply, 'I could never do your job' . . .
>
> [T]he man's words remain with me, well over two decades later. They were 'just the right thing to say' . . . In those words, he expressed his understanding of a difficult situation, his sadness at the death of the child, and his support for a stranger engaged in a wrenching task. Yet the philosophy I would later study would construe his words as 'merely pastoral', even irrelevant to the *real* issues of theodicy.[21]

Tilley's experience suggests that theodicists devalue human responses to evil and suffering. According to Tilley, 'explaining' evil, the traditional task of theodicy, is inadequate, as is the attempt to use emotionless, 'rational' language when confronted with the concrete reality of human suffering. Rather than clarify the meaning of evil, Tilley argues that the language of theodicy distorts the nature of human suffering by ignoring its reality and dealing instead with a pale shadow of suffering. So, a theodicist like Richard Swinburne can make an analogy between the extremes of suffering (for example, the death camps, cancer) and 'toothache'.[22] Tilley is not the only philosopher of religion to challenge the language of theodicy. Both D. Z. Phillips and Dorothee Soelle reject the theodicist's attempt to define the parameters of the debate concerning evil and the good God.

D. Z. Phillips: 'On Not Understanding God'

D. Z. Phillips is one of the fiercest critics of theodicy. According to him, philosophers of religion are misguided if they think there could ever be an adequate answer for evil; evil reveals to us a fact that few philosophers of religion are content to accept: that there are things beyond human understanding.[23] Moreover, to seek a sufficient explanation for the presence of evil and suffering is to distort the nature of that suffering. When a victim asks 'why is this happening to me?', it would be wrong to assume that a full and complete answer would satisfy that person. In the words of Rush Rhees:

> Suppose there has been an earthquake, and the geologists now give an explanation of it. This will not be an answer to the woman who has lost her home and her child and asks 'Why?' It does not make it easier to understand 'what has befallen us'. And the woman's question, though it may drive her mad, does not seek an answer. 'It was fate' may some day come to take the place of asking.[24]

Just as science cannot answer that woman's 'why?' neither can metaphysics. No reason will adequately explain away the pain

My heart grew sombre with grief, and wherever I looked I saw only death. My own country became a torment and my own home a grotesque abode of misery. All that we had done together was now a grim ordeal without him. My eyes searched everywhere for him, but he was not there to be seen. I hated all the places we had known together, because he was not in them and they could no longer whisper to me 'Here he comes!' as they would have done had he been alive but absent for a while . . . Tears alone were sweet to me, for in my heart's desire they had taken the place of my friend. (Saint Augustine, *Confessions*, IV:4, tr. R. S. Pine-Coffin, Harmondsworth: Penguin, 1961, p. 76)

Augustine, reflecting on the death of a friend, describes vividly the horror, pain and devastation of loss. Could any kind of explanation ever adequately ease the pain of grief? What sort of argument might?

of human loss. But Phillips goes further: it is not just that there is no answer which will satisfy the victim. If there is such a cosmic answer to the question evil poses, this would create greater problems for the God of theism. If God has foreseen from all eternity the torturing to death of one child, it would seem that that God is evil in the extreme. What kind of cosmic plan can be worth the weight of all this suffering?

If D. Z. Phillips's conclusion has implications for the way in which philosophers approach the problem of evil, it has wider ramifications for theism itself. The main thrust of Phillips's argument lies with his rejection of the God of the philosophers. In seeking to define and encapsulate the nature and being of God, Phillips argues that theists are 'relocating God in man's image. God is regarded as an agent whose activities, like those of any other agent, are capable of being understood, assessed and judged.'[25]

Behind the complex language of theodicy and its emphasis on rationality lies a God conceived as a supernatural human being. For Phillips, such an understanding of God is inadequate. Instead, he argues for a rejection of the God of theism, and a reinstigation of the ontological space and difference between God and humanity. A consideration of biblical passages suggests that God is quite different from a superhuman being: 'The Bible says that God is a spirit and they that worship him should worship him in spirit and in truth. Let's make the philosophical substitution: "God is a person without a body and they who . . ." On the other hand, let's forget it!'[26] If this radical difference between God and humanity is accepted, the conclusion is one which philosophers will find most difficult to accept: that is, that there are things which lie beyond human understanding, and that includes God.

Dorothee Soelle

In many ways, Dorothee Soelle's consideration of the problem of evil is not dissimilar to that offered by Phillips. Like Phillips, she rejects the theist's account of God. But while Phillips is hesitant at describing in any great detail his replacement (for the reasons outlined above), Soelle has no such reservations. In rejecting the idea of a supernatural God, she turns to the Bible. Citing the First Letter of John, she claims that, literally, 'God is love' (1 John 1:4). God is not some supernatural, other-worldly force, but rather 'our unending capacity to love'.[27] God is defined as a possibility inherent within human love.

Such an understanding of 'God' has implications for Soelle's approach to evil and the suffering that results from it. Rather than seek cosmic explanations for human misfortune, she argues that we should focus on forming practical responses to the problem of evil. For Soelle, such an approach involves solidarity with the sufferer. Whilst such solidarity involves sharing the victim's experience, it also involves aiding the sufferer's attempt to articulate that suffering. In Soelle's words: 'If people cannot speak about their affliction they will be destroyed by it, or swallowed up by apathy.'[28] When Soelle writes of the importance of finding a voice, she does not advocate the voice of the professional academic, versed in the language of theodicy. She is not advocating a discourse which rationalizes evil; her emphasis is with the victim. The task of the theologian/theodicist is to listen to the victim, and to help them find a voice to speak of their suffering. If Soelle offers a theodicy at all, it is a victim-centred one.[29]

The 'anti-theodicist' case has not gone unchallenged. James Wetzel has offered a highly critical appraisal of the anti-theodicist's stance.[30] According to Wetzel, anti-theodicists base their argument to a large extent upon the claim that the theodicist is insensitive to human suffering. While Wetzel accepts the need to be aware of the reality of human suffering, he argues that philosophical reflection upon evil and suffering is necessary if we are to make sense of our place in the universe. However, the critics of theodicy suggest that voices other than that of the professional academic must be heard if we are to come anywhere close to understanding the phenomenon of human suffering.

Understanding evil without God: Mary Midgley

If Phillips and Soelle have gone some way to challenging the concept of God which in part leads to the philosophical problem of evil, Mary Midgley offers an account of evil which denies that it is a theological problem.[31] She sees the theodical exercise as akin to a trial of God, an image which she finds singularly unhelpful. If God does not exist, the drama is pointless. If God does exist, 'he is surely something bigger and more mysterious than a corrupt or stupid official',[32] and therefore to question the ways of God seems a pointless exercise. Regardless of this, the problem evil poses for human beings remains. Midgley significantly shifts the focus of debate in the direction of the human, and, as such, is primarily concerned with moral evil. Why do people act in the way in which they do? If we can go some way to understanding that, Midgley hopes that we will be able to combat the wicked impulses in ourselves.

Midgley's account begins with a definition of evil surprisingly similar to Augustine's: 'Evil is . . . essentially the absence of good.'[33] Evil is a lack of goodness, rather than some thing in its own right. From this point, she goes on to argue that all have the capacity to do evil. The wicked do not form a separate group within society – would that they did, for then it would be easy to identify the wicked person! As it is, the wicked are just like 'the rest of us', and Midgley cites some words of Erich Fromm with approval: 'As long as one believes that the evil man wears horns, one will not discover an evil man.'[34] It is precisely this perceived connection between the good and the wicked that gives Midgley's account its impetus. If we are to avoid acting wickedly, it is important to identify that which motivates 'the wicked' themselves, for their motivations are not dissimilar to our own. In attempting to identify the wicked, Midgley accepts the difficulty of the task for precisely the reasons already given. She is hesitant about using examples like the Nazis to make her case, as such examples may lead to the belief that the wicked are 'foreigners with funny accents'. However, she feels that it is important at least to attempt such an identification, and in so doing she makes a distinction between two types of wickedness.

The first type of wickedness she identifies with 'the follower'. These are the people who let themselves become passive instruments of evil. They lack the imagination to see beyond their own petty concerns to the broader effects of their actions. As an example (somewhat at odds with her hesitance about using the Nazis), Midgley chooses Adolf Eichmann. One of the leading figures of the Nazi party, Eichmann was responsible for ensuring that the transports of Jews to the concentration camps arrived 'efficiently'. Hannah Arendt offered an account of Eichmann's trial which forms the basis for Midgley's discussion of the characteristics of the follower. In Arendt's words: 'It was sheer thoughtlessness – something by no means identical with stupidity – that predisposed him to become one of the greatest criminals of that period.'[35] From reading accounts of Eichmann's defence of his actions, it appears that his sole motivation was the furtherance of his own career; at no point does he seem to have considered the effect of those actions on the lives of others.

If the followers act from a lack of imagination, the 'instigators' of evil, who constitute Midgley's second group, initiate the evil act. According to Midgley the instigators act wickedly because one motive comes to dominate at the cost of other (balancing) motives. For example, pride and ambition are not qualities that are wicked in themselves; they only lead to evil action if they are not balanced by other qualities such as compassion and altruism:

> The positive motives which move [the instigators] may not be bad at all; they are often quite decent ones like prudence, loyalty, self-fulfilment and professional conscientiousness. The appalling element lies in the lack of the *other* motives which ought to balance these – in particular, of a proper regard for other people and of a proper priority system which would enforce it.[36]

Midgley's approach is compelling because it attempts to make a connection between our own lives and those of the people we might consider wicked. In so doing, she hopes that we might adopt a more thoughtful approach to life, dominated by a proper concern for others. If we can understand how humans might perpetrate evil acts, we might go some way to avoiding wickedness ourselves; and this, she argues, is a more important task than attempting the academic exercise of justifying in the face of evil a God who may or may not exist.

According to Mary Midgley: 'The problem of evil is not just a problem about God, but an important and difficult problem about individual human psychology' (*Wickedness*, p. 15). To what extent is it sufficient to address the problem of evil without recourse to God?

Conclusion: Evil and the Revision of God

In considering evil, considerable problems with the theistic concept of God emerge. At its most basic, the idea of God's power comes under question in the face of the reality of evil. Theodicists suggest different solutions, but invariably a strong emphasis is placed upon the importance of human freedom to combat the damaging idea that an all-powerful God may fail to act in the face of evil and suffering.

For the critics of theodicy, such an approach is not enough. The critics suggest that evil is not the only problem to be confronted: the theistic concept of God itself must be questioned for it cannot adequately address the reality of human suffering. This leads figures such as Phillips and Soelle to offer concepts of God which are quite different from that offered by the philosophical theist. Midgley's approach to the problem of evil opens the way to a further revision of God. She suggests that bringing God into the equation does little to solve the problem of wickedness and suffering; indeed, it may hinder attempts to come to terms with human responsibility for this phenomenon. This leaves the philosopher of religion with a further problem: to what extent can we talk meaningfully of 'God' in the face of evil?

Stewart Sutherland, whose ideas shall be considered in the next chapter, suggests a different correlation between God and evil.[37] Theodicists start their exploration of evil with the concept of God firmly in place. God is omnipotent, omniscient, immutable, impassible, benevolent, creator. Evil has to be shaped to cohere with this equation. Sutherland rejects such an approach, and argues that we should start with the fact of evil. Given that fact, what kind of God can we coherently talk about? Sutherland believes that if evil is taken seriously, the concept of God will be radically different from that offered by the theist. Evil, then, poses a major challenge to theism. In responding to it theologically, the attributes habitually assigned to God need to be reviewed, and the idea of divinity considered anew.

II Natural Histories of Religion

Introduction

Another significant way of discrediting religious belief is the attempt to show that it is founded, not on the laudable and virtuous human response to divine revelation, but, rather, in the frailty of human nature and intellect. A 'natural history of religion' constitutes precisely this. As the name (coined by David Hume) suggests, such a natural history will conceive of religion as having a natural, rather than a supernatural, origin: an origin as Hume says, 'in human nature'.[38] We will consider two such groups of natural histories: those which explain religion as the inevitable product of ignorance, an early and outdated form of science; and those which explain the idea of God as a projection of the human mind.

Religion as Mistake

Hume's *Dialogues Concerning Natural Religion*, as we have already seen, constitute Hume's attempt to undermine the rational foundations of religious faith. He castigates religion for having little evidence in its favour, and much against it. If we accept Hume's arguments, we can hardly contend that the religious view of the world is justified. The 'religious hypothesis' will seem to us to be a mistaken one, and once we have rejected the intellectual credentials of religion, we may wish to probe into its *causes*. In *The Natural History of Religion*, Hume pursues precisely this approach.

He begins by asserting that the earliest form of religion was polytheistic, the worship of many gods. When Hume considers such a system of belief he concludes that it cannot have arisen through the rational contemplation of nature (as in the teleological argument). Rather, it arises out of fear: 'the first ideas of religion arose not from a contemplation of the works of nature, but from a concern with regard to the events of life, and from the incessant hopes and fears, which actuate the human mind.'[39] So primitive human beings were moved by fear of death, of illness, of natural disaster; moved by the hope for food, for a good harvest, for fair weather. Through a process of personification, the objects of these fears and hopes become transformed into deities. Primitive humanity experiences awesome powers in the world: raging seas, destructive winds, a warming sun, a nourishing earth. They then proceed to ascribe divine personality to these powers and forces. Natural forces cease to be impersonal, inanimate things, and become gods.

Monotheists might feel entirely comfortable with this analysis of the origin and nature of polytheism, but what is most crucial (and subversive) in Hume's account is his argument that monotheism does not have a cause separate from polytheism, but is, rather, a *development* of it. Monotheism develops out of polytheism when one god in the pantheon receives more attention than the rest and becomes dominant. The primitives come greatly to fear this god, and praise him to the detriment of the other gods, until these others are finally forgotten altogether. Hume's conclusion is thus severe: monotheism, traditionally the focus of philosophy of religion, is not the product of reason at all, but is simply the final product of a long and unfortunate process of fear, ignorance and superstition.

Moreover, it is not just the origin of religion which is less than perfect. Just as religion is caused by fear and ignorance, so it thrives best in those conditions and consequently seeks to maintain and nourish them. Hence Hume's glum remark 'that in matters of religion men take a pleasure in being terrify'd, and that no preachers are so popular, as those who excite the most dismal and gloomy passions'.[40] So Hume, highlighting as typical of religion such features as bigotry, cruelty and persecution, concludes that religion stands in the way of human happiness and fulfilment, and constitutes a debilitating barrier to progress. Noting the detrimental effect of religion on morality – for religion promotes useless rituals rather than good life conduct – Hume remarks scathingly: 'Survey most nations and most ages. Examine the religious principles which have, in fact, prevailed in the world. You will scarcely be persuaded, that they are anything but sick men's dreams.'[41]

Hume's analysis of the origins of religion was groundbreaking, and his thoughts find an echo in the work of the Victorian anthropologists E. B. Tylor and J. G. Frazer.[42] These writers share with Hume the intention to explain religion by uncovering its origins, but they were also able to form their thoughts in the light of the most significant intellectual development of their time, for in 1859 Charles Darwin published his *Origin of Species*. This book expounded the theory of gradual evolution by natural selection, and the human species was placed squarely within this process. Fired with enthusiasm for this theory, anthropologists felt that they could apply the evolutionary schema to matters of human culture. So just as we see in biological evolution a process of progressive development, so anthropology could expect to chart the progress of the human mind and of human institutions from the earliest times through to the present. This provides, if you like, a warrant for Hume's pre-evolutionary account of religion, and presents to us a very radical idea. In the words of Eric Sharpe, 'viewed in Darwinian perspective, religion became something which it had never really been before. From being a body of revealed truth, it became a developing organism.'[43] It is this kind of evolutionary framework which forms the backdrop to Tylor's *Primitive Culture*. As an evolutionist, Tylor believes that human culture proceeds from lower to higher forms in mostly unbroken sequence, and he contends that so-called 'primitive' cultures provide us with surviving evidence of the earliest cultures. Existing primitive peoples, their institutions and psychology, constitute graphic evidence of what Tylor called 'the childhood of the species': in modern primitives we see the condition of primitive humanity. So when the question arises concerning the earliest form of religion, Tylor's response is to consider the form of religion practised by extant primitives. He locates this form of religion in what he calls 'animism', a belief in spiritual beings, and he suggests that the origin of animism lies in the mistaken explanation of two puzzling phenomena: dreams and death:

It seems as though thinking men, as yet at a low level of culture, were deeply impressed by two groups of biological problems. In the first place, what is it that makes the difference between a living body and a dead one; what causes working, sleep, trance, disease, death? In the second place, what are these human shapes which appear in dreams and visions? Looking at these two groups of phenomena, the ancient savage philosophers probably made their first step by the obvious inference that every man has two things belonging to him, namely, a life and a phantom.[44]

These, says Tylor, are perfectly rational inferences, based on the plain evidence of the primitive's senses. The earliest religion thus arises, not from irrational fantasies, but from empirical hypotheses, which just happen to be mistaken. They are mistaken because dreams are not to be accounted for by means of out-of-the-body experiences or the visitations of ghosts; nor is death to be accounted for by the soul's departure from the body. These things can be better explained materialistically. Animism is thus rational, but mistaken. From these mistaken inferences, the idea of animism progresses through polytheism until we eventually arrive at monotheism, which Tylor dubs 'the animism of civilized man'. But Christianity in the modern world is no more than a survival of a rude and mistaken belief, and animism's errors are its errors also. Religion has no meaningful role in modern culture, and is only found in varying degrees of decline as scientific progress robs it of its earlier prominence.

Tylor's thought epitomizes the nature of that stance in anthropology known as *intellectualism*. In Tylor's hands it takes the following form: how are we to understand the religion of primitives? Only by attributing to the primitive some measure of rational thought; the primitive is conceived as a philosopher, trying to make sense of the world. In this instance the primitive's conjectures concern the nature of the human person, and this leads to the mistaken belief that the world is peopled with spiritual beings. Essentially, Tylor credits the primitive with rational thought, but it is the thought of a child who might consider that its toys have souls. We in the west are less childlike: we have no need for childish religion.

Like Tylor, James Frazer also sets out to chart the history and development of religion. Furthermore, again like Tylor, he supplies an intellectualist analysis: religious beliefs are mistaken theories about the world, and religious rituals are mistaken and futile attempts to influence the course of nature. In his classic work *The Golden Bough* Frazer traces the development of three competing 'philosophies of life': magic, religion and science. Strictly speaking, these should be called 'philosophies of nature', as all three arise from a contemplation of the natural world. Just as Tylor thought that religion emerges as a result of philosophical deliberation on the nature of the human self, so Frazer sees it as a product of deliberation on the outside world. But religion is not, for Frazer, the earliest of mankind's philosophies, for it is preceded by *magic*. Magical action is, says Frazer, the result of a theory about the nature of causality; it is the product of theorizing about the nature of events as they happen in the world. The savage philosopher finds himself in a world which he wishes to understand and control. In an effort to explain the natural world the savage formulates two laws which are subsequently applied in the magical attempt to manipulate nature. The first law is called by Frazer the Law of Homoeopathy (or Similarity). It states that 'like produces like', meaning that causes resemble effects. So imagine that a magician wants to kill an enemy. Employing the Law of Homoeopathy, the magician will fashion an image of that enemy and proceed to destroy the effigy, either by burning it or by running a needle into its head or heart. As effects resemble causes, the person represented by the effigy will suffer a corresponding injury, and will be destroyed as the effigy is destroyed. Of course, homoeopathic magic can have less nefarious uses: if rain is required in times of drought, a magician may sprinkle water on the ground in the belief that this imitation of rain will produce the real thing.

The second law is called the Law of Contiguity, and states that things which have once been in contact with each other continue to act on each other at a distance after the physical contact has been severed. To illustrate the application of this law, someone wishing to harm an enemy may gather together some cuttings of that person's hair, some nail clippings, blood, spittle or clothing, and then burn them. The continued sym-

pathy between these items and the person to whom they be-
longed will produce in the latter a like result.

Homoeopathic and contagious magic can be brought together
under the rubric of 'Sympathetic Magic'. They are also alike in
that both are totally futile and hopeless. Frazer remarks: 'Magic
is a spurious system of natural law as well as a fallacious guide
of conduct; it is a false science as well as an abortive art.'[45] Magic,
then, for Frazer is mistaken. The belief which lies behind it is
that one can alter the course of nature simply by imitating it: this
is, of course, plainly wrong.

Inevitably, the inherent futility of magic is eventually dis-
covered by those sagacious enough to perceive that their cherished incantations and rites do not work – that, for example,
the 'victims' of effigy-burning continue to live – and they form
the opinion that what controls the course of nature is not a
system of impersonal laws which one can bend to one's own
needs, but rather certain gods or deities which one must appeal
to, make sacrifices to, pray to, and so on. Thus, religion is born
out of the recognized futility of magic. But like magic, religion
too is jettisoned once it is recognized that the gods are superflu-
ous, and that nature functions regularly rather than through
the capricious whims of supernatural agents: 'in short, religion,
regarded as an explanation of nature, is displaced by science'.[46]

The intellectualist explanation of religion is in many ways chari-
table to religion and its adherents, for despite the fact that it is
regarded as entirely fallacious, it is seen as a hypothesis which
was entirely rational in its own time. Hence Frazer's judgement
that the religious beliefs of our ancestors 'were not wilful ex-
travagances or the ravings of insanity, but simply hypotheses,
justifiable as such at the time when they were propounded but
which a fuller experience has proved to be inadequate'.[47] Nevertheless, there is little of comfort for the religious believer in what
Hume, Tylor and Frazer have to say. Religion is a mistake, and it
belongs to the past.

Projections, Illusions and Neuroses

To view religious beliefs as mistaken hypotheses about the nature of the world is to provide a fairly economical way of dispos-

ing of them. There is no truth in the religious view of the world: it is simply an antiquated and by now bankrupt way of explaining how things are. Hence, for Tylor and Frazer the true meaning of religious beliefs lies in their being outdated and futile 'proto-science'. There are, however, a number of other writers who have maintained that while religion, considered literally as a system of beliefs about supernatural realities, is most certainly false, it does contain an element of truth. This truth will not, nevertheless, be recognizable to the religious adherents themselves. In order to uncover the truth of religion, the philosopher has to sift through the surface confusions and errors of a religious system – what can be termed the *manifest* content of religion – in order to arrive at its true meaning, otherwise known as its *latent* content. While Tylor and Frazer were not much concerned with the meaning of the objects of religion (with the meaning of God), these other writers focus specifically on this issue.

For all these writers, God is ultimately seen as a *projection* of something of great concern to human beings. The pioneer in this approach to the meaning of religion is Ludwig Feuerbach (1804–72). Feuerbach's account of religious belief has as its starting point the firm conviction that religion as traditionally understood by the theologian is false. As a fairly radical empiricist, Feuerbach contends that human knowledge can only be reached through the evidence of the senses: 'But God is not seen, not heard, not perceived by the senses.'[48] There is a contradiction between those statements that are ceaselessly made about God – that he is omnipotent, omniscient, and so on – and a lack of evidence in favour of these claims: 'A necessary consequence of this contradiction is Atheism.'[49] As we will later see, this is a theme that resonates in the work of the logical positivists. Feuerbach's atheism is necessitated also by his profound materialism. His view is that thought is only possible because there are bodily creatures capable of thinking. If thought is thus dependent upon embodiment and if only bodily things can be said to exist, then it begins to appear suspect that theism posits belief in some non-material being. Driven by the complementary demands of empiricism and materialism, Feuerbach's position is that whatever 'God' means, it cannot refer to some supernatural entity which exists independently of human thought and imagination.

So, what is Feuerbach's conclusion about the meaning of God?

The answer to this question centres on the idea of a projection of what Feuerbach calls the 'human essence'. God must be re-interpreted so that it means simply the nature of the human species, projected outwards and conceived as a separate being:

> Religion is the dream of the human mind. But even in dreams we do not find ourselves in emptiness or in heaven, but on earth, in the realm of reality; we only see real things in the entrancing splendour of imagination and caprice, instead of in the simple daylight of reality and necessity. Hence I do nothing more to religion . . . than to open its eyes.[50]

In part, Feuerbach's analysis of the latent meaning of religion, and hence of the nature of God, implies a form of wish-fulfilment, such as we will find later elaborated by Freud. As a dream, religion has the status of something like a fantasy. It presents the world as humans would like it to be. The world in which people live is cruel, and yet here in religion, in the belief in God, humans can find compensation for all their sufferings. And it is in fact in the harshest of conditions, in the deepest of sufferings, that religion flourishes most: 'The more empty life is, the fuller, the more concrete is God . . . Only the poor man has a rich God.'[51]

It is worth at this point pausing in our presentation of Feuerbach's insights so as to note the influence of this last thought on Karl Marx (1818–83). Though Marx makes no attempt at a natural history of religion, he provides a significant contribution to the analysis of religion by contending that religion serves to prop up the *status quo*. It does this through the very feature highlighted above by Feuerbach: the poor in society are compensated for their sufferings and poverty by the promise of spiritual wealth in the life to come. The poor thus become resigned to their lot, and are numbed into a state of compliance with their oppressors. Emphasizing this drug-like capacity of religion, Marx writes: 'Religion is the sigh of the oppressed creature, the heart of a heartless world, just as it is the spirit of a spiritless situation. It is the opium of the people.'[52] Marx is in no doubt that this state of affairs must change if the people are ever to achieve real fulfilment: illusory happiness must be replaced with real happiness.

This can only be done through a revolutionary change in the social structure and the introduction of a communist state, in which the fulfilment of the people results in a withering away of the illusions offered by religion.

It would, however, be a gross misrepresentation of Feuerbach's account of religion if it were left simply that he viewed belief in God as a manifestation of all too human wishes. Alongside this feature of his analysis, there is considerable assessment of what the belief in God amounts to; and in our conclusion we will return to this aspect of his thought. Suffice it to say at this point that Feuerbach's account allows that religion does provide humans with a degree of knowledge, knowledge which is, albeit, indirect: 'Religion is man's earliest and also indirect form of self-knowledge. Hence, religion everywhere precedes philosophy . . . Man first of all sees his nature as if out of himself, before he finds it in himself. His own nature is in the first instance contemplated by him as that of another being.'[53] So the worship of God serves to provide humans with an image of their own nature. Viewed as the belief in a distinct being, religion is undeniably false, but as a picture of the essence of the human it is an accurate picture:

> Religion, at least the Christian, is the relation of man to himself, or more correctly to his own nature . . . The divine being is nothing else than the human being, or, rather, the human nature purified, freed from the limits of the individual man, made objective – i.e., contemplated and revered as another, a distinct being. All the attributes of the divine nature are, therefore, attributes of the human nature.[54]

So there is no distinction between the human and the divine. Once this is recognized, of course, belief in God must be surrendered. What we must do is say that such attributes as have been predicated of God actually belong to us, to human beings, and we – Prometheus-like – will take them for ourselves.

Feuerbach's picture of religious belief has been deeply influential, and we can see how it was applied in sociological analysis by turning our attention to the writings of Emile Durkheim (1858–1917). In his classic work *The Elementary Forms of the*

Religious Life, he sets out to examine the earliest form of religion in order to throw light on the essential nature of religion as such. Durkheim locates this earliest form of religion in *totemism*, a system of belief and societal classification, whereby tribes are divided into clans, each of which is identified with a separate totem animal, plant or other natural phenomenon (say, rain or thunder). In Australian Aboriginal society, there are a number of totemic groups, each of which is associated with a specific and peculiar totem, and emblems sacred to each totemic group or clan are portrayed on a number of sacred ritual objects. Durkheim's analysis shows how a specific group is identified by its objects of worship, and in such a fashion he establishes a significant link between the totem (the god) and the society which worships that god. This much is uncontentious. After all, Yahweh was significantly linked with the people of Israel. But Durkheim goes much further than simply saying that there is a link between the god and the society. Durkheim's connection between god and society is analogous to Feuerbach's connection between god and humanity:

> The totem is before else a symbol, a material expression of something else. But of what? . . . It expresses and symbolizes two different sorts of things . . . In the first place, it is the outward and visible form of what we have called the totemic principle or god. But it is also the symbol of a determined society or clan. It is its flag; it is the sign by which each clan distinguishes itself from the others . . . So if it is at once the symbol of the god and of the society, is that not because the society and the god are only one?[55]

In other words, 'the god is only a figurative expression of the society'.[56]

This is a prime example of projectionism. Some element of the human realm is pushed outward into a 'supernatural' realm and deified. As with Feuerbach's account, Durkheim's analysis of the nature of religion includes both cognitive and emotive elements. We saw how for Feuerbach the idea of God provided humanity with its first form of self-knowledge. Likewise for Durkheim, religion provides primitive man with an indirect form of knowledge concerning the nature of society. So there is some kind of truth in religion, in the idea of God, only it has to be recovered by the expert, recovered from its manifest clothing. On the manifest level, religion is of course plainly false. As Durkheim remarks, 'It is certain that religions are mistaken in regard to the real nature of things; science has proved it.'[57] An example may go some way to illustrate this point: people perform a rain dance; but rain does not follow as a result of that dance. We can, with Frazer, thus attribute to the ritualists a bizarre level of stupidity. But Durkheim is loathe to do this and suggests instead that the underlying purpose of that dance is to achieve something other than hastening rain. The real meaning of the rain dance is its function as the expression of a shared desire for rain. Here the emotive (or expressive) dimension of religion is brought into play: religious rituals serve to bind together a community in their hopes and fears, maintaining social stability.[58] Later sociologists and anthropologists have picked up on this dimension of Durkheim's account, and have left his more ambitious projectionist claims behind. Such writers stress the way in which performance of religious rituals can function as an important release of dangerous emotions, and serve to cement social ties. Hence, A. R. Radcliffe-Brown writes: 'An orderly social life amongst human beings depends upon the presence in the minds of the members of a society of certain sentiments, which control the behaviour of the individual in his relation to others. Rites can be seen to be the regulated symbolic expressions of certain sentiments.'[59] This is, however, some way removed from (though perhaps more plausible than) the boldest of Durkheim's claims, that the origin and nature of religion lies in a projection of society.

Finally, we turn to what is probably the most controversial natural history of religion. This can be found in the writings of the founder of psychoanalysis, Sigmund Freud (1856–1939). Freud's account is multi-faceted, and while much of it is reminiscent of writers previously considered, it constitutes a fascinating analysis of both the origins and the nature of religion. Firstly, in *The Future of an Illusion*, Freud presents religious beliefs as wish-fulfilling *illusions*. Freud means by this something like the following. Human beings find themselves in a world which is not at all conducive to their happiness. They have to suffer the pain and indignity of illness, angst, failure and, ultimately, death. How pleasant if things were different, if death were not the end to our strivings, if there were a powerful benevolent figure who cared about our fate! Religion offers us all of this, while at the same time having no evidence in favour of its truth. This leads Freud to claim that religious beliefs are 'illusions, fulfilments of the oldest, strongest and most urgent wishes of mankind'.[60] Freud is careful to state that an illusion is not an error, but it does mean that 'a wish-fulfilment is a prominent factor in its development',[61] and that it offers compensation for this-worldly sufferings. Freud even adopts a Marx-like tone when he likens the effects of religious beliefs to that of a narcotic. But there is a further dimension to Freud's account. When the religious believer personifies the threatening forces of nature, this gives him/her the apparent possibility of influencing the course of events: we are no longer helpless in the face of impersonal forces, for these forces are now seen as gods, and we can influence and appease them through prayer, ritual and sacrifice.

What is, however, most distinctive about Freud's account is his contention that religion is analogous to a neurosis. He stresses this in *Totem and Taboo*, significantly subtitled 'Some points of agreement between the mental lives of savages and neurotics'.[62] The most notorious aspect of this book is Freud's postulation of the historical starting point of belief in God. Taking up one of Darwin's conjectures, Freud suggests that human beings originally lived in small hordes, each of which was under the absolute rule of an older male who had exclusive sexual rights over all the females and who drove away all his sons as they grew up. The sons, resenting and fearing their father, one day used their combined strength to slaughter and – as cannibals – devour the despotic father. This primal act of parricide brought an end to the father's rule, but it also spawned something else: feelings of regret, remorse and guilt. The murderers had hated their father, but they loved and admired him too. And even though dead, the sons still feared the father, who became stronger than the living one had been. As an attempt to appease him, the sons instituted rites and moral rules, and as a commemoration of the terrible act they set up a meal in which a totem animal – the representative of the father – is eaten. The earthly father is projected outwards and becomes the god. Hence the beginnings of religion, founded on the remorseful actions of murderers and on an elevated father-fixation. For Freud, talk of God is no accidental symbolism, for 'at bottom God is nothing other than an exalted father'.[63] This idea of God also plays its part in the analysis of religion as wish-fulfilment, for, when children, we felt safe and protected by a super-powerful father. As adults, at the mercy of the world, we have a overwhelming desire for protection, and it is this notion of an eternal, omnipotent and loving father which fulfils this desire.

> Both Freud and Tylor, in their own way, suggest that religion is infantile in character. What aspects of religious behaviour might lead you to agree with them? How might a believer counter their charges?

It is Freud's conception of the 'Oedipus complex' which serves to liken these religious origins to a neurosis. In the Oedipus complex, which Freud maintains is universal, a boy around the age of four has the strong desire to murder his father and have sexual relations with his mother. This is, in other words, the exact same pathological phenomenon which brings about the primal parricide. Moreover, Freud is adamant that if we observe the actions of the religious we find that these actions are similar in character to the actions of people with obsessional neuroses. An example of this is what Freud calls 'the bed ceremonial': before he can go to sleep a particular neurotic must make sure that his chair stands in a particular place beside the bed; pillows and bedclothes must be placed or folded in exactly such and such a manner; and the neurotic's own body must lie in a precisely defined position. If these actions are not carried out in full and in the correct order the patient becomes seriously aggravated. Freud is impressed by the resemblance between such neurotic 'ceremonials' and ceremonials proper; for instance, the taking of the Eucharist or the recitation of formulaic prayers and incantations: 'It is easy to see where the resemblances lie between neurotic ceremonials and the sacred acts of religious ritual: in the qualms of conscience brought on by their neglect, in their complete isolation from all other actions and in the conscientiousness with which they are carried out in every detail.'[64]

So all these factors – the wish-fulfilling character of compensatory religious beliefs, the origins of religion in a pathological act, the father-fixation manifested in monotheism, and the close connections between ritual and obsessional actions – lead Freud to a damning conclusion about religion. It is condemned as 'the universal obsessional neurosis of humanity'.[65]

Conclusion: Assessing Natural Histories of Religion

So what can be concluded about these natural histories? Do they provide us with proof of the falsity of religion? Probably not. Most of the theories we have considered will not stand up to close scrutiny. We have not the space here to examine each one in detail, but common features will suffice to illustrate what is problematic in these accounts. These features concern the emphasis placed on the *origins* of religion. All the thinkers we have surveyed feel that the nature and validity of religion can be assessed by uncovering its origins. Hence, religion originated out of fear and ignorance, and is, consequently, fearful and ignorant; it grew out of a collective Oedipus complex and hence constitutes a father-fixation. The problem here is that to pursue such a line would be to commit a logical error known as 'the genetic fallacy'. It is a mistake to think that factors in the genesis of an institution or belief are relevant to its truth or falsity. So *even if* religion developed, say, out of some collective neurosis, this would have no bearing on the question of whether religious beliefs were true. Moreover, what on earth would possess us to be convinced that an account of religion's origins, such as that offered by Freud or by Tylor, was accurate? How could we ever know for sure that this corresponded to the true origins of religion? With Evans-Pritchard, we have to say that these natural histories have the quality of Rudyard Kipling's *Just So Stories*, like 'How the leopard got his spots': religion may have arisen in the way Hume, Tylor, et al. suggest, but we have no way of knowing for sure.[66]

On the other hand, it would be wrong to suggest that these

analyses of religion can have no value in our deliberations concerning its validity. It must surely affect our judgement as to the truth of religion to learn that religious ideas are more prevalent in cultures where knowledge is less advanced than it is the western world; or that ideas prevalent in religious thought, concerning spirits and disembodied agents, are typical of more primitive thought-processes. We cannot fail to be impressed by such material as it is presented to us by, say, Feuerbach, showing how closely the idea of God resembles a vastly magnified human being. And perhaps most significantly, and as Freud isolated, the fact that, in the absence of reliable evidence, religious beliefs express things *as we would like them to be* must give us cause to wonder whether such beliefs may indeed constitute wishful illusions.

III Religious Language and Verification

Introduction

We have so far surveyed two challenges to theism. The problem of evil highlights how the world as we encounter it constitutes some form of evidence against the belief in a loving God. Natural histories of religion contend that religion has a cause within human nature and that belief in God is either a mistake or else a disguised representation of something more mundane, be it human nature, society or an elevated father-figure. These are important challenges. A third challenge is no less important. It focuses on the language of religion, and contends that this language is meaningless. As with so many criticisms of religion, this challenge can be traced back in part to David Hume, who, in the closing words of his *Enquiry Concerning Human Understanding*, wrote:

> When we run over libraries . . . what havoc must we make? If we take in our hand any volume; of divinity or school metaphysics, for instance; let us ask, *Does it contain any abstract reasoning concerning quantity or number?* No. *Does it contain any experimental reasoning concerning matter of fact and existence?* No. Commit it then to the flames: for it can contain nothing but sophistry and illusion.[67]

Hume's point is that if we encounter a form of discourse which appears to make statements about the way things are but which has no grounding in experience, and is not checkable by experience, then it is worthless. Religion is just such a form of discourse. It must thus be 'committed to the flames'. In the twentieth century this attack on religion has received greater elaboration at the hands of radical empiricists, but before we examine their challenge, we should note the form of some earlier debates about religious language.

Maimonides and Aquinas on the Nature of Talk about God

The problem that was central to medieval philosophers and theologians largely concerned the extent to which it was possible to say anything descriptive of God. We learn words by their application in a worldly, human context. So we learn what the words 'wise' and 'kind' mean by seeing examples of wise people and by witnessing actions of kindness. But as well as saying that certain people are wise and kind, we also tend to speak of God as being wise and kind (and a whole lot of other things besides). This, however, results in a problem, for we are inclined to say that God is substantially unlike human beings, or other things in the world. If this is the case, and if our words are only designed to speak about worldly things, how can we use our worldly language to speak about something so otherworldly and different as God? One response to this problem was offered by the Jewish philosopher Moses Maimonides (1135–1204). Aware that the nature of God would be severely misrepresented if attributes taken from the human context were applied unambiguously to him, Maimonides maintains instead that God is entirely unknowable, and that one can talk meaningfully of him only to the extent of saying what he is not. This position, known as *negative predication*, avoids the unhappy consequence of treating 'God is wise' in the same way as 'Socrates is wise'. For Maimonides, when we say 'God is wise' we are saying nothing positive about God at all; rather, we are simply closing off certain unwanted conceptions. So when we say, for example, that God is a living god, we simply mean that

God is *not dead*. Maimonides believes that by such a system of predication we can eventually arrive at a sound conception of the nature of God. To this end, he supplies the example of finding out what a ship is by only being told what it is not. A person may be told a whole string of things about the ship; that it is not a plant, that it is not round, nor flat. Given enough of this negative information, Maimonides argues, one will eventually have arrived at the concept of a ship, even if one had never seen a ship. Likewise, it is possible to come closer to knowledge of God through consideration of what God is not.[68]

Against this, it has to be said that it is nowhere near self-evident that a person ignorant of the nature of ships will achieve sound understanding through Maimonides' method. If this is the case with regard to something worldly like ships, then how much more difficult must it be to arrive at an adequate notion of God (i.e. something entirely alien to us) by the same procedure? As a result, and though Maimonides was certainly right to point to the pitfalls of thinking that God could be described in the same manner as one would describe another human being, many other philosophers tried to find a way of speaking in a more positive manner about God. Perhaps the most important of these was Aquinas.

In the *Summa Theologiae*, Aquinas considers the nature of words traditionally predicated of God. Such predicates, for example wisdom and goodness, are of necessity drawn from the human realm. When applied to God, are these words used in a *univocal* or an *equivocal* fashion? To say that a word is used univocally is to say that it has the same meaning on each of two appearances (for example, the word 'politician' in 'Tony Blair is a politician' and 'William Hague is a politician'). To use a word equivocally, on the other hand, is to use that word in a completely different sense (compare the word 'bank' in the sentences 'She deposited her savings in the bank' and 'He walked along the river bank'). So if we now consider the statements 'God is wise' and 'Socrates is wise', is the predicate 'wise' being used univocally or equivocally?

Aquinas rejects both options, stressing that it is impossible to predicate anything univocally of God and creatures. The reason for this is that what God is not 'is clearer to us than what he is'.[69] Does this mean, then, that predicates must be applied equivocally? Certainly not. Aquinas argues against this position by appealing to St Paul's words in the Letter to the Romans: 'The invisible things of God are made known by those things that are made' (Romans 1:20). In other words, and parallel to the endeavour to argue from the world to God by means of the cosmological and teleological proofs, the nature of God is made known to us via the things we see in the world. In rejecting both univocal and equivocal predication, Aquinas argues for a middle way: *analogical predication*. The example Aquinas provides for this way is that of the word 'healthy': we say of a particular man that he is healthy, but we also say that his diet is healthy, and that he produces a healthy specimen of urine. In none of these three cases is the word 'healthy' being used in exactly the same sense, but neither is it used equivocally. Rather, both healthy diet and healthy urine have some relation to health in the man: the diet is the cause of the man's health, the urine a sign of it. The three uses of 'healthy' thus have an analogical or 'proportional' relation. Applying this to the case of God, then, we may say that if God is, as Aquinas maintains, the first cause of the world, then God is the cause of everything. So we may say 'God is love' because God is the cause of love.

> Write one paragraph which explains the difference between negative predication, positive predication and analogical predication.

Much more could be said about the medieval approach to religious language.[70] But our focus in this chapter is on challenges to religious belief, and this impels us to address more contemporary debates, which are not so much concerned with the meaning of the predicates typically applied to God; rather, the atheistic challenge to religion is whether its characteristic discourse has *any meaning at all*. The charge that religious language is meaningless is most generally associated with a group of scientifically minded philosophers called the Vienna Circle. Their philosophical position is known as logical positivism.

The Positivist Challenge to Religious Belief

The claim that religious utterance is devoid of meaning (that, for example, the statement 'God created the world' is meaningless and hence *incapable* of being true) can be seen to have its roots in the writings of Hume, but also in the early philosophy of Ludwig Wittgenstein (1889–1951).

In his *Tractatus Logico-Philosophicus*, Wittgenstein attempted to impose strict limits on what could meaningfully be said. Wittgenstein's theory of meaning stems in part from his being struck by an incident in a French court case, where a road accident was reconstructed in the court room by means of model vehicles and figures. It seemed to Wittgenstein that this model threw light on the way in which language related to the world: just as the model of the accident serves as a three-dimensional 'picture' of the actual accident, so the words and propositions of *language* must function as pictures of objects and facts in the *world*. It is not surprising, then, that this account of language has come to be known as the 'picture theory of meaning'. Hence: 'In order to understand the essential nature of a proposition, we should consider hieroglyphic script, which depicts the facts that it describes. And alphabetic script developed out of it without losing what was essential to depiction.'[71]

Given that language is essentially pictorial, then, the meaning of a statement (say, 'The cat sat on the mat') will be the fact that it depicts (a cat sitting on a mat). Apart from tautologies (analytic statements such as 'All bachelors are unmarried males'), it is such fact-depicting uses of language which alone constitute meaningful discourse. So 'the totality of true propositions is the whole of natural science',[72] and as a consequence, all that is uttered which is non-scientific, which cannot be reduced to a pictorial representation of a fact, is without meaning. Thus, when someone wants to talk about ethics (what is right or wrong), about aesthetics (what is beautiful), about metaphysics or about the objects of religion, then that person has 'failed to give a meaning to certain signs in his propositions'.[73] In other words, an ethical statement (for example, 'Stealing is wrong') does not picture any fact (contrast with 'Bill stole a car'), and the value judgement cannot be pictorially represented. It therefore signifies nothing and is without meaning. Wittgenstein's verdict is severe: 'Whereof one cannot speak, thereof one must be silent.'[74]

This account of language was deeply appealing to Rudolf Carnap, Moritz Schlick and other members of the Vienna Circle, and in the 1920s they and Wittgenstein added an empiricist element to it. The criterion of meaning which they developed became known as the *verification principle*. This principle admits both strong and weak formulations. Wittgenstein gave voice to a strong version of the principle when he said: 'If I can never verify the sense of a proposition completely, then I cannot have meant anything by the proposition either. Then the proposition signifies nothing whatsoever.'[75] What does this principle mean? Wittgenstein seems to be suggesting something like this. If I say to you, 'The sun will rise tomorrow', then the meaningfulness of that statement lies in the fact that I can conclusively verify (or prove) it. I can, in other words, show you the sun rising on the morning after I have made that statement. When the principle is applied to the language of religion, a diagnosis of meaninglessness is bound to follow. For how could a sentence such as 'God is one in three persons' be conclusively verified? The truth is, of course, that it could not. It is, then, without meaning.

The problem with the strong verification principle is that it disallows too much. There are many statements that are obviously meaningful which would be condemned as meaningless if the strong principle is applied. Take the statement, 'All mice like cheese'. This is surely meaningful, and almost certainly correct, but it cannot be conclusively verified, for it is beyond my powers to observe all mice (including all living mice, and those who lived in the past and those who will live in the future). Problems like this lead to the rejection of the strong principle, and reliance instead on a weaker version.

This weak verification principle is formulated and defended in the seminal work of A. J. Ayer (1910–89), *Language, Truth and Logic*. While the strong principle seeks conclusive verification, Ayer's version stresses only that a sentence is verifiable – and thus meaningful – 'if it is possible for experience to render it probable'.[76] Therefore:

We say that the question that must be asked about any putative statement of fact is not, Would any observations make its truth or falsehood logically certain? but simply, Would any observations be relevant to the determination of its truth or falsehood? And it is only if a negative answer is given to this second question that we conclude that the statement under consideration is non-sensical.[77]

This is certainly more acceptable and more amenable to common sense. All that my previous statement about the eating preferences of mice now depends upon is that some observation be relevant to its truth or falsity. I may, for example, observe a sample of twenty mice; and on the basis that they all happily consume cheese I conclude that all mice like cheese. So all that Ayer is saying is that for a sentence to be factually significant some evidence must be available which is relevant to the question of its truth status.

Though the weak verification principle makes these concessions to common sense, it makes no such concessions to religion. It is, indeed, just as damning of religious discourse as its more vociferous brother. Let us return to the trinitarian claim. What observations would be relevant to determining whether God was one in three persons? What sort of empirical evidence could we gather in favour of the truth of this contention? The truth of the matter is, of course, that we would be entirely at a loss to know what to do if asked to provide such evidence. Given that this is the case, there is, at the very least, a formidable question mark hanging over the factual significance of such religious contentions.

A related attack on the significance of religious language is to be found in the falsificationist challenge. Whereas a verificationist says that religious language is meaningless because it cannot in principle be verified (or because no evidence can count in its favour), a falsificationist claims that religious language is meaningless because it cannot be falsified (or because no evidence can count against it). Inspired by the work of Karl Popper in the philosophy of science, the falsificationist claims that in order for a statement to be meaningful certain factual states of affairs must be incompatible with that statement's truth. If I say, for example, that 'all fires are hot', the meaningfulness of that statement lies in the fact that if certain states of affairs prevail (if we notice that some fires are cold) then it will not be considered true; it will, in other words, have been falsified. If religious statements are to be meaningful, then, they must in principle be capable of falsification. The question is: are they?

It was Antony Flew who best argued the case for the meaninglessness of religious language on these principles. In his contribution to the famous 'University Discussion', Flew elaborates on a parable originally suggested by John Wisdom, in order to argue that because religious assertions deny nothing (in other words, are compatible with any state of affair), they signify nothing either:

> Once upon a time two explorers came upon a clearing in the jungle. In the clearing were growing many flowers and many weeds. One explorer says, 'Some gardener must tend this plot.' The other disagrees, 'There is no gardener.' So they pitch their tents and set a watch. No gardener is ever seen. 'But perhaps he is an invisible gardener.' So they set up a barbed-wire fence. They electrify it. They patrol with bloodhounds. (For they remember how H. G. Wells's *The Invisible Man* could be both smelt and touched though he could not be seen.) But no shrieks ever suggest that some intruder has received a shock. No movements of the wire ever betray an invisible climber. The bloodhounds never give cry. Yet still the Believer is not convinced. 'But there is a gardener, invisible, intangible, insensible to electric shocks, a gardener who has no scent and makes no sound, a gardener who comes secretly to look after the garden which he loves.' At last the Sceptic despairs, 'But what remains of your original assertion? Just how does what you call an invisible, intangible, eternally elusive gardener differ from an imaginary gardener or even from no gardener at all?'[78]

Flew characterizes the religious believer as akin to the explorer who believes in the gardener. Indeed, the religious believer's claims are just as vacuous. In a similar manner to the explorer, the theist begins by proclaiming an impressive cosmological assertion which is then whittled away to nothingness: it dies 'the death of a thousand qualifications'.[79] So a believer may say, for example, 'God loves us as a father loves his children'. This is a bold and indeed reassuring proclamation. Yet certain events make us doubt the truth of it. When we are confronted with abominable suffering we may ask the believer why it is that God stands by and lets his innocent children suffer. Surely no half-decent *earthly* father would allow that! But the theist might respond that God's love is inscrutable; his love is not an earthly love; and so on.[80] While some may find those words reassuring, others may be more sceptical. They may feel that the words lack content, because God's apparent love seems compatible with any situation, however dreadful. And if the statement 'God loves us' *is* so compatible, then it denies nothing and hence asserts nothing either. It is without meaning.

Responses to the Challenge I: Capitulation

Faced with the challenge variously presented by verificationists and falsificationists, some philosophers chose to capitulate, accepting that religion had been shown to be hopelessly faulty if construed as fact-asserting, and attempted to find it a foothold elsewhere. The first traces of such a response can be found in R. M. Hare's response to Flew's challenge. Hare openly concedes that 'on the ground marked out by Flew, he seems to me to be completely victorious'.[81] Nevertheless, he feels that religion is not altogether contentless, and to this end provides another parable which he hopes will throw light on the nature of religion. In the parable, a lunatic believes that all his university teachers want to murder him. Even when presented with the most genial and respectable of lecturers, he remains unconvinced, sure that this geniality is a mask hiding murderous intent. However many lecturers are presented as evidence that he is wrong, he keeps to his story.

If we apply Flew's test to this lunatic, we have to conclude that his theory asserts nothing and is thus without meaning. But it certainly does not follow that there is no difference between the lunatic and those with a more well-adjusted attitude to their teachers. This difference shows itself in the most explicit of ways: through the *behaviour* of the lunatic. Hare characterizes the lunatic's belief in the murderous intentions of lecturers as a *blik*, namely an unfalsifiable interpretation of one's experience. Another example of a *blik* would be the belief that everything happens by *chance*. And it is in terms of *bliks* that Hare says we should understand religious belief.

This has not been seen as a particularly positive way forward for religious belief, as it is simply characterized as a behaviour-influencing irrational fixation. There are, nonetheless, similar capitulating approaches which have a degree of promise. The most significant of these is the interpretation offered by R. B. Braithwaite in his essay, 'An Empiricist's View of the Nature of Religious Belief'. In order fully to understand Braithwaite's stance we need to know a little more about the positivist view of ethics.

Ethical statements, for a positivist like Ayer, pose a certain difficulty. 'Stealing is wrong' looks like a factual assertion, but it fails the verification test: how could one possibly prove that stealing was wrong? Ayer thus contends that ethical statements are not factual assertions; rather, such statements are *emotive* in character. 'Stealing is wrong' essentially means 'Stealing: boo!', or, to be more precise: 'I disapprove of stealing and urge you to do so as well.'[82] In this way, an ethical judgement expresses one's own feelings toward a particular action and attempts to make others feel the same. This analysis provides us with the clue to the positivist-capitulating account of religion offered by Braithwaite.

Braithwaite fully accepts the principle of verification and agrees that it rules out any account of religious discourse as fact-asserting (or *cognitive*). Instead, he claims that, as with ethics, it is best to view religion as having an emotive function. Characteristic religious statements serve, then, not to describe super-empirical realities, but to exhort one to follow a particular way of life, or pattern of acting. For example, the expression 'God created the world' will, on this analysis, not be seen as a cosmological claim, but as, rather, a means of leading one to a particular orientation towards the world. It will entail treating the world with respect, not polluting its rivers, nor exploiting its fruits. On this *non-cognitive* interpretation, one's embracing of the Christian religion does not amount to adherence to a theory of the world, but rather to the intention to lead a certain kind of life. The Christian religion simply is the enter-taining of a particular fictional narrative, which acts as a spur to moral action. Hence: 'A moral belief is an intention to behave in a certain way. A religious belief is an intention to behave in a certain way (a moral belief) together with the entertainment of certain stories associated with the intention in the mind of the believer.'[83] In such a manner, Braithwaite neatly provides a space for religion in the positivist world. Nevertheless, we might feel that his account is rather strained. It depends, of course, on accepting the emotive theory of ethics, and we may be reluctant to do this. After all, can reducing ethical statements to expressions of preference and disgust really capture the absolute character of these judgements? The positivist account makes it the case that ethical right and wrong *consists* in our preferences for certain actions. But it could be argued that we prefer those actions (and spurn others) *because* they are right (or wrong). Moreover, it seems bizarre that a believer's actions would be determined by the entertainment of *fictional* stories: the believer's attitude towards the world seems instead to be based on the conviction that the world is *in reality* the creation of God.

Responses to the Challenge II: Accommodation

Like Hare and Braithwaite, other philosophers and theologians were prepared to accept the positivist criteria of meaning, but nevertheless insisted that it does not disallow the cognitive character of religious language. In this section we will consider two such responses, those of Basil Mitchell and John Hick.

Mitchell responds to Flew's challenge initially by stating that it is untrue that the theologian does not allow the fact of suffering to count against belief in God. The problem of evil constitutes, as we have seen, a particularly difficult problem which the theologian recognizes as counting against theism. Nevertheless, it is true that the believer will not allow evil to count *decisively* against his/her beliefs. The reason for this is *faith*. Mitchell shows this by means of another parable:

> In time of war in an occupied country, a member of the resistance meets one night a stranger who deeply impresses him. They spend that night together in conversation. The Stranger tells the parti-

san that he himself is on the side of the resistance – indeed that he
is in command of it, and urges the partisan to have faith in him
no matter what happens. The partisan is utterly convinced at that
meeting of the Stranger's sincerity and constancy and undertakes
to trust him.

They never meet in conditions of intimacy again. But sometimes the Stranger is seen helping members of the resistance, and
the partisan is grateful and says to his friends, 'He is on our side.'

Sometimes he is seen in the uniform of the police handing over
patriots to the occupying power. On these occasions his friends
murmur against him: but the partisan still says, 'He is on our
side.' He still believes that, in spite of appearances, the Stranger
did not deceive him. Sometimes he asks the Stranger for help and
receives it. He is then thankful. Sometimes he asks and does not
receive it. Then he says, 'The Stranger knows best.' Sometimes
his friends, in exasperation, say 'Well, what *would* he have to do
for you to admit you were wrong and that he is not on our side?'
But the partisan refuses to answer. He will not consent to put the
Stranger to the test.[84]

The parable is comparable to that of the gardener. The partisan,
like the believing explorer, seems not to allow anything to count
decisively against his belief in the integrity of the Stranger. But
unlike Flew's explorer, the partisan bases his commitment to the
Stranger on a personal encounter and an evaluation of his character. The conclusion to be drawn from this is that one's committed belief in God is reached less by a process of observation
and experiment and more by a process akin to a judgement about
someone's character. With this latter case, of course, it is easy to
arrive at different conclusions ('He's a rat', 'No! He's wonderful!') even when faced with the same evidence. Consequently, a
debate about the existence of God can still be one about the
facts, and can escape the charge of meaninglessness. And, of
course, there is in the Stranger's case some hope of future verification: when the war is over, the truth about his role in the resistance may well be uncovered.

It is this prospect of future confirmation that is paramount in
John Hick's concept of *eschatological verification*.[85] In order to
expound this notion, Hick tells yet another parable. Two people

are walking together along a road which neither has travelled along before. One believes that the road leads to the Celestial City, the other says it leads nowhere. Along their journey they have pleasant moments as well as times of misery. The believer interprets the former as encouragements and the latter as trials, while the non-believer simply sees the variety as a sign of the meaninglessness of the journey. The issue between these two travellers is not an experimental one: no evidence can be gathered to count decisively for or against one of the travellers' views. Nevertheless, the believer's position is not vacuous, for there is here the possibility of verification; namely at the end of the journey. Hick's point is that Christianity lays great stress on the belief in a life after this earthly one, and this holds out the prospect of a post-mortem (or eschatological) verification. If we find ourselves – after death – in a heaven, then we will have the proof that Christianity is true. Of course, no conclusive evidence could be found for the falsity of Christianity (if we do not experience an afterlife, we will not be conscious to use that as a falsification). Hence, Christianity is verifiable if true, but not falsifiable if false.

The accounts of Mitchell and of Hick certainly provide some degree of rescue for the claim that religious language is cognitively meaningful. It seems that the question of the existence of God can be a genuine issue, though the question of future verification is certainly dependent on the intelligibility of the notion of an afterlife, a matter that will be addressed in chapter five.

Responses to the Challenge III: Repudiation

The two responses previously considered both broadly accept the positivist principles: Hare and Braithwaite try to find a non-cognitive place for religion, while Hick and Mitchell attempt to show how questions of verification and falsification need not count against religion's cognitivity. But there are other ways of responding, and these reject entirely the positivist criteria of meaning. One method of repudiation would be to employ a *tu quoque* argument. The verification principle may rule out the cognitive significance of religious language, but it also rules out itself. If we formulate the principle as 'the meaning of a statement is its method of verification', then how could one go about verifying this? Though this may be a useful response for the theologian, the verificationist could simply reply that the verification principle has intrinsic heuristic value, which, when applied, enables one to detect what is and what is not factually significant.

Another significant response can be found within the recent development known as reformed epistemology, associated with such philosophers as Alvin Plantinga and Nicholas Wolterstorff.[86] A positivist will not ask for verification of statements of immediate experience such as 'I am sitting in a chair' or 'I am looking at a white wall'. Such basic (or foundational) propositions are the building blocks of our experience from which we extend our knowledge of the world. The reformed epistemologist maintains that the statement 'God exists' is similarly basic. Just as I am directly aware of sitting on my chair or looking at my wall, so the religious believer is directly aware of the presence of God and hence of the truth of the statement 'God exists'. The problem with such an approach is self-evident: however explicitly a believer may (seem to) feel the presence of God, this experience can never be as certain as the fact that I am sitting in a chair, and can never thus be seen as properly basic. Moreover, the reformed proposal appears to allow for patently irrational beliefs (say, belief in the Great Pumpkin), something which we must surely want to guard against.

One final, and promising, way to counter the positivist charge is to reject the overall theory of language within which verificationism has its home. This, as we shall see in a later chapter, is what is effected in the later philosophy of Wittgenstein. Before considering the nature of this philosophy, however, we may note one significant Wittgenstein-influenced account of religious language offered in George Lindbeck's *The Nature of Doctrine*.[87] Lindbeck wants to argue against two major accounts of religious language, accounts which he terms the *cognitive-propositional* and the *experiential-expressive* respectively. According to the first, religious doctrines function as truth-claims about objective, supernatural realities. So the statement 'God is omnipotent' serves as a description of a superhuman being (God), just as the statement 'Jane is five-foot tall' serves as a description of a human being. The experiential-expressive approach, on the other hand, considers religious

doctrines to be non-informative symbols of inner feelings, attitudes or orientations, rough and groping articulations of a core
inner experience. Here, 'God is omnipotent' functions, not as a
description, but as a manifestation of some human experience;
for example, a feeling of human powerlessness in the world.

Lindbeck replaces these two accounts with a third, which he
calls a *cultural-linguistic* model. This model is based on an active
rather than a passive conception of language, for Lindbeck stresses
the power of language to *shape* the way we see the world, rather
than being simply the way in which we *describe* the world. So the
language of love, for example, *makes possible* the expression of
love and is not simply a verbal description of an inner, pre-linguis-
tic feeling. Applying these insights to religion, Lindbeck writes:

> It [a religion] is not primarily an array of beliefs about the true
> and the good (though it may involve these), or a symbolism ex-
> pressive of attitudes, feelings and sentiments (though these will
> be generated). Rather, it is similar to an idiom that makes possi-
> ble the description of realities, the formulation of beliefs, and the
> experiencing of inner attitudes, feelings, and sentiments. Like a
> culture or language, it is a communal phenomenon that shapes
> the subjectivities of individuals rather than being primarily a
> manifestation of those subjectivities.[88]

To what extent have the capitulators, the accommodators and
the repudiators dealt adequately with Flew's initial criticism of
religious belief? What do you consider to be the best way forward?

Conclusion

The problematic nature of religious language adds further cre-
dence to the atheistic contention that belief in God is unjustifi-
able. Indeed, the cumulative weight of the three challenges to
religious belief that we have considered in this chapter must force
upon us the conclusion that religion (as traditionally conceived)

is false. The fact of evil certainly contradicts the Christian's speculative claim that God is all-powerful and loving; a naturalistic
approach can reveal how religion is a function of human intellectual and emotional frailty; and a consideration of the peculiar
nature of religious language may well lead us to scepticism about
its informative status. While it is certainly true that none of these
three challenges is in itself conclusive and triumphant, they are –
taken together – far more persuasive than the arguments *for*
theism. As we saw, the traditional proofs are not convincing.
Hence, while theism has little evidence in its favour, there is fairly
strong evidence against its truth.

This evidence need not always lead to atheism. Some philosophers and theologians have felt that it entails only a rejection of a
particular kind of religious belief. For such thinkers, these challenges will function as a springboard for articulating alternative
accounts of religious belief. It is to such accounts that we now turn.

Suggested reading:

I   Evil

Marilyn McCord Adams and Robert Merrihew Adams (eds),
  The Problem of Evil, Oxford: OUP, 1990.
Hannah Arendt, *Eichmann in Jerusalem*, Harmondsworth: Pen-
  guin, 1977.
Stephen T. Davis (ed.), *Encountering Evil*, Edinburgh: T. and T.
  Clark, 1981.
John Hick, *Evil and the God of Love*, Basingstoke: Macmillan,
  1983.
Ann Loades and Loyal D. Rue (eds), *Contemporary Classics in
  the Philosophy of Religion*, Illinois: Open Court, 1991.
Mary Midgley, *Wickedness*, London: Ark, 1984.
Michael Peterson (ed.), *The Problem of Evil: Selected Readings*,
  Indiana: University of Notre Dame Press, 1992.
Dorothee Soelle, *Suffering*, London: DLT, 1975.
Kenneth Surin, *Theology and the Problem of Evil*, Oxford:
  Blackwell, 1986.
Richard Swinburne and D. Z. Phillips, 'The Problem of Evil', in
  S. C. Brown (ed.), *Reason and Religion*, Cornell: Cornell Uni-
  versity Press, 1977.

II Natural Histories of Religion

Peter B. Clarke and Peter Byrne, *Religion Defined and Explained*, Basingstoke: Macmillan, 1993.

Emile Durkheim, *The Elementary Forms of the Religious Life*, London: George Allen and Unwin, 1915.

E. E. Evans-Pritchard, *Theories of Primitive Religion*, Oxford: OUP, 1965.

Ludwig Feuerbach, *The Essence of Christianity*, tr. George Eliot, New York: Harper and Row, 1957.

J. G. Frazer, *The Golden Bough*, London: Macmillan, 1922.

Sigmund Freud, *Civilization, Society and Religion*, Harmondsworth: Penguin, 1985.

David Hume, 'The Natural History of Religion' in R. Wollheim (ed.), *Hume on Religion*, London: Collins, 1963.

Karl Marx, *On Religion*, Moscow: Progress Publishers, 1957.

Brian Morris, *Anthropological Studies of Religion*, Cambridge: CUP, 1987.

Daniel L. Pals, *Seven Theories of Religion*, Oxford: OUP, 1996.

E. B. Tylor, *Primitive Culture*, London: John Murray, 1891.

III Religious Language and Verification

A. J. Ayer, *Language, Truth and Logic*, Harmondsworth: Penguin, 1971.

Frederick Ferré, *Language, Logic and God*, Chicago: University of Chicago Press, 1961.

George Lindbeck, *The Nature of Doctrine*, London: SPCK, 1984.

Basil Mitchell (ed.), *The Philosophy of Religion*, Oxford: OUP, 1971.

I. T. Ramsey, *Religious Language*, London: SCM, 1957.

J. M. Soskice, *Metaphor and Religious Language*, Oxford: Clarendon Press, 1985.

Dan R. Stiver, *The Philosophy of Religious Language*, Oxford: Blackwell, 1996.

Ludwig Wittgenstein, *Tractatus Logico-Philosophicus*, London: RKP, 1922.

4

Alternative Approaches to the Philosophy of Religion

Introduction

So far, this introduction to the philosophy of religion has accepted the parameters for the subject set by philosophical theism. The previous chapter suggested some problems with the traditional focus of the subject by considering the problems raised by the presence of evil, and the difficulty of clarifying the nature of religious language. Theism presupposes that only a supernatural interpretation of the world can adequately explain the existence of the universe and the practice of religion; yet, as we saw, Hume, Feuerbach, Durkheim and Freud suggested that it is possible to advance naturalistic explanations for these phenomena. Rather than think in terms of a supernatural God responsible for all that is – including religion – they offered alternative this-worldly explanations for God.

The aim of this chapter is to offer some alternatives to the philosophical theism that dominates discussions in the philosophy of religion. Whilst theism may have determined the way in which philosophers approach the question of religion, other positions have been advocated. Some philosophers have sought to revise the concept of God; in this chapter the work of Don Cupitt and Stewart Sutherland will be used to exemplify this trend. Others have sought to appropriate the ideas of Ludwig Wittgenstein, and his impact on the philosophical study of religion will be considered. Feminist ideas and methodologies have come to influence approaches to theology in recent years, and this has had an impact on the way in which feminist philosophers of religion have approached the subject. In particular, attention has been given to the claim that religion reflects human desires and values, and consideration will be given to the effect this has on discussions of the concept of God.

I   Revisionary Accounts of God

Theism presupposes that 'God' is the name given to an existent being. This being is understood to be omnipotent, omniscient, perfectly good, immutable, etc. If God is defined in this way, the presence of evil and suffering in this world poses a real challenge to the possible existence of such a being. Don Cupitt and Stewart Sutherland are two philosophers of religion who accept the challenge that evil poses for belief in the God of theism. In response, they offer alternative accounts of the divine. For Cupitt, God becomes a symbol for the religious or spiritual life; for Sutherland, God becomes a way of living *sub specie aeternitatis* ('under a kind of eternity').

Don Cupitt: Taking Leave of God

> Man's last and highest parting occurs when, for God's sake, he takes leave of God.[1]

Cupitt's work has done much to popularize a concept of God which recognizes the connection between God and human values.[2] While his ideas on the nature of God and theology are constantly evolving, the concept of God outlined in his book *Taking Leave of God* remains his lasting contribution to the development of an alternative concept of God. In this work, Cupitt moves away from the traditional idea of God as an external, objective, existent being, to an understanding of God as a symbol for the religious and spiritual life. Cupitt is thus making a significant move away from considering God as an objective reality: the crux of a 'realist' position.[3] In its place he offers a non-referential and 'non-realist' account of religious language. Under such an account, God is not an existent being, but 'a unifying symbol that . . . personifies and represents to us everything that spirituality requires of us'.[4]

Cupitt's theology begins by challenging the claim that God is a reality external to human life and culture. He begins with the problem evil poses for belief in a God who is ontologically distinct from ourselves. Evil is not only problematic because God apparently fails to act in the world; it is also problematic if God *does* act in the world, for the limited nature of such action suggests a morally ambiguous God. As an example, Cupitt cites an air disaster in which many died, but some are 'saved': 'The air-crash survivor thanks God for his deliverance, but what of those who died? A God who schedules some to survive and some to die in a forthcoming air-crash is clearly repugnant.'[5] This raises a deeper issue. The God of theism is a God who can be described in the same way as a human being, albeit a *super*human being. The theist's God is an agent, powerful, all-knowing; a being amongst beings. Cupitt believes that if we take seriously the facts of this world, the existence of such a being is impossible to establish. Yet he goes further: it is not simply a case of the concept of God failing to fit the facts; Cupitt wants to argue that the needs of spirituality are not served by adherence to the theist's God. A God who is ontologically distinct from human beings would be 'spiritually oppressive',[6] for such a God would be opposed to what Cupitt believes to be the purpose of the religious life. According to Cupitt, religion requires an inner transformation. While morality deals with external actions, religion, he claims, deals with internal attitudes. In order for religion to be good religion – that is, the kind of religion that affects one's inner disposition – it must dispense with reliance on a God who is *external* to human experience. God must be understood as 'indwelling the believer'.[7]

In rejecting the efficacy of the external God, Cupitt also makes a plea for human autonomy. In order to be truly free, and thus truly creative, the external God must be rejected. We must find our own path through life, and the idea of a cosmic king issuing

divine commands on morality refutes the human endeavour to
decide that which is right: 'The modern person is no longer content to live his life so completely within an antecedently-prescribed
framework. He wants to define himself, to posit and pursue his
own goals and to choose for himself what to make of himself.'[8]
In offering an alternative understanding of God, Cupitt believes
that he is making possible the spiritual life for modern people.
Indeed, he argues that his analysis of the concept of God is simply making explicit the implicit trend within the history of religion. Consideration of the Old and New Testaments exemplifies
this movement. In the Old Testament, there is a gradual movement away from a focus on ritual, towards an understanding of
the importance of the inner life and the moral intentions of a
person. The prophet Jeremiah argued that the law written on
tablets had to be written on the hearts of the people of Israel.[9] In
similar vein, the New Testament contains a movement away from
the idea of external religious realities to the idea of importance
of the inner life. So, in the Gospels of Matthew and Mark, the
coming of the kingdom of God is viewed as an event which will
take place at the end of time.[10] In Luke's Gospel, the kingdom is
understood as a symbol for the everyday moral lives of the disciples. The kingdom is here and now, enacted in the lives of the
disciples.[11]

Acceptance of this interpretation has implications for the concept of God. Having rejected the notion that 'God' is the name
for a supernatural being, Cupitt offers an alternative definition:
'God is Christian spirituality in coded form, for God is a symbol
that represents to us everything that spirituality requires of us
and promises to us.'[12] Like Meister Eckhart, whom he cites at
the beginning of his work, Cupitt advocates a rejection of the
God of theism on the grounds that such a God hampers the development of human spirituality. Only a God who is not separate from human spirituality can be of help in the quest for the
integrated human existence.

Understanding God in this way has a profound effect upon
the way in which the nature of religious language is to be understood. The word 'God' only has meaning within the religious
life. In this sense, Cupitt's ideas are close to those of Wittgensteinians like D. Z. Phillips.[13] Language of God is not referential:

there is no ontologically distinct being called 'God' to whom such language refers. When the word 'God' is used, it is as a symbol for the reality and importance of a particular form of life; that is, the religious or the spiritual life.

Defining the meaning of 'God' in this way necessitates a reworking of the attributes traditionally and habitually ascribed to the divine; that is, power, knowledge, simplicity, aseity, eternity. Cupitt relates these apparent descriptions of the divine nature to human ideals and the values one needs to foster if committed to living the spiritual life. So, God is described as 'wise and all-knowing, in the way in which the religious requirement is experienced by us searching our hearts, because its demand for spiritual integrity will not allow us to keep any drawers locked'.[14] Likewise, 'God is powerful in the sense that the religious requirement recreates us from nothing (it reduces us to dust and then remakes us of dust).'[15] In this way, Cupitt allows the divine attributes to have meaning and power, despite his denial of the objective existence of God. Indeed, the divine attributes *only* have meaning in so far as they can be paralleled with the characteristics necessary for the pursuit of the spiritual life.

Consideration of Cupitt's work is valuable, not least because he shows what happens when religious language is not viewed descriptively, but as a symbolic way of exploring certain human values. Language used of God should not be understood as describing a divine being; rather, 'God' is that which symbolizes the spiritual life. Such an interpretation of the notion of God has been widely criticized. Keith Ward argues that Cupitt has simply reduced theological language to talk of the spiritual life.[16] Whilst the charge of reductionism is not in itself problematic, we might want to ask whether the word 'God', with the realist assumptions which surround it, is the most appropriate word for imaging Cupitt's account of spirituality. Likewise, is Cupitt's 'God' an appropriate object for worship? It seems that one would have significantly to reframe the idea of worship if this is to constitute a genuine possibility. John Hick has gone so far as to argue that such a concept of God is elitist; Cupitt's God is 'good news' for an intellectual elite, but 'bad news' for those whose lives need the hope of immortality in order to be meaningful.[17] Such negative points can perhaps be countered: the Sea of Faith movement within the Anglican Church suggests that there are people who wish to be religious – indeed, who profess to be 'Christian' – but who do not recognize the existence of an objective God.[18] It could be claimed that Cupitt offers a way in which religion can become relevant to our political and environmental concerns, helping us to respond to life in this world, not in some hypothetical other world.[19] In revising the concept of God Cupitt does seem to have offered a way of remaining religious for those who have rejected the theistic concept of God.

John Hick challenges the kind of non-realist account put forward by Cupitt in the following way:

> The non-realist faith starts from and returns to the naturalistic conception that we are simply complex animals who live and die, the circumstances of our lives happening to be fortunate for some and unfortunate for others. Probably half or more of the children who have been born throughout human history and pre-history have died in infancy, their potentialities almost entirely undeveloped . . . If the naturalistic vision is correct, that potentiality can never be fulfilled in the great majority, for at death they have ceased to exist . . . Thus the non-realist forms of religion, presupposing this naturalistic interpretation of the human situation, abandon hope for mankind as a whole. (John Hick, 'Religious Realism and Non-Realism: Defining the Issue', in Joseph Runzo (ed.), *Is God Real?*, Basingstoke: Macmillan, 1993, p. 13)

To what extent would you agree with Hick's assessment of non-realism? How might Cupitt respond to this charge?

Stewart Sutherland: A Revised Theism

Stewart Sutherland offers a rather different revision to the concept of God than that offered by Cupitt. In offering what could be called a 'revised realist' account of God,[20] Sutherland begins by suggesting a set of criteria for determining an acceptable form of belief. Criterion 2 runs thus: 'a religious belief which runs counter to our moral beliefs is to that extent unacceptable'.[21] This leads Sutherland, like Cupitt, to begin with the problem that evil poses for the theistic account of God. When confronted with the evil and suffering of this world, it seems impossible to accept the existence of an all-powerful creator God. Indeed, Sutherland argues that many theistic attempts to provide an answer to the problem of evil create more problems than they solve.[22] As he puts it, they highlight 'the dangers of attempting to fit one's view of evil and suffering to a preframed theology'.[23] Despite these reservations, Sutherland feels that, historically, theism has been an important instrument for offering ideas about how best to live. As such, he wants to offer a revised theism which maintains this positive ethical contribution, while dispensing with the 'unworkable' idea of a personal God.

In developing his idea of God, Sutherland begins by questioning the desire for an existent God. He takes two examples from the New Testament – the story of Christ's temptation (Matthew 4:8–10), and Christ's prayer in the Garden of Gethsemane (Matthew 26). A liberal theist coming across the first account where Christ is confronted by the devil will probably deny the existence of a personal devil. At the same time, however, they will want to maintain that the temptation narrative has real meaning. Denying the objective existence of the devil does not alter the fact that Christ is confronted in the wilderness with real choices about the way he is to carry out his ministry. In Sutherland's words: 'The religious or spiritual significance of the story does not depend upon a prior ontological commitment.'[24] The significance of the story is not tied to belief in the existence of a supernatural being – in this case, the devil. The importance of Christ's decision against certain ways of enacting his ministry can be accepted without acknowledging the existence of a devil who tempts him.

Sutherland goes on to apply this approach to the second story of Christ's prayer in the Garden. Why, he asks, should the objective existence of God be of fundamental importance to *this* story? If we can accept the significance of the choices facing Christ without referring to the existence of a devil in the temptation narrative, there seems to be no reason why we should not interpret Christ's prayer in a similar way. The choice Christ faces – the choice to accept or not to accept suffering – is a real choice *whether or not* we accept the existence of a supernatural being to whom Christ is speaking.

Sutherland is adamant that he is not trying to convince his reader that an objective, personal God does not exist; rather 'I am asking you what is meant in such a context either to claim that Satan does not *really* exist or to claim that God does *actually* exist.'[25] What does it *mean* to believe in God? For the theist, the emphasis appears to lie with making a reasoned commitment to an existent entity. So, attempts are made to establish the existence of God, to define God's characteristics. Sutherland's alternative account shifts the focus dramatically. What is the *significance* of believing in God? What effect does this belief have upon our lives and our actions?

The importance of the two narratives considered above, according to Sutherland, lies with the reality of the choices facing Christ – and, by implication, the choices facing Christ's followers today. The reality of these choices resides in the significance of the moral decisions that we make. This notion leads Sutherland to offer a reinterpretation of the concept of God. Central to Sutherland's ideas is the notion that there is a position from which we can make our moral decisions which is not determined by our individual desires and preferences, nor by the desires and preferences of human society as a whole. In the past, western theism has provided such an objective standpoint. Now, in a context in which belief in a personal God is waning, Sutherland wants to salvage this important idea and does so in formulating his ruling principle for ethical action – living *sub specie aeternitatis*.

The central concern for Sutherland is with the kind of life that springs from holding theistic beliefs. Theism suggests that there is a way of living which is not dependent upon individual human desires and preferences. There is an understanding of human life which is not relative to the outlook of human beings – and this outlook is what is meant by 'God'. In clarifying this idea, Sutherland takes an example from Robert Bolt's play, *A Man for All*

Seasons.[26] Sutherland considers a scene where Thomas More tells the ambitious young lawyer Rich to be a teacher. Rich wants to know what satisfaction there could be in such a lifestyle; it does not seem very glamorous or exciting. More's response is to focus upon the satisfaction to be gained in being a good teacher. If Rich is a good teacher, 'you will know it, your pupils will know it, and God will know it'. What, asks Sutherland, does it mean to say 'and God will know it'? Discussions of omniscience which we have hitherto considered would focus on defining the extent of God's knowledge: so, 'does God know the future?', 'to what extent does God know what it is to be human?', and so on. Sutherland offers a different account. He denies that the phrase 'and God will know it' means that More is drawing Rich's attention to a Celestial Intelligence Agency (CIA) in the sky reporting on his every move. According to Sutherland, this is an inappropriate understanding of that statement. Rather, this phrase draws attention to the idea that there is a way of life which is not dependent on external factors for its value. This offers the possibility of a life 'to which certain values are non-contingently related'.[27] If one is a good teacher, nothing could detract from that. If one follows a life of that kind, nothing could happen to Rich that would detract from the value of his life.

In suggesting the possibility of living *sub specie aeternitatis*, Sutherland is offering a significantly different account of God than that offered by Cupitt. God, in Sutherland's revised version, is not dependent on human beings for his existence:

> There are two jewels which lie at the heart of the possibility of a view *sub specie aeternitatis*: The first defines the hope, and indeed the belief, that there is an understanding of the affairs of men which is not relative to the outlook of individual, community or age. The second, which crowns that, is the implication that such a view is not even relative to the outlook of mankind.[28]

How could such a conclusion be established? Sutherland reverses this question: can such an idea be shown to be 'simply a product of human hopes and fears projected outwards'?[29] This is Feuerbach's conclusion, and, to an extent, that of Cupitt when considering the notion of God. In addressing this question, Sutherland admits that his argument could be vulnerable to the charge of unintelligibility. But he goes on to argue that his ideas do not contain a contradiction: 'my protection against the former will be an extreme reticence to define what the "content" of a view *sub specie aeternitatis* is.'[30] This might sound like sophistry: how can his idea be criticized if it is not defined adequately? However, Sutherland does suggest a way in which his argument could be explored: 'the appropriate procedure is to *exemplify* rather than *define* such a view.'[31]

Given the facts of this world, is the moral life possible? Sutherland suggests that it is, and that the *possibility* of the moral life constitutes the best evidence for his argument. God, then, is the principle for a way of life made possible by the way the world is. In other words, the world is such that the spiritual life, the moral life, is possible. If we could simply reduce human life to the survival of the fittest, there would be no examples of human heroism, self-sacrifice and bravery. But there are examples of these virtues. The world is thus capable of sustaining such qualities.

Richard Dawkins has argued that the theory of evolution suggests that humans possess 'selfish genes'. In his words:

> If we are told that a man had lived a long and prosperous life in the world of Chicago gangsters, we would be entitled to make some guesses as to the sort of man he was. We might expect that he would have qualities such as toughness, a quick trigger finger, and the ability to attract loyal friends . . . Like successful Chicago gangsters, our genes have survived, in some cases for millions of years, in a highly competitive world. This entitles us to expect certain qualities in our genes. I shall argue that a predominant quality to be expected in a successful gene is ruthless selfishness. This gene selfishness will usually give rise to selfishness in individual behaviour. (R. Dawkins, *The Selfish Gene*, Oxford: OUP, 1976, p. 2)

How does this contrast with Sutherland's view, and how might Sutherland respond to Dawkins's claims?

Under Sutherland's revised theism, 'God' is not the name of a supernatural being, but a way of living which is made possible by the way the world is. Sutherland is offering an essentially ethical interpretation of the concept of God which suggests that the word 'God' need not be understood simply as the name of an existent being. Like Cupitt, Sutherland could be accused of reductionism. Sutherland does not see this as problematic; after all, he is offering a *revised* account of theism. It could, however, be argued that his account of 'God' raises as many problems as it seeks to solve. What *is* this ruling principle for ethical action? Is it a transcendent ethic, akin to Plato's notion of the Good? In which case, where is it? While an intellectual might find Sutherland's interpretation of theism attractive, it is debatable that the ordinary believer would. Christian belief has tended to focus on the notion of having a personal relationship with God. It seems unlikely that such a relationship would be possible with an impersonal ruling principle. However, what Sutherland offers is a way of being religious which accepts the force of the arguments put against theism. His account of religion finds a peculiar resonance with a world which finds it hard to accept the reality of a personal God given the horrific instances of suffering and genocide experienced this century. Religion becomes less the belief in a set of propositions regarding a transcendent God, and more a way of being in the world.

Conclusion

Cupitt and Sutherland, then, offer alternative accounts of the divine to those offered by philosophical theism. While both views are somewhat different, both face the challenge that they are reducing the content of theism to an unacceptable extent. To what extent does the word 'God' still mean God if their ideas are taken on board? If the personal existence of God is to be jettisoned, it might seem better to do away with any reference to the idea of God. Would a believer identify 'their' God with either of the definitions offered by Cupitt or Sutherland? These problems are not insurmountable; it may be that they herald the way to a rethinking of what it means to formulate a concept of God and the spirituality attendant upon it. Rather than seek an overarching concept against which all others are judged, consideration of Cupitt and Sutherland might open the way to an acceptance of many different and varied accounts of divinity. In such a context, creativity comes to define the modern approach to religious belief.

II Wittgenstein and the Philosophy of Religion

Introduction

We have seen how the positivist attack on the meaningfulness of religious discourse stemmed in no small part from the work of Ludwig Wittgenstein.[32] Wittgenstein's claim that meaningfulness was restricted to the realm of scientific, fact-stating language was eagerly lapped up by atheistic thinkers keen to show religion to be nonsensical. On the other hand, while Wittgenstein's early work certainly lent itself to such an interpretation, it is not true that he himself was antithetical to religion. Indeed, even within the *Tractatus*, the framework of which looks so inhospitable to affairs of the spirit, Wittgenstein assigns a central place to religion. In this section, we shall outline that central place, referred to by Wittgenstein as the realm of 'the mystical', before moving on to a consideration of the impact on the philosophy of religion of his later (radically different) account of language and religion.

The Mystical

One element which might suggest to us that Wittgenstein was not a simple logical positivist concerns the attention he paid to questions of religion and value. When in his early period he speaks of such things he does this with a seriousness that no positivist – convinced of the worthlessness of such matters – could have done. We can witness this preoccupation with religious questions in his war notebooks, when we read passages such as the following, written in 1916:

> To believe in a God means to understand the question about the meaning of life.

> To believe in a God means to see that the facts of the world are not the end of the matter.
>
> To believe in God means to see that life has a meaning.[33]

'The facts of the world are not the end of the matter.' So while Wittgenstein has indeed circumscribed language so that its only subject-matter can be facts, he is keen to emphasize that 'the factual' is not all that should concern us. It is, of course, true that what goes beyond the clearly empirical cannot be spoken of ('Whereof one cannot speak thereof one must be silent'), but this does not mean that the unsayable is insignificant, or worthless. And it is this, more than anything else, that distinguishes Wittgenstein's account of language and religion from that of the positivists. Paul Engelmann brings this out well when he writes:

> A whole generation of disciples was able to take Wittgenstein for a positivist because he has something of enormous importance in common with the positivists: he draws the line between what we can speak about and what we must be silent about just as they do. The difference is only that they have nothing to be silent about. Positivism holds – and this is its essence – that what we can speak about is all that matters in life. *Whereas Wittgenstein passionately believes that all that really matters in life is precisely what, in his view, we must be silent about.* When he nevertheless takes immense pains to delimit the unimportant, it is not the coastline of that island which he is bent on surveying with meticulous accuracy, but the boundary of the ocean.[34]

If this is correct, then everything that is expressible in language is of secondary importance: what is crucial is what is unsayable, what Wittgenstein calls 'the mystical'.

In the mystical passages of the *Tractatus*, Wittgenstein turns his attention to such things as 'the sense of the world' and 'the problems of life'; he considers death, immortality and God. According to him, such matters are aspects of seeing the world in a particular way, seeing the world *sub specie aeternitatis*. Viewed 'under the aspect of eternity', the world becomes wondrous; we see it 'as a miracle'.[35] Wittgenstein's account lays great stress, not on the features of the world itself, but on how it is *viewed*.

The facts of the world are the same for Wittgenstein as they are for a positivist, but they are *viewed differently*. For the positivist: the world? Big deal! For Wittgenstein: the world? A miracle!

It is tempting to say that Wittgenstein's views on the mystical amount to a 'picture-preference', that he is admitting that, seen objectively, the world is non-miraculous (as the positivist holds), but that he then adds that it is aesthetically rewarding to look at the world in a quasi-mystical fashion. This, however, does not do justice to Wittgenstein's view. He really does hold the view that there is something outside language and outside the facts of the world which is of fundamental spiritual significance:

6.4   All propositions are of equal value.
6.41   The sense of the world must lie outside the world. In the world everything is as it is, and everything happens as it does happen: in it no value exists – and if it did exist, it would have no value.
6.421 Propositions can express nothing that is higher.[36]

Recall the picture theory of language considered in chapter three. We have language. It mirrors the facts of the world. But propositions can only handle humdrum states of affairs. They cannot express 'what is higher'. Words will only hold facts, just as, Wittgenstein says, 'a teacup will only hold a teacup full of water even if I were to pour out a gallon over it'.[37] Of course, this means that if we try to express in language what is 'higher', we will fail, we will end up talking nonsense. Wittgenstein recognized this; only he did not ridicule those who attempted to put the mystical into words. Indeed, this attempt is often applauded:

My whole tendency and I believe the tendency of all men who ever tried to write or talk Ethics or Religion was to run against the boundaries of language. This running against the walls of our cage is perfectly, absolutely hopeless . . . But it is a document of a tendency in the human mind which I personally cannot help respecting deeply and I would not for my life ridicule it.[38]

Wittgenstein's view, then, is this: trying to talk about 'higher things' is cognitively hopeless. What is mystical cannot be put into words. None the less, the attempt to speak of such things is not ludicrous: such an attempt will result, strictly speaking, in nonsensical utterance, but this is *important nonsense*, indicating something significant in human life.

This verbal nonsense is not the only way in which one can indicate the presence of the mystical. Note the following passage from the *Tractatus*: 'There are, indeed, things that cannot be put into words. They make themselves manifest. They are what is mystical.'[39] So how can what is inexpressible be manifested in a non-linguistic way? Wittgenstein's correspondence with Engelmann suggests one way. This suggestion emerges from Wittgenstein's reading of this poem by Ludwig Uhland:

> Count Eberhard Rustle-Beard
> From Württemberg's fair land
> On holy errand steer'd
> To Palestina's strand.
>
> The while he slowly rode
> Along a woodland way;
> He cut from the hawthorn bush
> A little fresh green spray.
>
> Then in his iron helm
> The little sprig he plac'd;
> And bore it in the wars,
> And over the ocean waste.
>
> And when he reach'd his home,
> He plac'd it in the earth;
> Where little leaves and buds
> The green Spring call'd forth.
>
> He went each year to it,
> The Count so brave and true;
> And overjoy'd was he
> To witness how it grew.

The Count was worn with age
The sprig became a tree;
'Neath which the old man oft
Would sit in reverie.

The branching arch so high,
Whose whisper is so bland,
Reminds him of the past
And Palestina's strand.

This simple poem makes no attempt to speak of grand meta-physical truths, and yet for Wittgenstein it gives witness to something significant in human life. As he put it: 'The poem by Uhland is really magnificent. And this is how it is: if only you do not try to utter what is unutterable then nothing gets lost. But the unutterable will be – unutterably – *contained* in what has been uttered!'[40] This is hardly the clearest of remarks, but Wittgenstein's point is that the words of the poem do not state what is of value: they show or mediate what is valuable, what is 'higher'. He is suggesting that we find in art and in literature a way in which the mystical is mediated; a way in which what is beyond the world penetrates the world. If we needed an image to help us understand this idea, we might think of a shaft of sunlight breaking through clouds, the brilliance of what is beyond our world casting its glow over what is mundane.

Another way in which the mystical is manifested might perhaps be found in a life lived ethically. By way of a good life, one can bring 'what is higher' into the world. But whether one locates the manifestation of the mystical either in ethics or in art, Wittgenstein has provided in his early thoughts on religion a way in which one can escape the attacks of positivists. Though religious discourse is indeed nonsensical, Wittgenstein argues that it is truly important. We may find in Wittgenstein's writings an attractive account of the nature of religion, one which finds its meaning not in the truth of speculative doctrines, but in a life well-lived and in a felt sense of the significance of human existence.

Wittgenstein's Later Thought

Wittgenstein eventually came to believe that the picture of language he had painted in the *Tractatus* was in error. Principally, he felt that all he had done was to describe one form of language – the language of science – and then to state dogmatically that *all* forms of language had to conform to this type or else be nonsensical. In his later book, the *Philosophical Investigations*, Wittgenstein attempts to overturn his earlier philosophy of language. Language, he argues, has no general form; rather, it is a loose relation of varying linguistic practices, termed by him 'language-games' (of which, more later). Because of the way language looks when it is written down, or how it sounds when it is spoken, we tend automatically to think that it serves always the same function. This, says Wittgenstein, would be like thinking that all those things we call 'games' have the same purpose, or at least manifest some common element. He attempts to undermine this:

> Instead of producing something common to all that we call language, I am saying that these phenomena have no one thing in common which makes us use the same word for all, – but that they are *related* to one another in many different ways. And it is because of this relationship, or these relationships, that we call them all 'language'.[41]

If we recognize that language may manifest itself in many varied forms – compare the language of poetry with the language of physics – then we may no longer be tempted to proclaim that if language does not serve to express facts then it is without sense.

We can see, then, that Wittgenstein's later account of language is less restrictive than the position he adopts in the *Tractatus*. There will be many spheres of discourse, as there are many games, each with their own rules, each with their own standards of truth, falsity and meaning. Of course, one consequence of this is that if religious discourse does not conform to the standards of the scientific, then it is no longer to be confined to the realm of the unsayable. Just because the language of religion does not 'picture' empirical facts, we should not presume that it is without meaning. For the later Wittgenstein, the meaning of a word or of a sentence is not always equated with the object or fact it represents. Language is no longer for Wittgenstein a static thing, whereby we describe states of affairs to each other. No, it is a dynamic practice, and the emphasis falls on the use of words, rather than what they represent. So: 'For a large class of cases – though not for all – in which we employ the word "meaning" it can be defined thus: the meaning of a word is its use in the language.'[42] If we are puzzled by the meaning of certain expressions in a particular sphere of discourse we should not automatically consider what that expression *depicts*. Rather, we should look to see how it is *used*, what role it plays in that linguistic activity.

Wittgenstein's response to Frazer's natural history of religion may help to clarify this. Frazer, recall, wants to say that religious practices are futile attempts to influence the course of nature, and that such rituals are the applications of an elementary, and erroneous, form of science. In other words, religion is false science.[43] For Wittgenstein, this is a bizarre conclusion, produced by the illusion that all human action and belief must be akin to one paradigm: the scientific. Hence Wittgenstein writes:

> Frazer's account of the magical and religious notions of men is unsatisfactory: it makes these notions appear as *mistakes*.
>
> Was Augustine mistaken, then, when he called on God on every page of the *Confessions*?
>
> Well – one might say – if he was not mistaken, then the Buddhist holy-man, or some other, whose religion expresses quite different notions, surely was. But *none* of them was making a mistake except where he was putting forward a theory.[44]

The contention is that it is only if we see religion as consisting of a set of theories, or hypotheses, about the nature of the world – that is, if we see religion as a species of science – that it begins to look mistaken. Wittgenstein is keen to stress that religion is precisely *not* theoretical in character. So belief in God is not to be equated with adherence to the hypothesis that somewhere or other there is a being called 'God'. To put it another way, believing in God is not akin to believing in the Loch Ness Monster.

Just as religious beliefs are misunderstood if conceived of as hypotheses, so *rituals* are misunderstood if they are thought to be attempts to manipulate the natural order. Wittgenstein rejects Frazer's view of the instrumental character of ritual by appealing to the numerous practical skills that members of primitive societies possess: 'The same savage who, apparently in order to kill his enemy, sticks his knife through a picture of him, really does build his hut of wood and cuts his arrow with skill and not in effigy.'[45] The force of Wittgenstein's point is this: Frazer maintains that the savage is so stupid that he cannot even conceive the distinction between the natural and the supernatural, so if he wants to kill his enemy, he kills him in effigy and does not resort to more practical means, like stabbing or poisoning him. Wittgenstein responds by saying that if this is the case, then these savages would surely hunt in effigy, build in effigy, marry in effigy, and so on. But they do not do this, and have, indeed, fairly sophisticated agricultural and technical skills. So when a member of a primitive culture wants to plough a field, he really does plough that field; he does not simply imitate the action of ploughing.

This suggests to Wittgenstein that magic and religion are not of a kind with scientific, or practical, activities; they are not collections of errors, nor are they 'proto-science'. So what character do they have? Here is one suggestion:

> Burning in effigy. Kissing the picture of a loved one. This is obviously not based on a belief that it will have a definite effect on the object which the picture represents. It aims at some satisfaction and it achieves it. Or rather, it does not aim at anything; we act in this way and then feel satisfied.[46]

Just like the primitive, we perform rituals; we kiss pictures of people we love; we sometimes kiss their names; we mutilate pictures of those people we despise or who have hurt us. But we do not perform these actions in order to achieve some concrete end. Rather, these actions satisfy some emotional need. For allied soldiers fighting in the Second World War, throwing darts at pictures of Hitler was not regarded as an easy or even possible method of assassination. Rather, such actions constituted an expression of their hatred for the enemy. Wittgenstein therefore writes:

When I am furious about something, I sometimes beat the ground or a tree with my walking stick. But I certainly do not believe that the ground is to blame or that my beating can help anything. 'I am venting my anger.' And all rites are of this kind. Such actions may be called Instinct-actions.[47]

This suggests a very different picture of the nature of religious belief, both from the account offered by Frazer, and from the philosophical theism considered in the early chapters of this book. Wittgenstein's view is that, far from being a theory concerning super-empirical entities or a metaphysical explanation, religion is an expression of human values, needs and desires.

Does Wittgenstein's critique of Frazer successfully defuse the intellectualist attack on religion? How convincing do you find his account of the nature of religious belief?

The logical distinctiveness of religion and science is again stressed in Wittgenstein's 'Lectures on Religious Belief', where he considers the status, not of primitive beliefs and rituals, but of certain Christian doctrines. Concerning the belief in a Last Judgement, Wittgenstein wants to know what is at stake between someone who does believe in such a Judgement, and someone who does not. So he considers two people, one of whom, whenever debating the course of action to take, or whenever something bad happens to him, thinks of punishment. If he is ill, he thinks, 'What have I done to deserve this?'; if he is ashamed, he thinks 'This will be punished.' The other person (the unbeliever) just does not think of punishment at all. But this is no contradiction of the believer, for they are not disagreeing over whether a particular event will occur. The belief in a Last Judgement is not a prediction:

Here believing obviously plays much more this role: suppose that a certain picture might play the role of constantly admonishing me, or I always think of it. Here, an enormous difference would be between those people for whom the picture is constantly in the foreground, and for others who just didn't use it at all.[48]

So, for Wittgenstein, belief in the Last Judgement is not a hypothesis, but rather a regulating or admonishing *picture*, in the same way that the 'all-seeing eye of God' might function as a picture which restrains us from our wicked inclinations.

It is important to recognize that Wittgenstein's account of religion, despite superficial similarities, diverges in an important sense from that of Braithwaite.[49] Braithwaite would agree that a belief in the Last Judgement amounts to the entertainment of a morally coercive non-factual 'picture': whenever we are about to act in an immoral fashion, thoughts of flames and punishment fill our minds and we try to pursue a better path of action. For Braithwaite, religious assertions can be reduced to moral assertions and simply are means to ends; if other fictional stories could serve equally well to induce us to act morally, then the Christian tales could be dispensed with without any great loss. Not so for Wittgenstein: religious beliefs are entirely non-reducible. To this end, he considers someone saying to another, 'we might see one another after death'. A student in Wittgenstein's class responds by saying, 'in this case, you might only mean that he expressed an attitude', but Wittgenstein is adamant that this is not the case: ' "No, it isn't the same as saying 'I'm very fond of you' " – and it may not be the same as saying anything else. It says what it says. Why should you be able to substitute anything else?'[50] These religious pictures, far from being reducible to other statements (e.g. ethical ones) actually *constitute* a particular way of looking at the world. If they are not used, then that view of the world is ignored; and if a religion dies, then that perspective dies with it.

For Wittgenstein, then, religion is not a speculative affair, and it is not the result of a cool contemplation of the world. It is, rather, grounded in a kind of instinctual reaction (which he calls a 'primitive reaction'). Out of such a reaction, a whole system of beliefs can develop. But these beliefs have no explanatory value and they are not theoretical. The character of religion, viewed this way, is best captured in a remark from *Culture and Value*: 'It strikes me that a religious belief could only be something like a passionate commitment to a system of reference. Hence, although it's *belief*, it's really a way of living, or a way of assessing life. It's passionately seizing hold of *this* interpretation.'[51]

Wittgenstein's Influence on the Philosophy of Religion

Wittgenstein's thoughts have had a profound influence on the shape of contemporary philosophy of religion; hence the considerable amount of time we have spent considering his views. It is the application of his concept of a 'language-game' to religion which has been the focus of most debate. When Wittgenstein speaks of language-games, he is, as we have already seen, arguing for the heterogeneity of language. A game such as football has radically different rules, methods and goals than a game like poker, and it would be a mistake to evaluate the one according to the rules of the other. Again, games are self-contained: we do not use, for example, a phrase such as 'leg before wicket' outside the context of the game of cricket. If we apply this framework to sectors of *language*, then we can say that different language-games will have different standards of truth, meaning, and so on. If we then proceed to say that *religion* is a language-game, our conclusion will be, firstly, that it cannot be judged by the standards of another language-game, such as science. In this way, the truth of Darwinian theory will not serve to undermine the creation narrative in Genesis. Secondly, if religion is a self-contained sphere of discourse, then its crucial terms (God, salvation, miracle, etc.) will have no application outside the language-game. God would here be akin to the piece called the 'king' in a game of chess: it has a pivotal role in the game, but has no value outside of it.

The view that religion constitutes a language-game has been severely criticized, for it can be seen to trivialize religious belief, making it seem something like an idle pastime. Moreover, it is seen to constitute a form of fideism, whereby religion is irrationally protected from sceptical attack. Many of the criticisms of the Wittgensteinian position are really criticisms of a parody of that position.[52] For a start, Wittgenstein never characterizes religion as a language-game; indeed, his own examples are rather more small-scale (such as telling a joke, play-acting, giving orders, etc.). And the appeal to language-games is best construed as imploring us to pay attention to the subtle differences of context which make religious discourse so unlike the discourse of the natural sciences. As Wittgenstein stressed in his remarks on

The Golden Bough, a formalized ritual may look as if it is an attempt to influence the growth of the crops (and would thus constitute primitive agricultural technology), yet in reality it may be something altogether different (say, an expression of hope that the crops will flourish). As we shall see in a later discussion, Wittgensteinians such as D. Z. Phillips produce similar analyses of central Christian themes, such as prayer and immortality.[53]

III   Feminism and the Philosophy of Religion

While feminist ideas and methodologies have had considerable impact on the area of theology, it is only recently that such ideas have begun to impinge on the subject-matter of philosophy of religion. In approaching the subject, feminist philosophers of religion have drawn upon the ideas of feminist theologians, and, more recently, have explored the contribution of feminist continental philosophy.[54] Much attention has been given to the connection between human values and the concept of God. There has been a tacit recognition that the theistic concept of God reflects masculine notions of what constitutes the good, which, in turn, have been used to define the concept of God.

Initially, then, it would seem appropriate to revisit Feuerbach's insight into the construction of the concept of God. Feuerbach directs us to the human values which are reflected in any society's conceptualization of God. From a feminist perspective, such an approach would appear to involve a twofold process: the deconstruction of God, and the reconstruction of the meaning of the divine.

Deconstructing the Concept of God

If Feuerbach's account of the concept of God as a human construction is accepted, an important question needs to be addressed. If 'God' stands for those qualities which human beings hold to be valuable, *whose* values does the philosophical concept of God reflect? Consideration of the God of theism goes some way to answering this question. The theist's God is defined in terms of power, knowledge and detachment. Furthermore, this God is described as impassible, unable to suffer – an attribute that has connotations of invulnerability. God is described as immutable, unable to change. If these factors are taken together, it seems that we have a telling picture of God made in 'man's' image. Replace the word 'God' with the word 'man' and one is left with the stereotypical picture of what constitutes masculinity in a patriarchal society.

Some of the earliest feminist analysis of the concept of God was concerned with exposing the way in which the notion of God is used to legitimate male domination. Mary Daly, a key figure in the quest for a female-centred approach to spirituality, began by outlining the extent to which the concept of God was derived from male experience of the world.[55] Writing of Christianity – although, arguably, she could have chosen any of the major monotheistic faiths – she notes that 'the myths and symbols of Christianity are essentially sexist'.[56] The language habitually used of God is distinctively male, both in terms of the attributes ascribed to God, but also in terms of the gender-language used of God: God is 'he'. According to Daly, this has a particular impact on human relationships: 'since "God" is male, the male is God. God the Father legitimates all earthly Godfathers'. [57]

> Drawing upon the account of philosophy of religion given so far in this book, what evidence might there be for Daly's claim that if ' "God" is male, the male is God'?

Much recent feminist analysis has continued Daly's work by exposing the way in which the concept of God has been used to valorize masculinist concepts and values. Sharon Welch has offered a fierce rebuttal of the desire for an omnipotent God. In her challenge to the contemporary atmosphere of 'cultured despair', she argues that the acceptance of an all-powerful God constitutes a real problem for human relationships.[58] According to Welch, 'the political logic of such doctrines [is] the glorification of domination'.[59] The idea of an all-powerful deity leads us to

glorify human examples of power. Moreover, the idea of omnipotence contains the belief that absolute power is an absolute
good: God, as perfect, is *all*-powerful. Consequently, human beings – or rather human rulers – are to aspire to such power. Welch
is concerned to refute the suggestion that absolute power is to be
desired; we only have to consider human history to see the legacy
of such an understanding of power. As Welch puts it, 'absolute
power *is* a destructive trait'.[60] If this is the case, should we continue to value a God defined as omnipotent?

Welch discerns a hierarchical structuring of society lying behind the notion of absolute power. If rulers are to aspire to the
power of God, the ruled are to submit to their 'masters' in the
same way as the Church is to submit to 'her' God. She writes:
'The result of the theological valorization of absolute power is
the erotics of domination, the glorification of submission to the
greatest power.'[61] Welch is suggesting a connection between theological language and human praxis, and, as such, demands a
review of the way in which God is conceptualized. Her analysis
has been built upon by James Nelson in his essay 'Embracing
Masculinity'.[62] Nelson draws upon feminist analysis of the concept of God in offering a critique of masculinist definitions of
power. He grounds his critique of power in an analysis of the
major patriarchal account of masculinity. In particular, he focuses on the penis as that which defines the male. The penis can
be described in two ways – as the phallus when erect, and as the
penis when flaccid. Nelson claims that the attributes of the phallus have been overvalued, whilst the penis and its 'teaching' has
been effectively ignored when determining values.

According to Nelson, patriarchal society has valued the phallus and its associated attributes of 'strength, hardness, determination, sinew, straightforwardness, penetration'.[63] It is interesting
to note the extent to which such words dominate academic discourse. An argument is deemed worthy of praise if it is 'straightforward', 'strongly worded', 'determined', 'penetrative'. While
phallic attributes are valued, the penis and the values which can
be derived from it are deemed of little importance. Nelson describes the penis as soft, vulnerable, in need of protection – curi-
ously 'feminine' traits which can be derived from the male body.

Nelson suggests that the emphasis on the phallus and its associated meanings has resulted in a definition of power as unilateral power.[64] He describes unilateral power as 'nonmutual and nonrelational. Its purpose is to produce the largest possible effect on another, while being least affected by the other. Its ideal is control.'[65] Nelson describes unilateral power as having the greatest effect on others without being affected oneself. Unilateral power does not arise from mutual co-operation with others; it involves remaining unaffected by the actions of others.

If we consider the philosopher's approach to divine power, the attributes Nelson highlights remain in evidence. In seeking to define omnipotence, philosophical arguments reflect underlying presuppositions about the nature of God. A key element within the concept of God concerns the nature of the divine existence. As we saw in our discussion in chapter two of the ontological argument, God's existence is necessary, rather than contingent. In other words, God's existence is *independent* of any other source. Divinity necessitates radical separation and independence. Does a notion of a God who is radically independent determine the conceptualization of power in unilateral terms? Nelson and Welch make a strong case for accepting this conclusion.

Like Welch, Nelson argues that the concept of God has an impact upon the structure of human relationships. When the concept of God has been linked with a unilateral model of divine power, it has tended to see 'God as omniscient, omnipotent, and controlling the world by divine fiat'.[66] Nelson describes this understanding of power as representative of 'a phallic definition of the divine'.[67] Qualities of strength and determination are applied to the divine, along with a notion of power which is 'heavily unilateral and one-directional'.[68] God is the Pantocrator, in control of the universe, radically distinct from human beings. Humans are powerless; God is all-powerful.

Analysing the attribute of omnipotence gives us a good example of the way in which feminists have attempted to deconstruct the theistic account of God. Welch and Nelson have attempted to expose the masculinist basis of much conceptualizing of God by drawing attention to the understanding of power which lies behind the notion of omnipotence. Other feminists have gone on to reconstruct the notion of God, or, to use a more inclusive term, 'God/ess'. It is to this development that we must now turn.

Reconstructing God/ess

Every man (according to Feuerbach) and every woman who is
not fated to remain a slave to the logic of the essence of man,
must imagine a God, an objective-subjective place or path whereby
the self could be coalesced in space and time: unity of instinct,
heart, and knowledge, unity of nature and spirit, condition for
the abode and for saintliness.[69]

In critiquing the concept of God, feminists argue that the concept of God traditionally accepted by philosophers of religion
divinizes patriarchal notions of what it means to be a 'real' man
in a male-dominated and male-defined society. Central to any
feminist account is the importance of stressing the 'full humanity of women'.[70] This has implications for the way in which God
is conceptualized. If human values and experience shape the concept of God, feminists argue that in order for the full humanity
of women to be accepted women's experience must be incorpo-
rated into this process. Male experience has constituted the norm
for philosophical discussions on the nature of God. In this section, emphasis will be given to women's experience and the effect that taking this seriously might have for the concept of God.
Particular emphasis will be given to considering an alternative
concept of God offered by thealogians, who argue that accounts
of the Goddess are the best way of incorporating women's experience into the concept of God.

Women's experience and the concept of God

In developing a theology, a fourfold pattern for the attainment
of truth has formed the basis for theological investigation. Tradition, revelation, hermeneutics of sacred texts, and experience
have to differing degrees and with differing emphasis provided
the basis for the truth content of specific theologies. In offering a
distinctively feminist approach to the concept of God, the importance of experience and particularly the reclamation of *wom-
en's* experience has been stressed by feminist theologians.[71] Yet
emphasizing experience is not without its own difficulties. In
developing a feminist theology or concept of God, *whose* experi-

ence is to be drawn upon? All too often in academic feminist theology, experience is defined as that pertaining to the educated, white, middle-class, professional woman. This would seem to exclude the experiences of women who do not fall into this category. As such, a theology based purely upon individual experience would seem inadequate.

A possible solution to the difficulties of basing any feminist concept of God upon experience might be overcome by considering experiences which unite, rather than divide, women. It has been suggested that the two experiences common to all women are the reality of oppression at the hands of a patriarchal society and the possibility of connection with other women. While this might provide a kind of unity in approaching the conceptualizing of God/ess, it may be that reflection on the problematic task of defining experience leads to a different way of thinking about the nature of theology. Rather than anticipate the construction of one overarching paradigm for the nature of God/ess, we have to recognize that there will be as many understandings of the divine as there are individuals. Diversity, rather than unity, needs to be emphasized. Just as there are a multiplicity of feminisms, so there will be many concepts of God.

Bearing in mind these difficulties, it is still possible to make some claims about the way in which feminist philosophy of religion might approach the concept of God. If the concept of God can be understood to embody those values that are most important for a group or society, the values which form the basis for a feminist understanding of God will differ from those habitually ascribed to God. For example, the idea of God as a superhuman agent has been challenged by feminists on a number of grounds. If God is understood as an agent, this God must presumably have a gender – with the consequences outlined by Mary Daly. At the same time, the idea of God as agent leads to the idea that divinity must lie outside of this world. Sharon Welch disputes this: 'Divinity is not a mark of that which is other than the finite . . . Divinity, or grace, is the resilient, fragile, healing power of finitude itself.'[72] A new emphasis on creation arises. Rather than see the world as the creation of an external deity, it becomes the place of divine possibilities. The shift away from an other-worldly concept of God to a this-worldly account of the divine affects the way in which divinity itself is described. The place given to the idea of absolute power in defining the nature of God, as we have seen, has been rejected; rather than think of divine power as intrusive and threatening (i.e. power *over* others), an alternative definition might focus on 'power' as the ability to *empower* others.

A feminist approach to the concept of God also requires a reappraisal of certain divine attributes which do not form the primary focus for philosophical discussions. Notions of divine justice become more important, although, again, a redefinition of what this might mean is needed. Rather than focus on understanding 'the justice of God', the emphasis would lie with developing accounts of how the divinization of justice might affect the human search for justice in this world. Justice becomes linked to the idea of liberation: how to achieve justice, and what it means in practice.

A feminist approach to the philosophy of religion raises challenging questions for some of the favourite ideas of theism. Rather than accept ideas about God and religion at face value and attempt to argue for the coherence or incoherence of such ideas, a feminist perspective offers a radical critique of the ideas of the discipline. For example, why might we want to argue for a personal immortality? To what extent might this be connected with patriarchal ideals of control over and dominance of the natural environment?[73] In critiquing the concept of God, feminists offer a wider critique of western society and its values. As Irigaray puts it:

> When women want to escape from exploitation, they do not merely destroy a few 'prejudices', they disrupt the entire order of dominant values, economic, social, moral and sexual. They call into question all existing theory, all thought, all language, inasmuch as these are monopolized by men and men alone.[74]

Thealogy and the concept of God

When faced with the apparent masculinism of the concept of God, feminists have responded in different ways. Some, like Mary Daly, have sought a redefinition of God which denies that God is a being (or noun), and argues for God as be-ing (or a verb).[75]

Others, like Sallie McFague, have argued that the language of God/ess needs to be developed to include female language and imagery, and also images which have no basis in gender.[76] According to McFague, such a process reveals the hidden and often revolutionary content of the Bible. A plethora of images is used to describe God. Drawing upon these images can lead to a concept of God which is more acceptable to the concerns of feminists. Others have argued for a different approach which seeks a return to the Goddess, and as such have embarked on *thea*logy as opposed to *theo*logy.

While this emphasis on a female deity might suggest that feminists are merely offering a reversal of the traditional God with its male language and dominance of male cultural forms, this need not be the case. This becomes clear when the nature of God/ess is approached from a feminist perspective. For most thealogians the attempt to establish the existence or otherwise of some divine being is not their primary concern. One of the most important thealogical insights concerns the lack of interest in the Goddess as a being whose existence could be proved. Starhawk, a radical feminist writer from the United States, makes this explicit:

> When I say Goddess I am not talking about a being somewhere outside of this world nor am I proposing a new belief system. I am talking about choosing an attitude: choosing to take this living world, the people and creatures in it, as the ultimate meaning and purpose of life, to see the world, the earth and our lives as sacred.[77]

Jane Caputi in her book *Gossips, Gorgons and Crones* reiterates this approach when writing of the Goddess as 'O-Zona' or the 'Lady of Slaughter'. For Caputi, this image of the Goddess of destruction describes her own sense of outrage at the wanton destruction of the environment. She is not describing a deity who could be discerned as an entity independent of human life. As she puts it:

> Now, I assure you, I am not proposing that there is a divine woman hanging out in the upper atmosphere. I am not suggesting that we worship O-Zona or try to establish a personal relationship

with her. Nor do I intend us to become supporters of ozone de-
pletion, seeing this phenomenon as a manifestation of divine will.
Rather, I am suggesting that the diminishment of the ozone layer
must be understood as a manifestation of female Powers, especially those raging, chaotic, creative, and destructive – essentially
transmutational – Powers associated with the Crone.[78]

Feminists such as Starhawk and Caputi accept and develop the
idea that concepts of God express human values. Starhawk writes
of 'Goddess' as a way of responding to the things of this world,
as a way of expressing the significance of human life and relationships. Caputi uses the image of the Goddess as 'the Lady of
Slaughter' to express her outrage at the destruction of the planet,
and the devaluation of female 'powers'. Caputi and Starhawk
use the language of the Goddess specifically as a way of exploring what it means to be a woman, and particularly what it means
to be a woman at this time in human history.

For some thealogians, the language of Goddess is employed to
make sense of their own individual experiences of womanhood.
Christine Downing employs the stories of the Greek goddesses
to make sense of her own experience of life.[79] Carol Christ sees
the Goddess as a symbol which enables women to come to terms
with their sexuality in a positive way. She writes of the Goddess
as a 'symbol [which] aids the process of naming and reclaiming
the female body and its cycles and processes'.[80] Christ points out
that, like the Christian God, the Goddess is often described in
triune terms. She is Virgin, Mother and Crone. Acceptance and
appropriation of the different stages of a woman's life in this
dramatic way enables women, Christ writes, 'to value youth,
creativity and wisdom in themselves and other women'.[81] Thus
the task of thealogy is intimately connected to issues of female
self-awareness and self-acceptance.

This ultimately individualistic appropriation of the Goddess
metaphor may seem unsatisfactory: not least to feminists concerned with the attainment of human liberation. It could be argued that the Goddess employed in the way suggested by
Downing and Christ encourages women – particularly middle-
class women – to ignore social inequalities in favour of private
'religious' experience. However, this does not mean that the im-

age of the Goddess is without the power to change human relationships. As Melissa Raphael points out, thealogy necessitates a
radical reappraisal of the notion of divinity.[82] If God/ess is not to
be understood as a cosmic force or agent outside of this world,
but as a way of endowing this life with meaning, a fundamental
change in human attitudes to the environment (and by implication to others) is needed. 'Order' does not come from without;
and that has implications not only for the God who is understood as the 'Prime Mover' and the 'First Cause', but also for the
western capitalist imposing 'order' on an apparently 'chaotic'
world: 'An ecologically harmonious culture that listened to the
rhythms of infinity would show patriarchal production to be the
dissonant negative chaos that it is.'[83]

Future discussion of the Goddess needs to focus on the social
and political implications of this image if it is to be a liberating
alternative to the abstract notion of the theist's God. Naomi
Goldenberg in her oft-quoted essay 'The Return of the Goddess'
suggests that the Goddess is an image which supports the idea of
the individual as part of a community.[84] As such, the idea of the
Goddess does have an impact upon the political realm as she
valorizes ideas of dependence and community. The Goddess is
an image for the connection between all things, and in emphasizing this sense of connection, the thealogian can go some way
to escaping the charge that the Goddess will only appeal to middle-class women. As Monica Sjöö and Barbara Mor write:

> (T)he Goddess [does not] 'live' solely in elite separatist retreats
> . . . The Goddess at this moment is starving to death in refugee
> camps, with a skeletal child clutched to her dry nipples . . . The
> Goddess is an eight-year-old girl being used for the special sexual
> thrills of visiting businessmen in a Brazilian brothel. The God-
> dess is patrolling with a rifle . . . trying to save a revolution in
> Nicaragua . . . the Goddess IS the world – the Goddess is *in* the
> world. And nobody can escape the world.[85]

In revisioning the nature of the world and the relationship of
human beings to their environment and each other, the image of
the Goddess may prove to be an important development in how
we understand the conceptualizing of the divine.

Drawing upon the examples given in this section, outline the strengths and weaknesses of thealogy. What might this approach suggest about the pursuit of theology more generally?

Liberating the Subject

Feminist approaches to the subject-matter of the philosophy of religion suggest a movement away from accepting the content of the discipline as traditionally defined. To this extent, it could be argued that feminists are attempting to liberate the subject itself. As befits an approach to the discipline which takes its lead from feminist theology – itself influenced by liberation theologies – the concern with liberation and empowerment is primary. This opens up philosophy of religion to a wider critique, for theological/thealogical discussions are of little interest if the social implications of such concepts are not of paramount importance. In approaching the philosophical study of religion, feminists are attempting to show the connections between academic debate and social values and structures. Under a feminist interpretation, the discipline becomes answerable to more than simply its own practitioners: philosophers of religion must also be aware of the way in which God and religion are integral features in the way in which human beings experience and structure their world.

Conclusion

This chapter has offered three separate approaches to philosophy of religion which challenge the way in which the discipline is habitually allied to philosophical theism. We have suggested that a different starting point might be possible, and have considered the ways in which various philosophers and theologians attempt this. At this point, we might want to ask ourselves if these alternative approaches have not in their own ways conceded too much to the sceptical attack upon religion. Cupitt and Sutherland specifically develop their accounts of religious

belief against a broader acceptance of the naturalistic interpretation of religion. An approach to the philosophy of religion
which takes its lead from Wittgenstein accepts the fundamental
difference between religious and scientific language. Feminist
thealogy specifically advances a view of religion as creative self-
expression. Do these alternative accounts capture something of
the significance of religious belief which is lost if the theistic
model is employed in the attempt to understand religion? Or
are these views merely expressions of the 'last gasp' of religion
in a world that can be well understood without recourse to
such a paradigm?

The remainder of this book will attempt to answer these questions. Our aim is to consider the way in which these various
approaches to philosophy of religion lead to different answers to
some of the central themes considered by practitioners of the
discipline. The next chapter focuses on precisely this point by
considering the different interpretations of miracle and immortality made by philosophical theists and by those offering revi-
sionist accounts of belief.

Suggested reading:

I   Revisionary Accounts of God

Beverley Clack, 'Stewart Sutherland and Belief in God', *Theol-
ogy*, July/August, 1996, pp. 290–5.
Don Cupitt, *Taking Leave of God*, London: SCM, 1980.
John Hick, *An Interpretation of Religion*, Basingstoke:
Macmillan, 1989, ch. 3.
Robin Le Poidevin, *Arguing for Atheism*, London: Routledge,
1996.
Stewart R. Sutherland, *God, Jesus and Belief*, Oxford: Blackwell,
1984.
Peter Vardy, *The Puzzle of God*, London: Collins Flame, 1990.
Keith Ward, *Holding Fast to God*, London: SPCK, 1982.

II   Wittgenstein and the Philosophy of Religion

Cyril Barrett, *Wittgenstein, Ethics and Religious Belief*, Oxford:
Blackwell, 1991.

Brian R. Clack, 'D. Z. Phillips, Wittgenstein and Religion', *Religious Studies,* 31, 1995, pp. 111–20.

Brian R. Clack, 'Wittgenstein and Expressive Theories of Religion', *International Journal for the Philosophy of Religion,* vol. 40, no. 1, 1996, pp. 47–61.

Brian R. Clack, *Wittgenstein, Frazer and Religion,* Basingstoke: Macmillan, 1998.

W. D. Hudson, *Wittgenstein and Religious Belief,* Basingstoke: Macmillan, 1975.

Kai Nielsen, 'Wittgensteinian Fideism', *Philosophy,* July 1967, pp. 207ff.

D. Z. Phillips, *Wittgenstein and Religion,* Basingstoke: Macmillan, 1993 (especially articles 'Philosophy, Theology and the Reality of God', 'Religious Beliefs and Language-Games' and 'Religion in Wittgenstein's Mirror').

Ludwig Wittgenstein, *Lectures and Conversations in Aesthetics, Psychology and Religious Belief,* Oxford: Blackwell, 1966.

Ludwig Wittgenstein, *Remarks on Frazer's Golden Bough,* Doncaster: Brynmill Press, 1979.

Ludwig Wittgenstein, *Culture and Value,* Oxford: Blackwell, 1980.

III   Feminism and the Philosophy of Religion

Pamela Sue Anderson, *A Feminist Philosophy of Religion,* Oxford: Blackwell, 1998.

Carol Christ and J. Plaskow (eds), *Womanspirit Rising,* New York: Harper and Row, 1979.

Beverley Clack, 'The Denial of Dualism: Thealogical Reflections on the Sexual and the Spiritual', *Feminist Theology,* September 1995.

Mary Daly, *Beyond God the Father,* London: Women's Press, 1986.

Christine Downing, *The Goddess,* New York: Crossroad Publishing, 1984.

James Nelson, 'Embracing Masculinity', in S. Longfellow and J. Nelson (eds), *Sexuality and the Sacred,* London: Mowbray, 1994.

Melissa Raphael, *Thealogy and Embodiment*, Sheffield: Sheffield Academic Press, 1996.

Rosemary Radford Ruether, *Sexism and God-Talk*, London: SCM, 1983.

Sharon Welch, *A Feminist Ethic of Risk*, Minneapolis: Fortress Press, 1990.

5

Divine Action and the Beyond

Introduction

In the previous chapter we explored some radical alternatives to the kind of philosophical theism which dominates discussions in the philosophy of religion. According to Cupitt and certain feminist thealogians, we should approach the concept of God creatively, viewing it less as a description of a transcendent being, and more as a creative interpretation of human values and concepts. Stewart Sutherland drew our attention to the connection between religion and morality, with all the implications that that has for how we are to live in this world. Feminist philosophy of religion suggested that we focus on issues of power: *whose* concept of God is that which forms the basis for debates in the philosophy of religion? And philosophy of religion which takes its lead from Wittgenstein suggests it is simply a confusion to think religion is centred on a realm of supernatural realities.

Having considered such radical views, we might expect the shape of debates within the philosophy of religion to change. If we take seriously these alternatives, can we still base our discussions upon a substantive definition of religion and the God who is attendant upon such an understanding? Surprisingly, philosophers of religion have tended to ignore, or to dismiss out of hand, such alternative approaches to the discipline. Our aim in this section is to consider the effect that taking seriously such challenges might have upon the shape of debates in the philosophy of religion. As such, we shall explore the way in which following either the 'traditional' theistic line or one of the alternative accounts affects the way in which key issues within the philosophy of religion are discussed. Of considerable interest to philosophers of religion have been the issues of the miraculous and immortality, and it is these themes that will test the efficacy of the different approaches to the philosophy of religion considered in this book.

1 Miracles

Classic Approaches to the Miraculous

If religious believers are asked to offer evidence in favour of the truth of their beliefs, they may often appeal to the occurrence of miracles, principally those attested to in the Bible. Historically, the questions that have principally concerned philosophers are: what is a miracle and what justification can we have for believing that such things occur or have occurred?

Defining 'miracle'

To take the first of these questions, what do we mean by the word 'miracle'? A helpful definition is offered by Richard Swinburne, who writes that 'a miracle is an event of an extraordinary kind, brought about by a god, and of religious significance'.[1] We can see that this definition consists of three clauses: 'extraordinary event'; 'brought about by a god'; 'of religious significance'. Most debate has focused on the first clause (what it means for something to be 'an extraordinary event'), but before we reach that controversy, we should take a brief look at the other two clauses.

When Swinburne says that a miracle will be something 'brought about by a god', this means that a given event can only be a miracle *if* there exists a super-empirical being (or beings) who brought about that event. No miracles occur in a universe conceived atheistically; extraordinary events would then be explained as flukes. Swinburne makes it clear that this clause may be interpreted tightly (it is only the Christian God who can work miracle) or loosely (a god other than the Christian one could perform such acts, or human beings might also work miracles by appealing to their god).

To say that an event must have 'religious significance' if it is to count as a miracle is to say that not just any remarkable occurrence will do. A putative miracle must reveal something about the nature of that supernatural being who has brought about the event; typically, it will attest to the god's compassion, love and goodness. For example, if a baby stricken with terminal cancer is suddenly and inexplicably cured, then it will perhaps be appropriate to describe this occurrence as a miracle. The parents of the child may praise and thank God for his benevolence and care. On the other hand, if that same baby mysteriously explodes into flames, then we are unlikely to refer to this as a miracle. The religious significance of a miracle, then, is that it offers us a glimpse of the love of God, and is an event which helps to better the world, furthering the divine purpose.

These preliminary points lead us to the central point: what do we mean when we say that a miracle is an extraordinary event? Many events might be extraordinary without being miraculous. It is, surely, extraordinary that a man has walked on the moon, or that a tree whose leaves fell in autumn is clothed again in spring. But we would probably be reluctant to call any of these miracles. This is because such happenings, extraordinary though they may be, are events *within the natural order of the world*. If we turn our attention to paradigm examples of miracles we find something very different: a sea parting to let people walk through it; water turned into wine; a man who has been dead for three days coming back to life. None of these events would occur naturally. Water, if kept undisturbed in a barrel will not transform itself into wine, and once a man has been dead for three days we can be sure that he will not walk and talk again. So if such events *do* take place, then we can say that something has taken place *against the natural flow of things*. Viewed this way, miracles break, or are violations of, natural laws.

David Hume's challenge to the belief in miracles

This violation conception of a miracle is expressed by David Hume in his *Enquiry Concerning Human Understanding*: 'A miracle may be accurately defined, a transgression of a law of nature by a particular volition of the Deity or by the interposition of some invisible agent.'[2]

Hume put forward the most important challenge to the belief in miracles. His attack is twofold: firstly, he offers an a priori argument against the very possibility of there being miracles; he then supplements this argument with four arguments designed to discredit all *reports* of miracles. In his main argument, Hume says that when conducting any enquiry, and in particular any historical enquiry, 'a wise man proportions his belief to the evidence'.[3] If it is claimed that some particular event (E) happened, an investigator will weigh the evidence in favour of E having happened against the evidence that E did not happen. This evidence will include such things as testimony, memories and our general experience of the world. The more commonplace an event, the more likely that it happened. So, for example, if I tell you that I have recently bought a new car, there will be no need for you to distrust my claim. On the other hand, if I then inform you that my car will travel at well over three hundred miles per hour, you would justifiably be sceptical. So the more commonplace an event, the more likely that it happened, and one is more justified in believing what is trivial and everyday than in believing what is fantastical.

Hume contends that this line of reasoning provides us with as strong an argument against the occurrence of miracles as we are ever likely to find. For a miracle, as we have seen, is considered to be the violation of a law of nature, and it is a crucial part of general experience of the world that such laws always hold true and are never broken:

A miracle is a violation of the laws of nature; and as a firm and unalterable experience has established these laws, the proof against a miracle, from the very nature of the fact, is as entire as any argument from experience can possibly be imagined . . . Nothing is esteemed a miracle, if it ever happens in the common course of nature. It is no miracle that a man, seemingly in good health, should die on a sudden: because such a kind of death, though more unusual than any other, has yet been frequently observed to happen. But it is a miracle, that a dead man should come to life; because that has never been observed in any age or country. There must, therefore, be a uniform experience against every miraculous event, otherwise the event would not merit that appellation. And as a uniform experience amounts to a proof, there is a direct and full proof, from the nature of the fact, against the existence of any miracle.[4]

So Hume's proof is this: we have knowledge of laws of nature, and we have faith in their constant functioning. We know, for example, that if I jump out of a window I will fall and not levitate. We know that when a person has died and been dead for a number of days that that person will not be revived. Thus, when someone tells us that a miracle has occurred – that a man who died a number of days ago has been seen walking about – then we have to weigh up the evidence for and against this occurrence. In favour of this peculiar event having happened we have someone's testimony, while, on the other hand, we have the whole weight of our experience of the constant functioning of the laws of nature. And, given the extraordinary nature of the event, it would seem more likely that the person reporting the miracle is mistaken rather than that a law of nature has been spectacularly broken. As Hume puts it:

No testimony is sufficient to establish a miracle, unless the testimony be of such a kind, that its falsehood would be more miraculous than the fact, which it endeavours to establish . . . When anyone tells me, that he saw a dead man restored to life, I immediately consider with myself, whether it be more probable, that this person should either deceive or be deceived, or the fact, which he relates, should really have happened. I weigh the one miracle against the other. . . and always reject the greater miracle.[5]

Given this reasoning, we must conclude that no rational person can ever be justified in believing in miraculous occurrences.

This is the case even if the person reporting the miracle is of outstanding character and is known to be impeccably honest. Indeed, Hume argues, it strengthens the sceptical argument further when we reflect upon the fact that reports of miracles tend to come, not from honest and reliable people, but from ignorant people whose intentions are open to question. Hume pursues this allegation in his subsidiary arguments, contained in the second part of his chapter on miracles. Just as we may wish to give our assent to certain questionable beliefs simply because they are held by reputable and trustworthy people, so we may refuse to ascribe to other equally questionable beliefs because these positions are held by people of dubious character and doubtful honesty. If I am told by a reputable authority on the subject that aliens may have visited earth, then I am more likely to entertain that view seriously than if the same piece of information is imparted to me by a drunk with a reputation for telling tall stories.

Such arguments against the reputation of people are often called *ad hominem* arguments. Hume's use of them in his account of miracles is masterly. Firstly, he observes that we never find miracles attested by a sufficient number of educated, sensible or reputable people. The corollary of this is found in his second argument: 'It forms a strong presumption against all supernatural and miraculous relations, that they are observed chiefly to abound among ignorant and barbarous nations . . . It is strange . . . that such prodigious events never happen in our days.'⁶ Is it really just a coincidence that miracles do not happen in modern times when we are vastly more educated, and far less credulous, than, say, the peasants of first century Palestine? What can it tell us about the character of 'the Miraculous' that its manifestations decline as knowledge increases? Hume's third argument focuses on the tendency of people to be superstitious and gullible, and to be titillated by stories of miraculous and remarkable events. This is so much the case that certain people lose control of their reason when tales of miracles are told to them. The tendency Hume describes is particularly true of religious people: 'A religionist may be an enthusiast, and imagine he sees what has no reality: he may know his narrative to be false, and yet persevere in it, with the best intentions in the world, for the sake of promoting so holy a cause.'⁷

We may see how such a line of thought may develop if we consider sceptical questionings of the resurrection of Christ. There have been a number of thinkers, notably Hermann Samuel Reimarus (1694–1768) who have maintained that the resurrection can be explained by the disciples stealing the body of Jesus from the tomb.[8] The disciples did this, not simply to be tricksters, but 'with the best intentions in the world, for the sake of promoting so holy a cause', namely Christ's ethical and political message. This may seem a fanciful speculation, and we might want to reject the explanation. But consider Hume's principles: unlikely as the grave-robbing scenario is, it is still *more* likely than accepting that a man has risen from the dead. We are then, from a rational point of view, duty-bound to accept *any* naturalistic account of the resurrection, for it will be more likely than the traditional miraculous version.

Hume's view has been immensely influential, and many philosophers have continued his sceptical approach.[9] Most notable of these continuations has been the standpoint discussed by R. F. Holland, who considers the contention that the very idea of a violation of a law of nature is incoherent, for it confounds a law of nature with a judicial law. Breaking a law of nature is not like breaking the law of the land. If I drive my car while intoxicated, or if I break into a person's house and steal from them, then my actions can be described as violations of a law. But a law of nature cannot be so flouted. If something, then, appears to break a law of nature, what this means is not that the event is miraculous, but that that law 'has been, not flouted or violated, but falsified'.[10] The law will then have to be revised (or discarded) in order to take account of this event. What the Humean tradition maintains, therefore, is that if a miracle is defined as a violation of a law of nature, then we can be sure that no event can be a miracle. We end up, then, with the following proof:

A miracle is 'a violation of a law of nature'.
A law of nature cannot be violated.
Therefore, no 'miracle' can occur.

In defence of the classic account of miracles

Hume has provided us with an extremely useful 'check to all kinds of superstitious illusion',[11] and we would be wise to adhere to his principles of reasoning whenever we are confronted with tales of miraculous occurrences. It would seem better to be sceptical than to be gullible. Of course, this does raise considerable difficulties for our acceptance of the gospel narratives: the miracles found in the Bible are not well attested, and the weight of evidence can never be in favour of their actual historical occurrence. On the other hand, it is the case that Hume is claiming far too much for his proof, which, it must be said, confuses improbability with *impossibility*. Miracles certainly are radically unusual events, but this can in no way mean that no miracle has ever occurred. Similarly, it may be true that most reports of miracles can be put down to the exercise of ignorance and credulity, to 'the knavery and folly of men',[12] but he is too quick to dismiss all miracles on these grounds.

Hume's argument, again, never touches on the question of what he would conclude were he *himself* to witness an apparently miraculous event. Here it would not be a knave's testimony he would have to consider, but the evidence of his own eyes. Of course, he could simply hold that in such circumstances his senses had deceived him, but what if the happening had been witnessed by countless other people? Would such sceptical questionings seem inappropriate? But here Holland's point comes into play: such a 'miraculous' event would not be a miracle at all, but something which showed that the laws of nature must be amended to accommodate that occurrence. So if a holy man were to levitate, this would not constitute a 'miracle'. Rather, the onus would be on *scientists* to reframe the law of gravity, including a condition that 'under such-and-such circumstances, a human being can rise up and float in the air'. But, as Swinburne rightly says, this seems a rather drastic course of action. If we have a law which has previously explained things well and has always led us to correct predictions about how things will function in the future, then it seems an over-reaction to reject that law because of one reported anomaly. Rather than revise the law and risk producing a worse one, it would be more sensible and economical to say that something bizarre and unrepeatable has occurred which appears to violate that law.[13]

To sum up our discussion thus far: Hume does not appear to have provided us with a conclusive proof against the possibility of miracles, and if we were presented with a well-enough attested example of an extraordinary event (say, of a man rising from the dead), we may have to withhold our disbelief and suggest that a natural law has indeed been broken. Of course, whether or not such a remarkable incident was 'brought about by a god' would be more difficult to prove. Indeed, it is perhaps the case that to describe something as a miracle is not to offer an explanation of that thing at all, but rather to confess our ignorance and awe in the face of it. This might lead us away from the violation conception altogether. For this is not the only way of understanding the miraculous: there is another way of looking at the subject, which has an equally distinguished history.

> Would you define a miracle as 'a violation of a law of nature'? If not, how would you define 'miracle'?

Alternative Accounts: Miracles as Signs and Coincidences

If the violation conception emphasizes the *features* of a miracle, then the alternative conception focuses on its *consequences*; in other words, on the effect it has on the person who witnesses (or hears about) it. B. R. Tilghman, for example, imagines two possible reactions to Jesus's raising of the dead man Lazarus. One observer finds it an extraordinary and marvellous event ('The darndest thing I ever saw in my life!'), while the other observer falls on his knees, crying 'My Lord and my God!' Only the latter of these two observers can be said to have experienced the event as a *miracle*. As it stands, this account can be accommodated within the violation conception, but Tilghman goes further, speculating that a medical examination of Lazarus might reveal that he was never dead in the first place, but perhaps only comatose, or else an accomplice in a confidence trick:

> The believer may be disillusioned and throw down his cross in disgust at what he takes to be a trick that was played on him . . .

But must that be the believer's response? Might we nevertheless imagine him acknowledging the doctors' conclusions and then setting it aside as not relevant to his life? For him it remains a miracle.[14]

The suggestion here, then, is that what counts as a miracle has little to do with its relation to the laws of nature, but to the impression it makes on a person; whether it leads them to change the direction of their life. This theme is uppermost in Paul Tillich's account of miracles, contained in his *Systematic Theology*. Defining miracles as 'sign-events', Tillich says that we cannot separate the occurrence of a miracle from its religious context. This is why Jesus refused to perform miracles when asked for a demonstration of his power. Tillich outlines three conditions that an event has to fulfil for it to be classed a miracle:

A genuine miracle is first of all an event which is astonishing, unusual, shaking, *without contradicting the rational structure of reality*. In the second place, it is an event which points to the mystery of being, expressing its relation to us in a definite way. In the third place, it is an occurrence which is received as a sign-event in an ecstatic experience.[15]

So Tillich's contention is that, without it violating any natural laws, an extraordinary event may serve as a revelation of God, and to that extent should be treated as a miracle. Though Tillich has moved a considerable distance from the violation conception, his account is still recognizably theistic. Miracles are not unconnected with God, and are, indeed, revelatory. When we turn to R. F. Holland's treatment of the subject we find something far more extreme.

Like Tilghman and Tillich, Holland wants to say that a particular event need not violate a natural law in order to be characterized as a miracle. All an event would need to have in order to deserve such an appellation is what he calls 'a kind of human significance'.[16] To this end, he tells the following story :

A child riding his toy motor-car strays on to an unguarded railway crossing near his house and a wheel of his car gets stuck down the side of one of the rails. An express train is due to pass

with the signals in its favour and a curve in the track makes
it impossible for the driver to stop his train in time to avoid
any obstruction he might encounter on the crossing. The mother
coming out of the house to look for her child sees him on the
crossing and hears the train approaching. She runs forward shout-
ing and waving. The little boy remains seated in his car, looking
downward, engrossed in the task of pedaling it free. The brakes
of the train are applied and it comes to rest a few feet from
the child. The mother thanks God for the miracle; which she
never ceases to think of as such, although, as she in due course
learns, there was nothing supernatural about the manner in
which the brakes of the train came to be applied. The driver had
fainted, for a reason which had nothing to do with the presence
of the child on the line, and the brakes were applied automatically as his hand ceased to exert pressure on the control
lever.[17]

Though such a coincidence may, says Holland, be regarded as
a miracle, 'it cannot without confusion be taken as a sign of
divine interference with the natural order'.[18] The upshot of
this is that a miracle should be seen simply as a remarkable and
beneficial coincidence interpreted in a religious fashion. To say
that something which has happened to me is a 'miracle' amounts
to much the same as thanking my lucky stars; I am expressing
the intensity of my relief when I use that word 'miracle'. Holland's account certainly captures the sense of 'miracle' as it is
used colloquially. When we hear of people escaping from burning buildings or from the wreckage of an air crash, we often
hear these exploits described as 'miracles'. But the inverted com-
mas are used here intentionally. We do not tend to think of
these 'miracles' as in the same league as the miracles of the
New Testament, what we might call 'miracles-proper'. If this
is the case, then what right does Holland have to say that
his 'coincidence conception' is a worthy recipient of the title
of miracle? It is one thing to say that a religious *response* is
crucial to anything counting as a miracle; it is another thing to
say that the response is all and that divine action is no part of
the event.

Nevertheless, aspects of the sign conception do grasp something of the way in which a religious believer looks at the world. If we observe the phenomena of the natural world, we may be overcome with emotions such as these, expressed by D. H. Lawrence:

> The one universal element in consciousness which is fundamental to life is the element of wonder. You cannot help feeling it in a bean as it starts to grow and pulls itself out of its jacket. You cannot help feeling it in the glisten of the nucleus of the amoeba. You recognize it, willy-nilly, in an ant busily tugging at a straw; in a rook as it walks the frosty grass.[19]

If, suffused with religious feeling, a believer looks around at the world, it may be their natural reaction to describe those things Lawrence speaks of as miracles.

Consider this example from Wittgenstein, who thought it characteristic of the religious sensibility that it viewed the world as a miracle:

> The miracles of nature.
> One might say: art *shows* us the miracles of nature. It is based on the *concept* of the miracles of nature. (The blossom, just opening out. What is *marvellous* about it?) We say: 'Just look at it opening out!' (*Culture and Value*, p. 56e)

To what extent is such an understanding of the miraculous adequate? Is there anything you would want to add?

Such things we do – habitually – describe as miracles. The question is: are these called miracles because we see the hand of God in them, or can they, *irrespective* of such a commitment, be described as such? Certainly, these 'miracles of nature' do not violate any natural law, so again our central question is paramount: must an event be contrary to a natural law, and caused by a god, in order to be classed as a miracle? Similar issues about the action of a god are raised when we consider a central feature of the religious life: prayer, described by William James as 'the very soul and essence of religion'.[20]

Petitionary Prayer: Classic and Alternative Accounts

Francis Galton once suggested an experiment to test the concrete effects of prayer. Prayers for rain were to be made over one half of England, while prayers for fine weather were to be made over the other half. When rainfall measurements for the two halves were compared, we would be able to see whether the prayers had had any noticeable effect. To some people, Galton's suggestion may seem futile and stupid. But if praying to God is believed to usher in results, then surely these effects could be charted in the manner suggested by Galton. Or are these kind of results – concrete, empirical results – not the fruits of prayer? Once again, two conceptions of prayer are apparent: one sees prayer as an attempt to achieve some end, while the other views it as in some sense expressive.

The former is perhaps the most natural position to adopt. People pray for relief from illness, for good examination results, for an end to wars, and so on. By engaging in prayer, the believer is hoping that God will heed the prayer and help to achieve the end which is so desired. Indeed, there are thousands of Christians who believe that God has indeed acted in response to their requests. There are, however, problems with holding such an opinion. God, as we have seen, is supposed to be omniscient. So why does he need to be told, say, that the people of Bosnia are enduring suffering? And why does he need to be asked to help them? Surely an omniscient, omnipotent, loving God would do so without being asked. Yet even if God did act in answer to the prayer and brought stability to Bosnia, why could he not do so elsewhere, bringing peace to all parts of the world?

For advocates of a less traditional account of petitionary prayer, such problems arise because God is here figured to be something like a politician, forced to act by the weight of public opinion. For a philosopher like Peter Winch, the roots of the problem lie just in this, in confusing the nature of petitionary prayer with the requests we might make of another human being:

> [Prayer] cannot be elucidated by starting simply with the function 'making requests to x', substituting 'God' for 'x', and then asking what difference is made by the fact that God has different characteristics from other xs. 'Making requests of x', that is, is not a function which retains the same sense whether 'God' or some other name or description of a human being is substituted for 'x'.[21]

What this means is that, although it may superficially *look* as if a prayer of petition is an attempt to achieve a desired end, an attempt to persuade God to do something, it in fact has a radically different character. For Wittgensteinians such as Winch and Phillips, this character can only be uncovered by paying attention to the *use* of the language of prayer. When this is attended to, when we examine the role that such prayers have in the lives of believers, what we see is that far from being attempts to cajole, prayers of petition are in fact the means whereby a believer can express and reflect upon deep and troubling elements in his/her life:

> When deep religious believers pray for something, they are not so much asking God to bring this about, but in a way telling Him of the strength of their desires. They realize that things may not go as they wish, but they are asking to be able to go on living whatever happens. In prayers of confession and in prayers of petition, the believer is trying to find a meaning and a hope that will deliver him from the elements in his life which threaten to destroy it: in the first case, his guilt, and in the second case, his desires.[22]

Phillips is keen to emphasize that a petitionary prayer which really intended to bring about a change in anything other than the believer himself would be 'superstitious'. Prayer, then, has nothing to do with influencing the outcome of events, and everything to do with reflecting upon the character and purpose of our lives.

What are we doing when we pray for a situation, like the conflict in Northern Ireland, to be resolved? What implications might our answer have for the concept of God?

If James is right to equate prayer with the essence of religion, then Phillips's view certainly takes us right back to the heart of those alternative approaches to the philosophy of religion we considered in the previous chapter. Religion is not a speculative explanation of the nature of the world, but a way of reflecting upon our human condition and improving our moral and spiritual sensibility. When we review these differing approaches to the nature of miracle and prayer, it is hard not to feel that it is certainly more acceptable to believe in miracles if they are conceived as something other than violations of natural law, and hard also not to think that prayer is more credible if it is a species of meditation rather than a form of manipulation. On the other hand, one must be aware of the nagging suspicion that some crucial element of religious belief is being stripped away when miracles are seen only as remarkable coincidences or else as the marvels of nature. Similarly, the Wittgensteinian accounts of prayer, though certainly not ungrounded in the language of prayer, do tend to excite the impression that what is being attempted is something akin to the salvaging of wreckage: prayers once thought to be able to move mountains have been shown to be futile, and as a last resort believers present them as sources of self-reflection. The decision which one must reach is whether this indeed is the case, or whether this model actually presents what is essential about prayer and the miraculous. Of course, one could always maintain that the traditional model is the right one. One would then have to provide good examples of miracles and of answered prayers. And that might not be an easy task.

II Immortality

Introduction

Though wise men at their end know dark is right,
Because their words had forked no lightning they
Do not go gentle into that good night.

Human beings are the only animals which know that they will die. How are they to come to terms with the knowledge of mortality? Dylan Thomas's poem, cited above, suggests one response to this knowledge. Written for his dying father, he encourages him to fight against death, to resist the pull of mortality. An alternative approach has been suggested by different religious traditions: death should not be viewed as the end of life, but the gateway to further life which lies beyond the grave.[23] When philosophers of religion have considered this claim, they have focused on establishing the coherence – or otherwise – of this belief in immortality. The aim of this section is to consider the different forms these discussions have taken, and to consider some of the recent contributions to the debate by those who would refute the coherence of philosophical theism.

Classic Approaches to Immortality

Discussions of immortality in traditional philosophy of religion have tended to focus upon two interconnected areas which are vital to establishing the coherence of the belief in a life after death: survival and personhood.

'Surviving death'

The implication behind the idea of immortality appears to be that we will 'survive' death. As D. Z. Phillips points out, this is problematic. We know what happens to human bodies after death – they rot and decay. As such, the meaning of the term 'surviving death' seems far from straightforward. Indeed, it seems illogical, for to talk of survival in ordinary contexts implies that death has been avoided. To say that I have 'survived' a horrific accident, for example, means that I did not die. What meaning, if any, can be ascribed to this contradictory phrase, 'surviving death'?[24]

Different philosophers have approached this issue in different ways. John Hick, for example, offers one solution to this apparent problem. According to Hick, God will save human beings from death. Hick argues that God has the ability to create a complete blueprint of our personality which appears in a different spatio-temporal dimension when we die.[25] He offers this 'Replica' theory as a means of showing the *logical possibility* of surviving death. His chief concern is to challenge the claim that it is logically impossible for the human individual to survive death. If my body rots after my death, how can I (in any real sense) be said to survive? What of my foibles and peculiarities: how can these things survive without the body that defines me as a person?

In everyday situations, we recognize a person by their physical shape; personal identity is thus connected to bodily continuity. At death, this primary means for personal identity is broken. Hick's argument rests on his claim that it is logically possible for the self to survive the radical discontinuity of personal identity caused by death. He begins by defining resurrection as the belief in the divine creation in another space of an exact psycho-physical replica of a deceased person. We might not be convinced that such a 'replica' could be us in any real sense. Hick attempts to convert us to his way of thinking by relating three examples which show the logical possibility of maintaining that this replica is us:[26]

1 Whilst giving a lecture in London, I vanish. At the precise moment that I cease to exist in London, an exact replica of myself comes into existence in New York. The New York B. Clack is exactly similar to the London B. Clack in every respect. Mentally and physically she is exactly like the person who disappeared in London. The memories, fingerprints, hair, stomach contents, beliefs, habits and mental propensities are identical to those of the B. Clack who disappeared in London. Now, Hick asks, would we say that the New York B. Clack is the same as the person who disappeared in London? The person involved is conscious of being 'the same'; their family and friends think that they are 'the same' (so this is a rather different state of affairs than that faced by the pro-

tagonists of the film *Invasion of the Body Snatchers*!). Soon we would extend our use of the term the 'same person' to cover the facts of this case. *Despite* the radical break in bodily continuity, we would eventually come to accept the New York B. Clack as the London B. Clack.

2   For his second example, Hick offers the same instance, only this time, in London, the person dies. Hick believes that even with a corpse on our hands, we would still come to think of the New York B. Clack as being the same person as the London B. Clack.

3   This time, replication takes place in another space. B. Clack dies, and reappears not in America, but in another world. Hick argues that if we are prepared to accept the validity of the previous illustration, we should accept that B. Clack is the same person in this new world as the person who had died in London.

Hick believes that by using these examples, he has shown the logical possibility of thinking that our personality could survive death. His critics have not been so sure. Terence Penelhum objects that in examples (2) and (3) it is far from mandatory that we will accept the New York B. Clack to be the same as the B. Clack in London. We need to *decide* if they are the same. According to Penelhum, there can only be automatic and unquestionable identity where bodily continuity is maintained.[27] Hick accepts the fact that we need to decide but does not believe this to be a problem. All instances which fall outside our normal experience need decision. Hick is only concerned to show that *it is logically possible to speak of ourselves being resurrected* to a new life in a new world.

> How convincing do you find Hick's argument for the logical possibility of surviving death? What issues might you want to raise with him?

Consideration of Hick has shown us that the notion of immortality is closely connected with our understanding of what it is to be a person. This issue forms the second focus for discussions of immortality.

The question of personhood

What is it that constitutes the human person? Am I simply a highly developed mammal (to use Gilbert Ryle's phrase[28])? Do I consist of body and mind/soul (the distinction made classically by Plato and Descartes)? Am I a unity of the spiritual and the material (the claim ascribed to Aristotle by Antony Flew,[29] and traditional Church doctrine)?

The kind of answer we give to these questions will in many ways determine our answer to the question 'will I survive death?' If we think of ourselves in naturalistic terms as highly developed mammals, it is difficult to think in terms of a life after death. Death, when it comes, will mark the end of our existence. If we think of ourselves as a duality of soul and body, it would seem consistent to imagine a life outside the confines of the body. Our soul (or mind) could survive death, for it is not material and therefore is unaffected by the destruction wrought by death. The important point to grasp here is not the specific answers given to the question 'will I survive death?', but the importance of the concept of personhood for understanding the idea of immortality.

Indeed, the way in which we understand the notion of personhood will affect the understanding of post-mortem existence which we hold. If we define the human self as essentially the mind/soul, it will be consistent to hold to a notion of immortality. According to the classic account of this theory in Plato's writings, the mind/soul constitutes the essential self, and when death destroys the body, the mind will be free to escape from the physical world to its rightful place in the world of ideas or forms.[30] As we shall see when we consider H. H. Price's ideas on the next world, such a mind-dependent notion of personhood will mean that we must look forward to a non-physical form of post-mortem existence with all that that implies. Alternatively, if we hold to the view that the body as much as the mind shapes what it is to be a human person, we would consistently hold to the idea of resurrection; if I am to exist after my death, that existence must include some form of physical extension. John Hick's account of the afterlife provides just such a picture of what that might entail. Having decided upon their understanding of the self, and accepted the account of the afterlife that it implies, some philosophers have attempted to formulate speculative accounts of what the afterlife might be like. Consideration of these accounts can be informative, for they may suggest something of the difficulty of imagining a life outside the normal constraints of human existence.

How do you think of yourself? To what extent does your account of the self inform your understanding of the possibilty – or otherwise – of life after death?

H. H. Price takes as his starting point the account of the self offered by Plato and Descartes.[31] Under this dualistic view, the soul/mind will survive death as it is an immaterial entity. Price accepts this concept and considers the attributes that such an immaterial entity might take with it into the next world. According to Price, the mind or soul consists of consciousness, memory, volition and the capacity for emotions. These qualities will survive death. If Price is correct, what will a mind-dependent state be like? Most obviously, as we will have no sense organs, we will have no sense-experiences. In order to have experiences, we will use our memories. In itself, this may prove problematic. We might find that our concerns were either so trivial or so wrapt up in the sensual that this new mind-based life would be purgatorial. This may bring a sense of judgement into the equation, although Price's new world does not seem particularly just: for some people who have experienced great suffering, the idea of playing around with their (horrific) memories seems far from fair.

According to Price, our experience of this new world will be akin to the experience of dreaming, with one significant difference: it will be a dreamscape that we can control. And just as in a dream we have the experience of physical realities, so in this world we will have the sensation of physical life, including a dream body. This might suggest a rather lonely existence; however, Price argues that we will be able to communicate with other minds through telepathy. It is at this point that Price appears to be developing the philosopher's dream of the mind, of thought, and of the intellectual world. For those who are not philosophers, such a world may seem limited in its appeal. Price agrees, but says 'even though it is unsatisfying, it may be all that we are going to get'.[32]

In religious terms, the next life has usually been viewed as a realm of eternal bliss.

> And I saw a new heaven and a new earth; for the first heaven and the first earth had passed away, and the sea was no more. And I saw the holy city, new Jerusalem, coming down out of heaven from God, prepared as a bride adorned for her husband; and I heard a loud voice from the throne saying, 'Behold, the dwelling of God is with men. He will dwell with them; and they shall be his people, and God himself will be with them; he will wipe away every tear from their eyes, and death shall be no more, neither shall there be mourning nor crying nor pain anymore, for the former things have passed away.' (Revelation 21:1–4)

How does Price's account compare with such a vision?

John Hick offers a rather different account of the human self than that suggested by H. H. Price. While Price is at pains to remove physical experience from the afterlife, Hick believes that the account of the self that Price assumes is inadequate. For Hick, there is more to the self than simply its mental processes. Hick understands the self to be a combination of both the physical and the mental, and therefore wants to conceive of a new body in the next life.

According to Hick, we will be replicated in the next world at the last moment of conscious life. This suggests that the senile will not enter the new world as senile – surely a good thing! Indeed, Hick offers a vision of the next world as a kind of cosmic sanatorium where all are restored to good health:

We must suppose that in its new environment it is subjected to processes of healing and repair which bring it into a state of health and activity. In the case of old people – and most people die in relatively old age – we might even conceive of a process of growing physically younger to an optimum age.[33]

Consistent with his view that human life involves the process of 'soul-making', Hick believes that the next world will continue this process of education. The next life, just like this life, will involve a process of becoming.

> The afterlife presented by Hick seems very similar to the world we currently inhabit. Bernard Williams argues that 'an endless life would be a meaningless life' (Bernard Williams, *Problems of the Self*, Cambridge: CUP, 1973). Would an eternal life which is much like this one prove boring?

Discussions of survival and personhood have, then, constituted the focus for traditional discussions of the concept of immortality. The discussion of immortality has taken place against the backdrop of philosophical theism. This world is a prelude to a further life outside the physical realm. The emphasis in such discussions has been placed upon establishing the coherence of 'life after death', and, occasionally, upon offering speculative accounts of what the 'next world' might be like. Contemporary accounts of immortality have significantly shifted the focus of the discussion. Instead of defining immortality as 'more life after death', emphasis has been placed upon locating the idea of immortality within certain religious and moral attitudes towards human life and experience.

Alternative Approaches to Immortality

If classic accounts of immortality have focused on the coherence of the claim that the self will survive death, recent discussions of this concept have offered an alternative vision of what immortality might mean. In particular, two main themes have come to dominate accounts by philosophers of religion unconvinced by the central arguments of theism. Morality and critiquing the relationship between a particular understanding of the self and the notion of immortality form the focus for these kinds of discussion.

Morality

D. Z. Phillips has given the most comprehensive account of immortality as it relates to notions of morality. Phillips is concerned to move our thinking of immortality away from an understanding of it as 'more life after death' towards an understanding of it as 'eternal life'. Why is this different? Phillips claims that the notion of eternal life has been falsely understood as referring to a further quantity of life after death, when it actually refers to a *quality* of existence to be found in the here and now. As such, Phillips claims that the theistic discussion of immortality rests on a mistaken interpretation of the meaning of religious language.[34]

A Wittgensteinian, it should come as no surprise that Phillips's account is dependent upon an analysis of language, and particularly the way in which language is used. By focusing on the way in which language is used, it is possible to uncover the mistaken metaphysical language which informs the speculations of philosophers. If we look at the everyday use of words like 'soul', 'body', etc. we see that metaphysical speculation misunderstands the nature of the language. 'He would sell his soul for money' does not mean he would sell some kind of metaphysical entity which makes him up as a person. Likewise, 'I only wanted her for her body' does not mean that the would-be seducer is only interested in her corpse. By focusing on the way in which language like this is used, Phillips shows that the language of immortality/eternal life has moral significance.

Grounding his account in an analysis of the language of religion, Phillips argues that when Christ talks of 'eternal life', he is proclaiming a new way of living, rather than offering his listeners more life after death. For example, when the Rich Young Ruler asks Christ what he must do to inherit 'eternal life', Christ gives him practical advice on how to live; he tells the young man

to 'sell all you have and give to the poor' (Mark 10:21). Christ is
not offering the man advice about how to get into heaven, but
about how to live on a practical level. Eternal life relates to a
quality of existence open to all, rather than a further quantity of
existence after death. Thus Phillips defines eternity in the following way: 'Eternity is not more life, but this life seen under
certain moral and religious modes of thought.'[35]

Such an understanding can be challenged. If immortality is
not about more life after death, why bother to live a religious or
a moral life? After all, death would seem to be the end for all,
regardless of our beliefs or the lives we have led. Phillips's response is to turn to the New Testament:

> When Jesus saw men eaten up by pride, he said that they have
> their reward; that is, that is all their lives amount to; they are
> wedded to the temporal . . . For a person to die unaware of his
> distance from God would not, for the believer, be a matter of that
> person escaping anything, but of his dying in the worst possible
> state.[36]

So reward and punishment are terms which only make sense in
the here and now. It is better to live the moral life than not to live
the moral life. Such a message seems to lie behind Woody Allen's
film, *Crimes and Misdemeanors* (1989). The plot revolves around
Judah, a man who has his blackmailing mistress murdered. He is
initially riddled with guilt, but his crime goes undiscovered and
unpunished. Yet although he may have 'got away' with murder
the question seems to be whether we would want to be a person
like that, a person who is utterly devoid of principle.

How convincing do you find Phillips's claim that to think of immortality as life after death is to mistake the logic of the language?

Phillips's account of immortality locates the concept of immortality firmly within his understanding of eternal life. How
am I to live in a meaningful way in this world? The language of

immortality is thus a dramatic way of stressing the importance of morality, and should not be understood as describing some future post-mortem existence. The connection which Phillips makes between morality and immortality is also to be found in the work of Stewart Sutherland. In many ways, Sutherland's ideas are similar to those offered by Phillips.[37] At the outset Sutherland admits that he is agnostic about the possibility of life after death, and so will not be attempting to argue for or against such a concept. Instead, his aim is to offer a different understanding of immortality which is not based upon the question of whether or not we survive death. Sutherland is unhappy with the definition of immortality as surviving death for one main reason: what, he asks, does it mean to claim that immortality is 'endless life'? He suggests that there is a contradiction here, for 'to speak of life, of what is living, is to speak of what is temporal'.[38] That which is 'alive' must contain the possibility of being 'dead'. So to exist is to be open to the possibility of non-existence. 'Endless life' is thus a contradiction in terms.

Having rejected the normal grounds for discussing immortality, Sutherland goes on to offer his own account of this concept. Religious belief, he argues, is about making life meaningful. How might belief in endless life make life meaningful? Sutherland suggests that it does not, and, like Phillips, goes on to postulate a difference between endless life and eternal life. Of particular interest to Sutherland are some words from Kierkegaard: 'Only in the ethical is there an immortality and an eternal life.'[39] If we take this idea seriously, we do not need to look beyond this world for an understanding of immortality. Eternal life is not more life after death, but is a quality of existence to be found in the here and now. Thus, 'we must be speaking not of a post-mortem appendage to life (not even if it is endless) but of human life as such, and of what, if anything, in human life is independent of chance and change'.[40]

The last part of that sentence is crucial. What in human life is independent of chance and change? We might wonder why this matters. Sutherland feels that finding this eternal quality is crucial. He believes that the major fear which we encounter in human life is the fear of triviality, and that finding this 'eternal' element will quell that fear. So much of what we value as human

beings is dependent upon contingent matters that are not subject
to our control – or even to the control of other human beings.
Many of our objectives in life can be rendered meaningless or
trivialized by events outside our control. Money, power, success,
reputation can all, for example, be rendered meaningless by the
things that happen to us. If the significance of one's life is based
upon these transitory values, then, to an extent, one is vulnerable.
Say I base my life on the acquisition of money, power and privi-
lege. Such a life is ultimately based on poor foundations, for it is
always possible that something may happen which means I lose
all my money, I am no longer powerful and I lose my privileged
position.[41] All my life's work, in such an eventuality, will be rendered worthless. All that I have lived by will be shown to have
been false.

Having considered this option, Sutherland seeks an alternative
lifestyle. Is there a way of living by which we can avoid having life
rendered trivial and meaningless by the things that happen to us?
Sutherland suggests that we can live by certain eternal ethical values. He defines these values as the commitment to goodness, justice and truth. If we live according to these values our lives could
never be rendered trivial, because these values will be seen to have
more importance than the things that happen to us in human life.
In exploring this idea, Sutherland draws upon the example of Franz
Jäggerstätter, an Austrian peasant-farmer beheaded by the Nazis
in 1943 for refusing to pay his taxes or to be conscripted into the
Nazi army. Jäggerstätter acted like this because he believed that
Nazism was evil, and therefore he could not participate in sup-
porting the regime *in any way*. Friends pointed out to him the
suffering that his inevitable death would bring to his family – and
for what? His death would have no effect on the outlook or for-
tunes of the Nazi government.

Yet for Jäggerstätter the answer was simple – one cannot serve
God and Hitler. It was a case of right and wrong. Sutherland
focuses on this clear-cut distinction. Jäggerstätter's commitment
to goodness shows that it is possible to transcend the limits of
finite existence. A commitment to such fundamental notions
renders what happens to us in life ultimately meaningless. What
matters are the values we live by. If we consider the lives of those
who do not live by such values we see that the fear of death plays

a prominent role in their thinking. They are rendered vulnerable by the need to preserve their lives at all costs.[42] The alternative is the kind of life lived by Jäggerstätter, with its commitment to the eternal values of goodness and justice.

> To what extent would you agree with Sutherland that the fear of 'triviality' is the major fear human beings face? What about the problem of evil and suffering? Does the way in which some people have little or no choice about their lives significantly undermine Sutherland's emphasis on living by certain values?

Phillips and Sutherland both offer an interpretation of immortality as morality. For Phillips, the concept of eternal life is best interpreted in a moral sense: eternal life is possible, here and now, in the way in which we live. For Sutherland, the language of immortality suggests the importance of certain eternal ethical values. Both are interpreting and redefining what it means to talk of immortality.

The self and immortality

We have already suggested a connection between concepts of the self and notions of immortality. The history of religions suggests that as human beings gained a stronger sense of their own individuality, the idea of death became more frightening, and thus the need for some form of survival more urgent.[43] In the west, with its emphasis on individuality, the idea of a mind which could escape death because it is not part of the corporeal self has become the dominant way of considering the self. The western concept of the self, which has come from Plato via Descartes, has not been without its critics. It is possible to isolate two main attacks to this notion and the accompanying view of personal immortality. The first suggests a religious motive for criticizing the idea of immortality. The second arises from feminist and ecologist reflections on human structures.

The idea that there might be a religious motive for criticizing the idea of immortality seems incongruous: it could be argued that the belief in immortality forms the bedrock for the monotheistic faiths. Writers such as Simone Weil have suggested that the belief in immortality does not marry with the religious concern to move away from self-centredness.[44] It would seem inconsistent to eradicate selfishness in oneself during this life only to reinstigate the self at death. Under this approach, the notion of immortality is itself ultimately selfish. It is based upon the notion that I am at the centre of the world, that the world could not possibly survive without me. Yet this is not the case. Indeed, it is this very self-centredness which appears to create the fear of death.

Miller Quarles, a retired 82-year-old oil tycoon, has financed scientific research to isolate the gene which causes ageing.[45] His aim is to 'end this cringing death march into oblivion'. To accommodate the numbers of old people who would not die, he argues for selective reproduction: 'we may have to rethink the idea of reproduction as a right'.[46] In the past he has argued for the compulsory sterilization of children. It is difficult not to accuse such a person of selfishness; especially as there seems to be little regard for the young or those yet to be born.

P. D. James gives a frightening picture of what such a world might be like if Miller Quarles's research is successful. Her novel *The Children of Men* describes a world in which a mystery virus has destroyed the possibility of human reproduction.[47] The human race faces extinction. James paints a disturbing apocalyptic picture of human society. Universities have to decide whether to refurbish libraries; kittens are christened in the stead of babies; disturbed women push prams which house beautiful dolls. James revealingly shows how much of human endeavour is dependent upon the hope of a future generation which will develop current ideas, and find new solutions to old problems. Perhaps death is not the problem, but how we are to live and to come to terms with the reality – and rightness – of our own mortality.

It is telling that in Leo Tolstoy's classic novel on this theme, *The Death of Ivan Ilyich* (1886), Ivan is only able to overcome the fear of death when he comes to terms with the idea that he is dying. This happens when he shifts the focus away from his own suffering and considers the suffering of his family. After three days of screaming, he realizes that his death is causing them pain, and seeks to end their suffering as quickly as possible:

> He felt sorry for them, he had to do something to keep from hurt-
> ing them. To deliver them and himself from this suffering. 'How
> good and simple!' he thought. 'And the pain?' he asked himself.
> 'Where has it gone? . . .' . . . Where was death? What was death?
> There was no fear because there was no death. Instead of death
> there was light. 'So that's it!' he exclaimed. 'What bliss!' [48]

In recognizing his responsibility to his family, and in accepting
death, Ivan's fear of death is conquered. The lesson seems to be
that rather than fear death and seek to avoid it, we should accept
our fundamental mortality and seek to live in the most fulfilling
way possible. It seems strange that religions that seek to raise us
above self-centredness should wish to reincorporate the self in
an afterlife existence. Fulfilment, it is claimed, does not lie with
selfishness but with dying to the self on a day-to-day basis. Accepting the reality of our mortality would seem to be the logical
development of such an account of the religious life.

> What grounds might there be for claiming that the hope for im-
> mortality is selfish?

The contention that a critique of immortality might be con-
structed on religious grounds has not gone unchallenged. John
Hick claims that religion without the belief in immortality would
be no real religion at all.[49] He argues that the belief in immortality is integral to religious thinking, principally because it offers
hope in situations where there apparently is no hope. Would a
religion which failed to offer some kind of personal immortality
be an appropriate form of religious belief? Of course, some east-
ern forms of religion suggest precisely that. Hick seems to take
the western account of the individual as the universal way of
considering the self.[50]

A rather different criticism of the belief in immortality has
been raised by some feminist writers. Fundamental to the notion
of immortality is the belief that it is possible to transcend the
physical self and the physical world. Feminists, and particularly
those concerned with ecological issues, have high-lighted the con-

nection between the ideal of self-transcendence and the patriarchal attempt to dominate the physical realm.[51] Feminists have focused on the way in which women have been oppressed by masculinist attempts to dominate the physical world. Ecofeminists such as Sherry Ortner have made the connection between the attempted domination of women and the attempted domination of the physical world.[52] They point to the way in which, historically, women have been identified with nature. In such a critique, the claim that the physical can be transcended is associated with the patriarchal desire to dominate and suppress the natural world and women. A good illustration of this connection can be found in the little-known writings of Otto Weininger. In Weininger's writings, the common identification which philosophers as diverse as Aristotle, Kant and Schopenhauer have made between women and nature is brought to its ultimate conclusion. For Weininger argues that woman, because of her corporeal nature, is not and cannot be immortal.

In his work *Sex and Character*, Weininger brings to fruition the philosophical understanding of woman as nature and man as reason.[53] In so doing, he builds upon the claims of Aristotle that the male is the active force in the procreative act, the female providing the passive matter which is to be shaped by the male.[54] He takes to its logical conclusion Kant's view that women were to be identified with beauty, intuition and spontaneity, while men were to be identified with the higher moral values of duty and reason.[55]

In developing such ideas, Weininger claims that masculine and feminine qualities are radically polarized. All positive achievements are associated with the masculine, all destructive ideas with the feminine. Man is understood as monad, gloriously individual, the embodiment of reason, who is capable of transcending the physical realm. Woman, on the contrary, is identified with sexuality, and as such is so subsumed by nature that she is incapable of transcending the physical world. Thus, man has the possibility of immortality, woman does not. In Weininger's words:

> As the absolute female has no trace of individuality and will, no sense of worth or of love, she can have no part in the higher, transcendental life. The intelligible, hyperempirical existence of the male transcends matter, space, and time. He is certainly mor-

tal, but he is immortal as well. And so he has the power to choose between the two, between the life which is lost with death and the life to which death is only a stepping-stone.[56]

The identification of man with reason and woman with nature supports Weininger's claim that only the male is capable of immortality. He argues that women do not have the qualities necessary to the transcendence of the physical realm; moreover, they do not even aspire to immortality: 'That the woman has no craving for perpetual life is too apparent; there is nothing in her of the eternal which man tries to interpose and must interpose between his real self and his projected, empirical self.'[57]

What makes this so interesting is that from a feminist perspective Weininger may be on to something. Admittedly, his ideas are located in a deep-rooted misogyny, but they are also surprisingly close to some women's views of life and death. In a television programme, six elderly women from the Hen Co-operative talked of their experience of the ageing process.[58] Their views on death were particularly interesting. A common theme ran through their discussions: life was viewed as cyclical. We are all part of the cycle of life, and death is part of the wheel of life, death and rebirth. But not rebirth in the sense of new life in a heavenly realm. It is enough to be part of nature and reclaimed by the great natural processes. Rosemary Ruether picks up on this theme in her book *Gaia and God*. Like the women of the Hen Co-op, she wants to argue for a different kind of immortality. Rather than think of immortality as involving an escape from the natural world, she suggests that we think of it in a more ecological way. We should see ourselves as part of the great cycle of the natural world. She writes:

> Like humans, the animals and plants are living centers of organic life who exist for a season. Then each of our roots shrivels, the organic structures that sustain our life fail, and we die. The cutting of the life center also means that our bodies disintegrate into organic matter, to enter the cycle of decomposition and recomposition as other entities.[59]

This is a form of immortality, for 'the material substance of our bodies live on in plants and animals';[60] but there is no conscious survival for the self. This may seem frightening, but Ruether argues that as we are one with the physical world we must accept our fundamental mortality. There is no escape from this world, and, rather than seek Weininger's transcendence of the physical, we should embrace our mortality joyfully, finding our kinship with all of creation.

It is this notion of kinship which ecofeminists like Ruether have adapted to critique the concept of immortality. What are the ecological implications of the belief that human beings can escape from the confines of this world at death? Does such a notion of the distance between ourselves and the physical world contribute to the ecological destruction of this world? If we are to save this planet, it would seem that we need to rethink our relationship to the physical world. Creating a false distinction between ourselves and the planet suggests that our abuse of the natural resources of this world will continue. Ecofeminists like Ruether suggest that the belief in the immortal self which will survive death contributes to this lack of care for our environment.

Jane Caputi, in her book *Gossips, Gorgons and Crones* (Bear Books, 1993, p. 65), quotes David Wilkerson, an Assemblies of God minister:

> Are we so blind, so earthbound, that we want God to keep us alive physically, only to live in a contaminated, hostile environment? Why can't we see that a holocaust can only dissolve this earthly body; but that dissolving brings us into a celestial one . . . I died to the world – its pleasures, its pains, its destruction – so that a meltdown simply brings me into the fulness of an inheritance I already possess in measure.

What might such words suggest about the way in which belief in immortality can contribute to our abuse of the planet? Can you develop an argument for immortality which seeks to safeguard this world too?

Immortality in a Human Context

We seem to have come a long way in the course of this section. We began with the traditional discussion of immortality as the belief that the self will survive death, and then considered the alternative accounts of immortality offered by D. Z. Phillips and Stewart Sutherland. In considering the critique of feminist writers, the suggestion was made that the very notion of immortality contributes to our destruction of the planet. Rosemary Ruether suggested that if we are to save the planet for future life in all its diverse forms, we must do away with the notion that our real home is beyond the stars.

The acceptance of mortality may initially seem rather depressing. One is put in mind of medieval tombs which picture death as obscene in its finality. The corpse and its inevitable decay are shown in graphic detail and haunt the mind. Yet need the acceptance of mortality necessitate morbidity? Two writers suggest that this need not be the case. Don Cupitt offers a positive account of mortality. He writes of the human self 'as a miniature counterpart of the world. It too burns, pours out and passes away. We should burn brightly, all out.'[61] He goes on to argue that the 'purest affirmation of life is also a thoroughgoing acceptance of transience and death'.[62] We throw ourselves fully into the transience of existence, joyously living in relation to others and to the world itself.

The playwright Dennis Potter offers a similarly positive acceptance of mortality. Suffering from cancer and close to death, in his final interview he spoke of his greater appreciation of the sheer beauty of contingent, passing human life and the natural world since his recognition of his own mortality:

> Below my window in Ross, when I'm working in Ross, for example, there at this season, the blossom is out in full now . . . it's a plum tree, it looks like apple blossom but it's white, and looking at it, instead of saying 'Oh that's nice blossom' . . . last week looking at it through the window when I'm writing, I *see* it is the whitest, frothiest, blossomest blossom that there ever could be, and I can see it. Things are both more trivial than they ever were, and more important than they ever were, and the difference between the trivial and the important doesn't seem to matter. But

the nowness of everything is absolutely wondrous, and if people could *see* that, you know. There's no way of telling you, you have to experience it, but the glory of it, if you like, the comfort of it, the reassurance . . . not that I'm interested in reassuring people, bugger that. The fact is, if you see the present tense, boy do you see it! And boy can you celebrate it.[63]

The belief in the personal existence of the self after death need not be the only way of living with the fact of mortality. Living in the light of the knowledge of our mortality, experiencing every moment, every experience, every joy, as something fleeting and beautiful, may be just as fulfilling.

Conclusion

In this chapter, then, we have considered different approaches to the idea of miracle and immortality. These approaches presuppose particular understandings of the nature of religion and the task of the philosophy of religion. So for philosophers like Swinburne, Hick and Hume, religion and its attendant features are associated with an account of religion based upon theism. For philosophers like Holland, Phillips and Sutherland, the theistic concept of God is not the only focus for religion and religious enquiry. For feminist philosophers, we need to locate religious ideas in their wider social context, and this will necessitate a rather different approach to an issue like immortality. In the final chapter, the distinction between the kind of philosophy of religion based on philosophical theism and the alternative approaches to the discipline will be put into a broader perspective. Given the world in which we live, what is the future for religion, and, by implication, which approach offers the best way forward for the philosophy of religion?

Suggested reading:

I   Miracles

Baruch Brody (ed.), *Readings in the Philosophy of Religion*, New Jersey: Prentice-Hall, 1974, section on 'Miracles' (especially

papers by Patrick Nowell-Smith and R. F. Holland).
Brian Davies, *An Introduction to the Philosophy of Religion*, 2nd edition, Oxford: OUP, 1993, ch. 10.
David Hume, *Enquiry Concerning Human Understanding*, ed. L. A. Selby-Bigge, Oxford: Clarendon Press, 1975.
D. Z. Phillips, *The Concept of Prayer*, London: RKP, 1965.
W. L. Rowe and W. J. Wainwright, *Philosophy of Religion: Selected Readings*, Orlando: Harcourt Brace Jovanovich, 1989, section on 'Miracles' (especially papers by R. Swinburne and P. Tillich).
Richard Swinburne, *The Concept of Miracle*, Basingstoke: Macmillan, 1970.

II Immortality

Ray S. Anderson, *Theology, Death and Dying*, Oxford: Blackwell, 1986.
Dan Cohn-Sherbok and Christopher Lewis, *Beyond Death: Theological and Philosophical Reflections on Life after Death*, Basingstoke: Macmillan, 1995.
Don Cupitt, *Solar Ethics*, London: SCM, 1995.
Antony Flew, *The Logic of Mortality*, Oxford: Blackwell, 1987.
John Hick, *Death and Eternal Life*, Basingstoke: Macmillan, 1985.
Julia Neuberger and John A. White (eds), *A Necessary End: Attitudes to Death*, Basingstoke: Macmillan, 1991.
D. Z. Phillips, *Death and Immortality*, Basingstoke: Macmillan, 1970.
Dennis Potter, *Seeing the Blossom*, London: Faber and Faber, 1994.
Rosemary Radford Ruether, *Gaia and God*, London: SCM, 1992.
Stewart Sutherland, 'What Happens After Death?', *Scottish Journal of Theology*, 1969.
Stewart Sutherland, *God, Jesus and Belief*, Oxford: Blackwell, 1984.
Simone Weil, *Waiting on God*, London: Fontana, 1959.

6

The Future of Religion

Introduction

When we began our exploration of the philosophy of religion we noted the extent to which exploring and defining the nature of God dominates the discussions of philosophers of religion. It should be noted, moreover, that many of the arguments for the existence of God which continue to inform the thoughts of philosophers of religion were originally propounded by medieval theologians and philosophers, such as Anselm and Aquinas. In the period in which these writers put forward their ideas, religious belief was far less problematic than it is in our time. In advanced, industrialized societies such as ours, the status of religion has been drastically undermined. The thought processes of modern people are no longer predominantly religious in character; they are, rather, 'secular'. The process of secularization is one in which religion loses its social significance: where once religion would have been fundamental in, for example, the running of government or education, it is marginalized in modern society.

In this chapter we shall consider the effect that secularization has had upon the nature of religious belief. Rather than attempt to 'turn back the clock', so to speak, to a more religion-friendly era, our aim is to take on board the changed situation in which we find ourselves, and to seek an understanding of religion appropriate to the modern age. In this sense, we are developing the claims of the German theologian Dietrich Bonhoeffer, who, during his imprisonment at the hands of the Nazis, came to believe that rather than attempt to 'change' secular people into 'religious' people, the Church should come to terms with a humanity which has 'come of age' and does not need the 'tutelage of "God" '.[1] However, embracing the reality of secularization need not sound the death knell for religion, but may, as we shall explore in the second part of this chapter, suggest a future direction for the understanding and practice of religion, and, consequently, for the shape of the philosophy of religion.

I   Religion and Secularization

The declining number of people regularly attending church services attests to the process of secularization. And even where people *do* firmly hold religious beliefs, these are held in a more individualistic and flexible manner. This is what sociologists mean when they refer to the *privatization* of religious belief. Here, belief or, more loosely, spirituality, ceases to be tied to formal religious institutions. A person's religion need have no relation to a church, nor, indeed, need it have any social context whatsoever. It becomes a 'private affair' rather than a social confession, and individuals may choose which beliefs and practices appeal to them in order to pursue their own personal spiritual quest. No longer bound by cultural inheritance, an individual may wish to combine certain Christian beliefs with elements drawn from other religions, like Buddhism or neo-paganism.[2] The fact that this would be deemed heretical by the Church is no longer of any significance: the individual is now paramount, and free to explore his or her own spirituality. It follows that Ronald Hutton's accurate comment that modern-day paganism does not have direct links to the ancient religions of the British Isles is of little significance.[3] Consideration of contemporary paganism suggests that it is in part a creative rendition of particular attitudes to the earth and to others. Religion arises from the creative impulses of individuals: thus the kind of revisions of religion made by Cupitt and certain feminist thealogians can be viewed as aspects of this process of secularization.

Along with privatization, another central element of the secular society is what is called the *disenchantment* of the world. Religion holds certain things in awe; there are holy objects and elements of the natural world which are held to have special, supernatural qualities. It is now hard to view the world in such an enchanted way. The growth of science can explain natural phenomena without reference to supernatural agency. Things that would previously have been seen as miracles or signs can be rationally explained. Such remarkable occurrences as rainbows and eclipses of the sun are no longer seen as divine signs or disastrous omens, but can be explained in a mundane fashion. Such disenchantment brings with it a sense of personal loss: a loss of belonging in a world which has meaning and significance. Our world seems barren in contrast to the spiritualized world of the 'primitive', a world which is perhaps beautiful, like a fairy-tale land. Spirits live in the boughs of trees, dead ancestors eat food with us, fairies dance in rings.[4]

Of course, one's judgement on disenchantment may be less mournful if one adopts the perspective of certain thinkers considered earlier in this book. Frazer, for example, sees little to regret in the passing of beliefs so obviously erroneous. At the close of *The Golden Bough*, he describes how magic and religion have been mistaken attempts to understand and manipulate the world, and how, with science, humankind now possesses the possibility to turn its back on ignorance and move toward genuine understanding. Frazer's optimism is here undisguised:

> The abundance, the solidity, and the splendour of the results already achieved by science are well fitted to inspire us with a cheerful confidence in the soundness of its method. Here at last, after groping about in the dark for countless ages, man has hit upon a clue to the labyrinth, a golden key that opens many locks in the treasury of nature.[5]

Frazer has thus set the decline of religion in an historical framework. He is not alone in doing this. As Gordon Graham has illustrated,[6] the secularization thesis is itself grounded in a particular philosophical view of the nature and purpose of history, one that is adopted from G. W. F. Hegel.[7] According to Hegel, history is not, as Macbeth had bleakly thought, 'a tale told by an idiot, full of sound and fury, signifying nothing'. Rather, it has a purpose and a goal. For Hegel, this goal is *freedom*. But more generally, we can say that the Hegelian conception presents history as the story of the progressive development of human intelligence and culture. The dawn of religion, and its subsequent decline, are factors in this process.

Gordon Graham comments on two consequences of the application of Hegel's historical picture for the secularization thesis:

First, the decline of religion is inevitable – it is a phase through which human beings have passed and which they have outgrown. Secondly, the decline of religion is desirable – in leaving religion behind we discard more primitive beliefs and practices and move toward more enlightened ones. ('Religion, Secularization and Modernity', in *Philosophy*, vol. 67, no. 260, p. 185)

Is the decline of religion something to be welcomed? What benefits might flow from living in a purely secular society?

If these comments are taken seriously, the future of religion looks grim. The phenomenon of secularization has exacerbated the difficulties of maintaining a 'religious' position, in the traditional sense of the word. As we have seen throughout this book, consideration of the philosophical approach to religion reveals significant difficulties with the habitual way in which the nature and function of religion is understood within a western context. The arguments for the existence of God, as traditionally formulated, raise more problems for theism than they are meant to solve. While there may be a case for accepting the cumulative force of the arguments for belief in God, in the way in which Swinburne suggests,[8] it seems far from self-evident that these arguments will convince the sceptical or thoughtful person, imbued in the culture of secularism, of the truth of theism. If religion is to be equated with worship of a divine being, a diminishment in its influence and validity seems increasingly likely. Against the backdrop of a society which defines itself as secular and thus rejects the idea that humans can transcend the physical world, belief in the theist's God becomes evermore untenable. From a philosophical perspective, the theist's case is far from unassailable; indeed, it could be argued that the paucity of evidence for the theist's God makes the rejection of such an account of religion inevitable.

Yet at the same time it is important to note the extent to which new and creative religious responses to the world are being explored. Tanya Luhrmann has documented one element of this trend in her study of contemporary witchcraft, or 'Wicca'.[9] The secularization thesis contends that as science explains more and more of the world around us, so the need for religion abates. The growth of those who practise magic suggests a more complex relationship between a society which defines itself as 'secular' and the religious beliefs of the individual. This need not lessen the strength of the arguments against philosophical theism, but it does suggest that the notion of what it means to be 'religious' will have to be revised against the backdrop of life in the contemporary world. However, if, as is surely the case, the life of religion is to do with the shared experience of a culture, rather than with the idiosyncratic wants of the individual, it is far from clear that the emphasis on privatized spirituality is not itself a further sounding of the death knell for religion.

In concluding this introduction to the philosophy of religion, we will offer some suggestions as to the possible shape of religion in the future. If we take seriously some of the objections made against a theistic account of religion, what kind of religion is best suited to survive into the third millennium?

II   The Future for Religion?

One initial response to the problems facing religion might be to reject the need for any kind of religious or spiritual dimension to life. But to do this is perhaps to miss the important place religion has held historically as a way of exploring and examining the human condition. As we saw in our discussion of the design argument, even a sceptic such as David Hume recognized the extent to which the religious response is almost 'natural' when faced with the beauty and profundity of human existence.[10] Yet to accept this response does not mean that we have to approach religion in an irrational, purely emotive way.[11] What it might mean is a return to the focus of natural theology: that it is by reflecting upon the natural world (and the human realm) that we can come to know what it means to speak of the divine. In this sense, natural theology is this-worldly and human-centred, and an account of religion which takes this focus seriously must reflect the human – in particular, the creativity that so defines human life. If such an understanding of religion as rooted in the natural world is accepted, and if we go on to see religion as the outpouring of human creativity, what (and who) might be the sources for future developments in religious thinking?

Positively Feuerbachian

In considering the naturalistic interpretation of religion we focused upon the negative parts of Feuerbach's critique of religion: most notably, we considered his theory of projection.[12] According to Feuerbach, God is a projection of the values that humans hold most dear. Yet to limit a discussion of Feuerbach to this element of his thinking is to miss a great deal of what he has to say about religion. If Feuerbach deconstructs the supernatural account of religion, he also offers more positive suggestions for how religion might be reconstructed.

Of particular importance to a human-centred account of religion is Feuerbach's contention that divinity and humanity are not poles apart but can be assimilated into the unified human existence. In exploring this idea, he offers a reinterpretation of the Christian doctrine of the incarnation. For Christians, God is revealed in the person of Christ who is both human and divine. Feuerbach revisits this doctrine, and argues that its significance lies in revealing the 'real' relationship between God and humanity. Rather than focus on the Christological debates of the early Church which sought to establish the coherence of merging God and humanity, Feuerbach gives the doctrine a radical reading. Presaging non-realists like Cupitt, he argues that in the incarnation, God and humanity are revealed as identical: 'In the Incarnation religion only confesses, what in reflection on itself, as theology, it will not admit; namely, that God is an altogether human being.'[13] Once this 'truth' is recognized, all aspects of religious belief are open to reinterpretation. Talk of divine love 'is only human love made objective, affirming itself'. Ideas of the personal God revealed in Christ refer to the fact that 'God is a human being, God is a man'.[14]

> 'The secret of theology is anthropology' (Feuerbach, *The Essence of Christianity*, p. 270). How convincing do you find Feuerbach's argument that the incarnation 'reveals' the reality of the connection between divinity and humanity? Find examples of how this interpretation might affect other religious doctrines and beliefs.

It is not altogether clear what effect Feuerbach anticipated that his theories would have on religion. In places, he suggests that if we take seriously his claim that the essence of religion is found in the imagination of human beings we will ultimately be led to reject the need for any kind of religion at all. Instead, we can find in our own lives meaning and fulfilment. In this sense, Feuerbach reflects Voltaire's suggestion in *Candide*, that the meaning of human life is to be found not in the super natural but in the natural world: ' "We must work without arguing," said Martin; "that is the only way to make life bearable." '[15] However, in his 'Concluding Application', Feuerbach suggests a rather different approach to religion. Rather than reject any kind of religious interpretation, he gives his reader a taste of what a religion might be like that takes its humanity seriously. He focuses upon the fundamentally human and natural quality of religious rituals and beliefs. Christian baptism and the celebration of the Eucharist are transformed into acts that celebrate nature and humanity. In baptism, the life-giving and sustaining quality of water is celebrated. It cleans the body and cleanses the mind; thus it represents to us the 'wonderful but natural effect of water on man'.[16] We do not need a super-natural interpretation of this ritual to maintain a sense of wonder at the natural world around us. In baptism, we are not accepting an invitation to become part of some heavenly community, but are celebrating our grounding in this world.

Likewise, the Eucharist becomes a celebration of the ordinary acts of eating and drinking. In drinking wine and eating bread, we celebrate the fruits of nature and human ingenuity at the cultivation of nature.[17] Issues of how the bread and wine 'become' the body and blood of Christ are irrelevant and pointless. Instead, a natural interpretation of religion is revealed that is no less grounded in a sense of awe and wonderment than is the supernatural account. While Feuerbach may have rejected the notion of a supernaturalist God, he maintains a sense of the spiritual which can only be found in humanity and in nature.

If this more positive strand in Feuerbach is accepted, what might it mean for our understanding of religion? In focusing our attention upon the connections between religious practice and the things of this world, Feuerbach offers a fresh emphasis upon human creativity. If natural theology as traditionally practised suggested that we could find God *through* the things and processes of the natural world, Feuerbach argues that 'God' is *in* the natural world. In other words, God (or the divine) is to be found in the everyday things of human life. 'God' is found in human reflection, and is created through the countless things and activities which give shape and purpose to human life.

Of course, this suggests a very different approach to theology. Rather than think of theology as the attempt to find and define the (one) meaning of God, theology itself must embrace the need to be creative. God (or gods) are not found, but *created*. It is perhaps here that feminist reinventions of the Goddess are of importance. Just as feminists explore what it means to be a woman through employing and creating images of the Goddess, so theology could benefit from new and varied attempts to explore what it means to talk of 'God'.[18] The theologian is less like a scientist, seeking some kind of objective fact, and more like an artist, endlessly seeking to express different ways of giving meaning and purpose to human life.

Don Cupitt: *Solar Ethics*

Cupitt is perhaps the one modern theologian who has fully appreciated Feuerbach's analysis. He also consciously seeks to define the work of the theologian as the work of the artist, writing thus: 'Think of yourself not as a soldier, but as an artist who has chosen to work mainly within a particular tradition. That is faith, the production of one's own life as a work of religious art.'[19] Throughout Cupitt's work, emphasis is placed on the importance of accepting the transience of life. Drawing on the ideas of the nineteenth-century thinker and self-styled prophet Friedrich Nietzsche, he feels that we must accept the full extent of 'the death of God'. In using this phrase, Nietzsche is pointing not only to the death of the idea of the objective God; he is also using it to allude to the death of all objective and absolute moral values.[20] In the face of nihilism (nothingness), we are left with the task of creating our own meaning and our own values.

In one of his most recent works, *Solar Ethics*, Cupitt combines this need to create our own values with a thoroughgoing acceptance of the transitory nature of human life. He argues that the human self, like the world itself, is constantly moving towards nothingness. This is not a cause for alarm, but for celebration, for it means that the self is 'a miniature counterpart of the world. It too burns, pours out and passes away. We should burn brightly, all out.'[21] Rather than fear change and the inevitable death which awaits us all, we should seize the moment, live life to the full, and glory in the transience of life.

In arguing for an acceptance of change and transience, Cupitt explicitly rejects the dualism that has underpinned much thinking in the western tradition. Like Feuerbach, he explicitly rejects the dualist's distinctions between the physical and the spiritual, this world and the next, God and the self. While this necessitates the rejection of any attempt to define the self in terms of spiritual and physical, mind and body, it also leads to an explicit acceptance of mortality. Living and dying are part and parcel of what it means to be a human being. Cupitt's refusal to accept any attempt to escape the reality of death does not mean that religion is no longer necessary. Quite the reverse: Cupitt wants to argue that 'the unity of living and dying . . . is eternal life'.[22] Religion that is grounded in the human has no need for a flight from such harsh realities. Rather, the fact of death 'concentrates the mind wonderfully', and forces us to live wholly in the present.[23]

The rejection of dualism also necessitates a new approach to accounts of what it means to be spiritual. In his earlier writings,

Cupitt tends to focus upon the importance of the internal for an appropriate understanding of the religious and spiritual life.[24] Now, his emphasis on living wholly in the present forces him to rethink this idea. He comes to realize that we need to reject the flight from the external to the internal which has been understood as the religious quest. Having exposed the human roots of religion, a new kind of spirituality is required. Now 'we reverse the movement, setting out instead a solar ethic of uninhibited self-publication'.[25] Cupitt uses the sun as a symbol for this process of externalization: 'we should love life and pour out our hearts – and that is emotivism, or solar ethics'.[26] For Cupitt, 'true' religion must be understood as the fruit of human self-expression. In rejecting the realist claims of theism, he establishes the centrality of human creativity for a contemporary account of religion. Religion becomes a matter of individual self-expression, rather than the acceptance of a core set of beliefs which are binding and authoritarian.[27]

'As a general ethical maxim, then, it is rational for us to love and to value every aspect of the world and our lives as highly as is consistently compossible. To Live like that is to live as the sun does, purely affirmatively' (Cupitt, *Solar Ethics*, p. 35). Compare Cupitt's words with these from William Blake's *Songs of Experience*:

O rose, thou art sick!
The invisible worm
That flies in the night,
In the howling storm

Has found out thy bed
Of crimson joy,
And his dark secret love
Does thy life destroy.

Both Cupitt and Blake accept the transitoriness of time, yet Cupitt is far more positive about its implications. Which attitude do you feel comes closest to a religious position, and why?

If the validity of Cupitt's approach is accepted, our attitude towards the concept of God will change. Rather than seek to give accurate accounts of the nature of God which correspond with the divine reality, we accept that there is no external God. Such an acceptance means that we are given the freedom to create our own image of the divine; or, if you prefer, we are free to decide what has the quality of divinity for us. In creating such images, the crucial factor will be the kind of impact that these ideas have on us and those around us.

The Artist as Theologian

If Cupitt equates religion with the development of human creativity, it would seem that the artist is likely to have a significant role to play in the future shape that religion takes. This is not a particularly new or original idea. The great nineteenth-century liberal theologian Friedrich Schleiermacher offered a similar understanding in *On Religion*, in which he addresses 'the cultured despisers of religion' who believe that the Enlightenment has shown religion to be false and pointless.[28] Schleiermacher's argument is simple. He does not seek to convince them of the 'truth' of religion, in the sense that there is an existent God before whom they should bend. Rather, he argues that in order to be fully human, in order to live the cultivated human life, they need religion. Religion for Schleiermacher is fundamentally associated with human creativity. Hence he writes: 'A man's special calling is the melody of his life, and it remains a simple, meagre series of notes unless religion, with its endlessly rich variety, accompany it with all notes, and raise the simple song to a full-voiced, glorious harmony.'[29] Far from limiting the extent of human creativity, religion is viewed as adding colour and vibrancy to human life. Similar ideas can also be found in the writings of Paul Tillich, who argues that religion deals with the 'depth experiences' of human life. Even God is to be redefined and understood in relation to these experiences. So:

> The name of this infinite and inexhaustible depth and ground of all being is God. That depth is what the word God means. And if that word has not much meaning for you, translate it, and speak

of the depths of your life, of the source of your being, of your
ultimate concern, of what you take seriously without any reser-
vation . . . He who knows about depth knows about God.[30]

It seems strange that these rich and evocative views of the meaning and purpose of religion should be viewed by many as
'reductionist'. For those theologians concerned with the creativity which stems from a religious appreciation of the world, a
natural interpretation of religion need not diminish human life,
but can, rather, enrich it.

Schleiermacher, of course, was writing in a very different age
from ours. The twentieth century has experienced two world
wars which have challenged this idea that human beings are in-
nately good, in touch with their own selves and spirituality. In
such a context, Schleiermacher's words might ring rather hollow
with an optimism about the human condition which we do not
share. In offering his views of religion, Tillich, by way of contrast, was more aware of the dark depths of the human psyche.
In the remainder of this chapter we need to explore the extent to
which this idea of the theologian as artist is viable in an age such
as ours.[31] As a way of exemplifying what this idea might mean,
we will consider two writers whose work frequently involves
religious themes. In different ways and with different emphasis,
Iris Murdoch and Dennis Potter confront the question of what it
means to be religious in a world which has lost a sense of the
transcendent.

Iris Murdoch: being good without 'God'

As a philosopher, Iris Murdoch is best known for her explora-
tions of what it means to be good.[32] Influenced by Plato's writings, her concern is with the notion of 'the Good', rather than
with the idea of an objective God. Her novels, which themselves have been critically acclaimed, also deal with these themes,
and with what it means to be religious in a secular world. However, Murdoch contends that philosophy and fiction are distinct disciplines, and that it is fiction that constitutes her chief
concern.[33] Despite this claim, her novels deal in some depth
with religious and philosophical themes. *The Time of the*

Angels and *The Good Apprentice* provide good illustrations of the scope of her writing, giving us an indication of the way in which the theologian might be an artist in the modern age.

The Time of the Angels

What happens when a religious man loses his faith in God? This is the question that dominates this early novel by Iris Murdoch. The central character is the rather mysterious and dark figure of Carel Fisher, an Anglican priest. An eccentric pastor, he has recently been moved from his last parish where he was given to delivering controversial sermons in which he would confront the congregation with questions like 'what if I told you there is no God?'.[34] His own response to this question is forthright: he has lost his faith, and Murdoch's concern is to portray the bleakness of trying to live without God. Through the character of Carel she seems to be asking whether it is possible to be good without 'God'. The answer is by no means certain or positive. Carel is an unpleasant, manipulative character, whose malign influence affects the other characters, despite the rarity of his actual presence. Murdoch seems to use him as a catalyst for chaos and destruction. In many ways this is not surprising: Carel has realized the true meaning of the death of God. It is not just that the concept of God as habitually framed is dead; rather, *all* forms of morality are now open to question. There is no transcendent guarantor for an objective moral code. Self-centredness seems the only response; in realizing the non-existence of God, Carel claims to feel like God himself: 'When I celebrate mass, I am God.'[35]

This identification of the self with God is portrayed as far from healthy, Carel acting at best amorally and at worst immorally throughout the novel. It is the concern with morality which underpins the diverse parts of the book. Carel's brother Marcus is writing a book on morality in a secular age – with little success and decreasing enthusiasm. Unlike Carel, Marcus still believes that it is possible to construct a morality if the death of God is accepted. However, by the end of the book he is unsure of whether this exercise is profitable or possible: ' "Carel's right about the absurd optimism of all philosophy up to the present, and he's right that people who pretend to dispense with the idea of God don't really do so. One's got to learn to live without the idea of the Good being somehow One. That's what's hard." "[36] If it is difficult to visualize the shape of morality after the death of God, it is even more difficult to conceive of religion without the transcendent God. Minor characters pass judgement on the death of Christianity: 'All those stories are simply false, and the oftener it's said the better.'[37] Even a Bishop whom Marcus meets shares his conviction that the old symbolism of the faith must die. Marcus finds this disturbing, for while he does not believe, 'he wanted other people to believe'.[38]

At the end of the book, the reader is left no clearer as to the way forward in a world without the God of theism. Carel has committed suicide, implying that it is not possible to live without some kind of belief in a transcendent deity or truth. While critics have complained that *The Time of the Angels* is not a successful piece of work,[39] there is in this dark, ominous novel an almost barely perceptible hint of a possible way forward. Muriel, Carel's neglected daughter, is a poet who feels that 'the only salvation in this age is to be an artist'.[40] While this coheres with the argument of this chapter, it would be an overstatement to claim that Murdoch herself is offering this idea as a positive message. In part, it is a rather poignant reflection on the sorry state of Muriel's life: her poetry is rejected by her cousin Elizabeth as clichéd and overlong. Yet in her description of Muriel's commitment to poetry, Murdoch suggests something of the attention and commitment required for living the moral life: 'She was no longer a scribbler down of random inspiration. She knew how to work, steadily and for hours on end, like a carpenter or a shoemaker.'[41] While the book leaves the reader with a sense of hopelessness, it is in these small indications of a possible way forward that the stage is set for a more positive analysis of the way in which one might live the good life after the death of the transcendent God.

The Good Apprentice

If *The Time of the Angels* presents us with the vision of a world without God, *The Good Apprentice* offers a vision of the moral life as a quest for truth and goodness. The central character of the book, Edward, is suffering from a complete mental breakdown, caused by his extreme guilt following the death of his best friend, Mark. Edward gave Mark LSD without his knowledge, leaving him alone when he was called unexpectedly away. On his return, Edward discovers that Mark has jumped out of the window and is dead. Edward – rightly? – feels responsible. Those around him, particularly his stepfather Harry, seek to show him that what happened was simply an accident, that he was not responsible, that he is ill and will recover.[42] Edward dismisses such rationalizations, and attempts to find atonement through seeking out his natural father, Jesse Baltram, an eccentric artist. The book follows his attempt – often thwarted – to find redemption for his 'crime'.

Edward's stepbrother Stuart is also on a quest. He is seeking a 'religion without God'.[43] The rejection of the theist's God is central to Stuart's revised form of spirituality. In rejecting the God of theism, Stuart argues that the very concept of God is too small to accommodate the truth of the spiritual path:

> 'God' had always seemed to Stuart something hard and limited and small, identified as an idol, and certainly not the name of what he found within himself . . . Christ was a pure essence, something which, as it were, he might have kissed, as one might kiss a holy stone, or the soil of a holy land, or the trunk of a holy tree: something which was everywhere, yet simple separate and alone. Something alive; and he himself was Christ.[44]

In many ways, Stuart is a positive version of Carel. Like Carel, Stuart identifies self-knowledge with the knowledge of God. Likewise, Stuart acts as a catalyst for the events of the novel. His appearance often marks disturbing, sometimes destructive events. In this sense, it seems that Murdoch is making a point about the disturbing nature of goodness and the moral/spiritual life. So, Midge's quest for a useful life is initiated by her encounter with Stuart, which itself has ramifications for those about her – most notably, it necessitates the end of her affair with Stuart's father Harry.

Throughout the book, Murdoch recognizes the difficult nature of finding the good life. For Edward, this seems to be achieved through a process of gain and loss. At Seegard, the home of his natural father Jesse, his stepmother and stepsisters, Edward initially finds that work can form a framework for the 'good life'. However, this ideal is later shown to be false, for, just as the relationships between the protagonists at Seegard collapse, so the house itself deteriorates. Yet even this situation is far from clear: for Edward, the structured life seems to form the basis for his recovery. For Stuart, the gradual recognition of the difficulty of being good without the personal God is resolved in practical action: he eventually decides to become a teacher.

Again, the literary landscape devised by Murdoch is complex, and it would be misleading to suggest that one answer is being offered to the question of how one is to live in the religionless world. Yet what we do have is a plethora of voices, giving different suggestions as to how one should live. This, it would seem, is the strength of the novel over works of philosophy and theology. The nature of the novel allows for diverse accounts of the nature of God, and what constitutes the good life: so for Thomas, the psychotherapist, 'God is a belief that at our deepest level we are known and loved'; for Harry, 'abstract good and bad are just fictions'; and so on.[45] A novel, unlike a consistent piece of philosophical theorizing, offers the reader alternative approaches to key moral and spiritual issues. The emphasis is placed upon the need of individuals to choose for themselves. Murdoch thus confronts the reality of a world which rejects the presence of God, but also presents the need for some sort of continued discussion concerning the Good/God.

> How helpful is literature in the attempt to consider the spiritual/
> religious/moral life? Have you any examples of novels, poetry or
> films which have confronted you with the need to decide on the
> meaning of life, the reality of God, the need for morality?

Dennis Potter: priest of our time

The controversial playwright Dennis Potter provides a further example of the way in which art might provide a model for religious discourse. D. Z. Phillips describes Potter as a 'priest of our time';[46] not, it should be noted, a priest *for* our time, but as someone born at a particular point in human history, when the old religious truths are gone. It is this sense of the loss of the transcendent which characterizes much of Potter's work. Yet this does not mean that one can no longer write about religion or concern oneself with what until recently would have been seen as primarily religious themes. As Potter explains in the introduction to his play *Brimstone and Treacle*: 'The sort of "religious drama" that I want to write will not necessarily mention the word "God" at all. Perhaps, too, it will be based on the feeling that religion is not the bandage, but the wound.'[47]

This sense that religion is not the bandage but the wound needs to be unpacked, as it is an image which dominates much of Potter's thinking on religion. In reflecting on this image, Phillips interprets it in the following way: 'Religion has, nevertheless, created a wound, a wound caused by the longing for some kind of perfection, for something more than the merely human.'[48] This interpretation suggests more about Phillips's own approach to religion than it does Potter's concerns. Indeed, it could be argued that Potter is suggesting that, far from religion offering the believer a taste of the transcendent, it is best understood as giving expression to the nature of human life and experience. Good religion, he seems to suggest, will not attempt to cover up the wounds of life, but will confront and involve all aspects of human existence.

Brimstone and Treacle

> There resides infinitely more good in the demonic man than in the trivial man.[49]

Described by the then Director of Programmes at the BBC as 'brilliantly written and made, but nauseating', *Brimstone and Treacle* is one of Potter's most controversial plays. The Bateses are struggling to care for their comatose daughter Pattie, when they are visited by Martin, a strange, possibly 'demonic' young man. Martin offers them support, yet abuses Pattie. It is during one such rape that Pattie recovers consciousness. Much of the play concerns the relationship between the Bateses, and the character of their strange visitor.

The 'visitation motif' is a popular one in much fiction. A supernatural visitor disrupts the lives of those visited, his presence leading to a needed release of violence, sex or emotion. In *Brimstone and Treacle* it is a devil, not an angel, who constitutes the heavenly visitor. In response to the question, 'why a devil?', Potter provided an interesting answer: 'If it had been an angel visiting a troubled house, you wouldn't have had to think at all about it. It would be like one of those coloured religious postcards – it would have been religiose instead of religious.'[50]

This returns us to the key image suggested at the beginning of this section: religion is not the bandage, it is the wound. Religion should not be a sop to the hardship of life, but a way of thinking critically about the human condition. Potter goes on:

> One writes a Christmas card without looking at the verse or the picture; whereas if you have a Christmas card in front of you that was obscene or shocking or utterly astounding you'd think twice before you signed it, and you'd start to think about Christ, Christmas, images, your nature, your feelings and so on.[51]

It is precisely this shocking image which dominates the play. A fundamental ambiguity is present concerning what is 'good' and what is 'evil'. This is most obviously reflected in the character of Martin: his actions might be 'evil' (i.e. raping Pattie) but the outcome is 'good' (i.e. she is restored to consciousness through this brutal act). Yet this ambiguity is also represented in the character of Bates. A casual fascist, Bates has leanings towards the National Front. In a conversation surrounding this issue, Martin presses Bates about the lengths to which he would go in his desire to see 'England for the English':

MARTIN: Thank God for the National Front.
BATES [*uncomfortable*]:   Yes.
MARTIN: They won't take any namby-pamby nonsense. The blacks don't want to go . . . Only possible answer – put them into camps . . . Camps. Any camps for the time being. Oh, think of it! Think-of-it! Hundreds of people. No, thousands of people. Hundreds of thousands. Millions. Rounded up from their stinking slums and overcrowded ghettos . . . Think of all the hate they'll feel! Think of all the hate we'll feel when they start killing us back. Think of

all the violence! Think of the pain and the de-grad-at-ion and in
the end, in the end, the riots and the shooting and the black corpses
and the swastikas and the –

BATES: No! Stop it!

[*Martin stops dead, and surfaces*]

MARTIN [*subdued*]:   No?

BATES: That – that's going too far.

MARTIN: But – pardon me if I've – I thought you wanted to get rid
of the blacks. I mean, you seemed very keen on –

BATES [*snapping*]:   Not if it means that!

[*Pause*]

MARTIN [*deflated*]:   No. Suppose not, really. But you must admit it's
logical, sir.[52]

Bates's attitude is challenged by Martin's logical outworking of
his ideas, which seems to suggest that whatever 'the good' might
be, it is associated with clear thinking. In exposing the logical conclusion of his attitudes towards ethnic minorities, Bates is forced to
reconsider his moral commitments and attitudes. This says much
about the attitude to religion expressed in the play. As Potter writes
in the introduction to *Brimstone and Treacle*: 'The play tries to
mock sanctimoniousness, which has too become the substitute for,
or the last sickly residue of, religious feelings.'[53] At one point, Martin
'prays' with Mrs Bates in a mocking parody of contemporary religious styles. He starts with the voice of an American evangelist,
then as an Irish priest. Mrs Bates's response to this travesty of a
prayer is to murmur 'lovely'.[54] A sickly sweet view of God and
religion is rejected, replaced by clarity, clear-sightedness and vision.

> What does it mean to be 'religious'? What might it mean to sug-
> gest that religion is the wound, not the bandage?

Conclusion: Seeing the Blossom

We have already considered some of Potter's comments from his
last interview when we discussed the meaning of immortality.

To conclude, it seems appropriate to consider what religion might mean if we take seriously the 'nowness of everything',[55] the sheer transitory 'thisness' of human existence. And this most human of dramatists offers us some interesting thoughts on the subject.

Often castigated for the supposedly 'blasphemous' nature of his work, in his last interview Potter talks of the importance of the spiritual. Yet he is quick to point out that the spiritual should not be juxtaposed with the physical: God is not to be understood in contradiction to the human. He is careful not to frame his understanding of religion in the language of theism. Indeed, he is at pains to reject the traditional view of God:

> I mean, the kind of Christianity, or indeed any other religion, that is a religion because of the fear of death, or hope that there is something beyond death, does not interest me. I thought, what a cruel old bugger is God, if it's terror that is the ruling edifice, if you like, of the structure of religion? And too often for too many people it is. Now that to me isn't religion.[56]

Instead, Potter reiterates his sense that 'religion to me has always been the wound, not the bandage'.[57] Religion is not there to ornament human life, to apply salve to the hurts and pain which invariably afflict us. Philosophers of religion have tended to see religious belief as one hypothesis among many; one way – perhaps the most plausible way – of explaining the existence and character of the world. Religion here becomes something cool and dispassionate, in its essence something divorced from our emotions. But the reverse is true: a phenomenon predominantly of the emotions, religion arises out of the turbulence and anguish of human life, the apparent hollowness of the human condition. It is a sign of our all-too-human longings and frustrations. This need not leave us feeling hopeless in the face of a heartless universe, but may, in fact, enable us to immerse ourselves in the transient nature of human existence, knowing that it is our fate to live 'like a star / That shoots and is gone.'[58] One might feel that this view of human life is antithetical to religious sensibilities, yet other possibilities present themselves. While we may no longer have recourse to a fully systematized and coherent theology, a new religious sensibility may emerge, focused on an intuitive sense of the significance of our brief lives and our human associations: 'I see God in us or with us, if I see at all, as some shreds and particles and rumours, some knowledge that we have, some feeling why we sing and dance and act, why we paint, why we love, why we make art.'[59]

Suggested reading:

Colin Crowder (ed.), *God and Reality*, London: Mowbray, 1997.

Don Cupitt, *Solar Ethics*, London: SCM, 1995.

Ludwig Feuerbach, *The Essence of Christianity*, tr. George Eliot, New York: Harper and Row, 1957.

David Jasper, *The Study of Literature and Religion*, Basingstoke: Macmillan, 1992.

Iris Murdoch, *The Time of the Angels*, Harmondsworth: Penguin, 1968.

Iris Murdoch, *The Good Apprentice*, Harmondsworth: Penguin, 1985.

Iris Murdoch, *The Sovereignty of Good*, London: Ark, 1985.

D. Z. Phillips, *From Fantasy to Faith*, Basingstoke: Macmillan, 1991.

Dennis Potter, *Brimstone and Treacle*, London: Samuel French, 1978.

Friedrich Schleiermacher, *On Religion*, tr. J. Oman, New York: Harper and Row, 1958.

Paul Tillich, *The Shaking of the Foundations*, Harmondsworth: Penguin, 1962.

Richard Todd, *Iris Murdoch*, London: Methuen, 1984.

T. R. Wright, *Theology and Literature*, Oxford: Blackwell, 1988.

Notes

Chapter I Religious Belief and the Philosophy of Religion

1 See chapter 3, section II, 'Natural Histories of Religion'.
2 See Peter B. Clarke and Peter Byrne, *Religion Defined and Explained*, Basingstoke: Macmillan, 1993, pp. 3–27.
3 E. B. Tylor, *Primitive Culture*, vol. I, London: John Murray, 1891, p. 424.
4 For a full consideration of these dimensions of religion, see Ninian Smart, *Dimensions of the Sacred*, London: Collins, 1996.
5 See Emile Durkheim, *The Elementary Forms of the Religious Life*, London: George Allen and Unwin, 1915. Durkheim's definition of religion runs thus: 'A religion is a unified system of beliefs and practices relative to sacred things, that is things set apart and forbidden – beliefs and practices which unite into one single moral community called a Church, all those who adhere to them' (p. 47).
6 J. M. Yinger, *The Scientific Study of Religion*, New York: Macmillan, 1970.
7 Ibid., p. 7.
8 To be considered in chapter 3.
9 This line will be pursued in chapter 6.
10 Brian Davies, *An Introduction to the Philosophy of Religion*, 2nd edition, Oxford: OUP, 1993, p. ix.
11 J. C. A. Gaskin, *The Quest for Eternity*, Harmondsworth: Penguin, 1984, p. 24.

12 See W. L. Rowe and W. J. Wainwright (eds), *Philosophy of Religion: Selected Readings*, Orlando: Harcourt Brace Janovich, 1989, pp. 96–127; and Baruch Brody (ed.), *Readings in the Philosophy of Religion*, New Jersey: Prentice-Hall, 1974, pp. 12–63, for examples of this approach.
13 Robin Le Poidevin, *Arguing for Atheism*, London: Routledge, 1996, pp. xvii–xviii.
14 Peter Vardy, *The Puzzle of God*, London: Collins Flame, 1990.
15 M. Peterson, W. Hasker, B. Reichenbach and D. Basinger, *Reason and Religious Belief*, Oxford: OUP, 1991, p. 5.
16 Brody, *Readings in the Philosophy of Religion*, p. viii.
17 See Richard Swinburne, *The Coherence of Theism*, Oxford: Clarendon Press, 1977; and *The Existence of God*, Oxford: Clarendon Press, 1979.
18 J. L. Mackie, *The Miracle of Theism*, Oxford: OUP, 1982.
19 For feminists working in this area, this question is of particular importance. Has the concept of God been used to valorize masculinist values? See chapter 4 for full discussion of this issue.
20 This difference in approaches will be made plain in chapter 4.
21 See Hesiod, *Theogony*, and Ovid, *Metamorphoses* for examples of the 'human' traits of the gods.
22 See Plato, *The Republic*, chs 24 and 25.
23 See H. Chadwick, *The Early Church*, Harmondsworth: Penguin, 1967, for a succinct account of these controversies.
24 For a discussion of this comment, see Don Cupitt, *The Sea of Faith*, London: BBC, 1984, pp. 52–5.
25 See the discussion in chapter 5 of D. Z. Phillips's approach to the philosophy of religion.

Chapter 2   Natural Theology

1 In using the male pronoun and its derivatives for God, this chapter reflects the masculinized form of God common to philosophy of religion. As we shall see in the section concerned with feminist philosophy of religion, this usage has not gone unchallenged, but to use inclusive language for God at this stage would mask a significant feature of the traditional concept of God.
2 Anselm, *Proslogion*, ch. 2, in *The Prayers and Meditations of St. Anselm*, tr. B. Ward, Harmondsworth: Penguin, 1973, p. 245.
3 See Baruch Brody (ed.), *Readings in the Philosophy of Religion*, New Jersey: Prentice-Hall, 1974, pp. 14–28.

4   See René Descartes, *Meditations on First Philosophy*, Third and Fifth Meditations.
5   René Descartes, *Discourse on Method and the Meditations*, tr. F. E. Sutcliffe, Harmondsworth: Penguin, 1968, p. 145.
6   See Immanuel Kant, *Critique of Pure Reason*, edited by N. Kemp Smith, Basingstoke: Macmillan, 1950, pp. 500–7.
7   Ibid., p. 505.
8   Norman Malcolm, 'Anselm's Ontological Arguments', in Brody (ed.), *Readings in the Philosophy of Religion*, pp. 37–52.
9   Ibid., p. 43.
10 J. N. Findlay, 'Can God's Existence be Disproved?', in Antony Flew and Alasdair MacIntyre, *New Essays in Philosophical Theology*, London: SCM, 1955, pp. 47–56.
11 See Anthony O'Hear, *Experience, Explanation and Faith*, London: RKP, 1984, p. 151.
12 Thomas Aquinas, *Summa Theologiae* 1a, tr. Dominican Fathers of English Province, in Brody (ed.), *Readings in the Philosophy of Religion*, p. 65.
13 David Hume, *Dialogues Concerning Natural Religion* (1779), edited by N. Kemp Smith, Indianapolis: Bobbs-Merrill, 1947, p. 188.
14 Ibid., p. 189.
15 Ibid.
16 Ibid., p. 188.
17 Ibid., pp. 190–1.
18 Bertrand Russell, 'The Existence of God: A Debate with Father F. C. Copleston, S.J.', in *Why I Am Not a Christian*, London: George Allen and Unwin, 1967, p. 139.
19 Ibid., p. 140.
20 See William Paley, 'The Analogy of the Watch', in Brody (ed.), *Readings in the Philosophy of Religion*, pp. 112–26.
21 This is the issue that is developed by David Hume in his critique of the design argument in *Dialogues Concerning Natural Religion*.
22 Richard Swinburne, *The Existence of God*, Oxford: Clarendon Press, 1979, p. 136.
23 Ibid.
24 Hume, *Dialogues Concerning Natural Religion*, p. 176.
25 See James Lovelock, *Gaia: A New Look at Life on Earth*, Oxford: OUP, 1995.
26 See Hume, *Dialogues Concerning Natural Religion*, part V.
27 Ibid.
28 Writers like the Marquis de Sade and Charles Baudelaire have

based their ideas precisely on these aspects of human life.

29 From Alfred, Lord Tennyson's poem 'In Memoriam', LV.
30 Hume, *Dialogues Concerning Natural Religion*, part XI, p. 211.
31 David Hume, *Enquiry Concerning Human Understanding* (1777), edited by L. A. Selby-Bigge, Oxford: OUP, 1975, p. 136.
32 Ibid., p. 137.
33 See D. Z. Phillips, *Religion Without Explanation*, Oxford: Blackwell, 1976, ch. 2.
34 Brian Davies, *An Introduction to the Philosophy of Religion*, Oxford: OUP, 1993, pp. 101–19.
35 Hume, *Dialogues Concerning Natural Religion*, part X, p. 202.
36 Swinburne, *The Existence of God*, p. 244.
37 William James, *The Varieties of Religious Experience*, London: Fontana, 1960, p. 366.
38 Ibid., p. 367.
39 'Lines composed a few miles above Tintern Abbey'. Many more examples of this sporadic kind of experience can be found in James, *The Varieties of Religious Experience*, pp. 369–85.
40 See Swinburne, *The Existence of God*, pp. 249–52.
41 Ibid., p. 250.
42 Ibid., p. 251.
43 Ibid.
44 See C. B. Martin, 'A Religious Way of Knowing', in Brody (ed.), *Readings in the Philosophy of Religion*, p. 517.
45 See for example R. B. Braithwaite, 'An Empiricist's View of the Nature of Religious Belief', in Basil Mitchell (ed.), *The Philosophy of Religion*, Oxford: OUP, 1971, pp. 72–91, where he argues that religious language can be verified by considering the effect that it has upon the life of the individual. By extension, religious experience can be verified by the impact it has upon the individual's way of life.
46 See C. B. Martin, '"Seeing" God', in W. L. Rowe and W. J. Wainwright, *Philosophy of Religion: Selected Readings*, Orlando: Harcourt Brace Jovanovich, 1989, p. 352.
47 Swinburne, *The Existence of God*, p. 254. My emphasis.
48 Antony Flew, *God and Philosophy*, London: Hutchinson, 1966, p. 127.
49 Paul Tillich, *Systematic Theology*, vol. I, London: SCM, 1978, p. 237.
50 R. Swinburne, *The Coherence of Theism*, Oxford: Clarendon Press, 1977, p. 1.
51 These issues will be pursued in the discussion of Feuerbach in

chapter 3, and the discussion of feminism in chapter 4.
52 Aquinas, in Brody (ed.), p. 337.
53 Nelson Pike, 'Omnipotence and God's Ability to Sin', in Brody (ed.), *Readings in the Philosophy of Religion*, pp. 349–63.
54 Ibid., p. 361.
55 George Mavrodes, 'Some Puzzles Concerning Omnipotence', in Brody (ed.), *Readings in the Philosophy of Religion*, pp. 340–2.
56 See, however, Anthony Kenny, *The God of the Philosophers*, Oxford: OUP, 1979, pp. 15–37.
57 Swinburne, *The Coherence of Theism*.
58 Ibid., p. 174.
59 See discussion of process thought in chapter 3.
60 For a contemporary discussion of this issue, see R. E. Creel, *Divine Impassibility*, Cambridge: CUP, 1986.

Chapter 3 Challenges to Theism

1 'Theodicy', the term coined by G. W. Leibniz, from the Greek for 'God' (*theos*) and 'justice' (*diké*).
2 David Hume, *Dialogues Concerning Natural Religion* (1779), edited by N. Kemp Smith, Indianapolis: Bobbs-Merrill, 1947, p. 198.
3 See for example Dorothee Soelle, *Suffering*, London: Darton Longman and Todd, 1975; P. T. Forsyth, *The Justification of God: Lectures for War-Time in a Christian Theodicy*, London: Duckworth, 1916; Dietrich Bonhoeffer, *Letters and Papers from Prison*, London: SCM, 1971; Jürgen Moltmann, *The Crucified God*, London: SCM, 1974.
4 See John Roth, in R. Rubenstein and J. Roth, *Approaches to Auschwitz*, London: SCM, 1987, for an example of this approach.
5 See John Hick, *Evil and the God of Love*, Basingstoke: Macmillan, 1983, p. 6, for a discussion of the roots of this subject.
6 Augustine, *City of God*, book XI, ch. 22.
7 See Genesis 3.
8 For Hick's development of Irenaeus, see his *Evil and the God of Love*, part III.
9 For Swinburne's theodicy, see R. Swinburne, 'The Problem of Evil', in S. C. Brown (ed.), *Reason and Religion*, Cornell: Cornell University Press, 1977, and R. Swinburne, *The Existence of God*, Oxford: Clarendon Press, 1979, ch. 11.
10 Swinburne, in Brown (ed.), p. 90.
11 Hick, *Evil and the God of Love*, p. 308.

12 John Hick, *Death and Eternal Life*, Basingstoke: Macmillan, 1985, p. 294.

13 See Moltmann, *The Crucified God*, pp. 267–9.

14 See Kenneth Surin, *Theology and the Problem of Evil*, Oxford: Blackwell, 1986.

15 See John Hick's account of process in *Evil and the God of Love*, and David Griffin's 'Creation out of chaos and the problem of evil', in S. T. Davis (ed.), *Encountering Evil*, Edinburgh: T. and T. Clark, 1981. For critique, see Peter Hare and Edward Madden, 'Evil and Persuasive Power', in M. Peterson (ed.), *The Problem of Evil: Selected Readings*, Indiana: University of Notre Dame Press, 1992.

16 Griffin, in Davis (ed.), p. 105.

17 Ibid., p. 112.

18 Ibid.

19 A. N. Whitehead, quoted by Lewis Ford in 'Divine Persuasion and the Triumph of Good', in Peterson (ed.), *The Problem of Evil: Selected Readings*, p. 258.

20 See William Hasker, 'On Regretting the Evils of This World', in Peterson (ed.), *The Problem of Evil: Selected Readings*, pp. 153–67; Robert Merrihew Adams, 'Existence, Self-Interest and the Problem of Evil', in A. Loades and L. D. Rue (eds), *Contemporary Classics in the Philosophy of Religion*, Illinois: Open Court, 1991, pp. 217–29.

21 T. Tilley, *The Evils of Theodicy*, Washington DC: Georgetown University Press, 1990, pp. 1–2.

22 See for example, Swinburne, in Brown (ed.), pp. 81–2.

23 See D. Z. Phillips, 'On Not Understanding God', in D. Z. Phillips (ed.), *Wittgenstein and Religion*, Basingstoke: Macmillan, 1993, pp. 153–70.

24 Quoted in ibid., p. 166.

25 Ibid., p. 154.

26 D. Z. Phillips, *Faith after Foundationalism*, London: Routledge, 1988, p. 7.

27 Soelle, *Suffering*, p. 92.

28 Ibid., p. 76.

29 See ibid., pp. 76–8. Also Surin's analysis of her work in Surin, *Theology and the Problem of Evil*, pp. 112–24.

30 J. Wetzel, 'Can Theodicy Be Avoided? The Claim of Unredeemed Evil', in Peterson (ed.), *The Problem of Evil: Selected Readings*, pp. 351–65.

31 See M. Midgley, *Wickedness*, London: Ark, 1984.

32 Ibid., p. 1.

33 Ibid., p. 14.
34 From Fromm's *Anatomy of Human Destructiveness*, quoted in ibid., p. 4.
35 Hannah Arendt, *Eichmann in Jerusalem*, Harmondsworth: Penguin, 1977, pp. 287–8, quoted in Midgley, *Wickedness*, p. 64.
36 Midgley, *Wickedness*, p. 67.
37 See Stewart R. Sutherland, *God, Jesus and Belief*, Oxford: Blackwell, 1984, ch. 1.
38 David Hume, 'The Natural History of Religion', in Richard Wollheim (ed.), *Hume on Religion*, London: Collins, 1963, p. 31.
39 Ibid., p. 38
40 D. Hume, *A Treatise of Human Nature* (1740), edited by L. A. Selby-Bigge, Oxford: Clarendon Press, 1888, p. 115.
41 Hume, in Wollheim (ed.), p. 97.
42 See E. B. Tylor, *Primitive Culture*, London: John Murray, 1891; J. G. Frazer, *The Golden Bough*, London: Macmillan, 1922.
43 Eric Sharpe, *Comparative Religion*, London: Duckworth, 1986, p. 48.
44 Tylor, *Primitive Culture*, vol. I, p. 428.
45 Frazer, *The Golden Bough*, p. 11.
46 Ibid., p. 712.
47 Ibid., p. 264.
48 Ludwig Feuerbach, *The Essence of Christianity*, tr. George Eliot, New York: Harper and Row, 1957, p. 200.
49 Ibid.
50 Ibid., p. xxxix.
51 Ibid., p. 73.
52 Karl Marx, *On Religion*, Moscow: Progress Publishers, 1957, p. 37.
53 Feuerbach, *The Essence of Christianity*, p. 13.
54 Ibid., p. 14.
55 Emile Durkheim, *The Elementary Forms of the Religious Life*, London: Allen and Unwin, 1915, p. 206.
56 Ibid., p. 226.
57 Ibid., p. 83.
58 This is, of course, consonant with the etymology of the word 're-ligion', which, as we mentioned in chapter 1, may have its roots in the Latin *religare* ('to bind').
59 A. R. Radcliffe-Brown, *Structure and Function in Primitive Society*, London: RKP, 1952, p. 157.
60 Sigmund Freud, 'The Future of an Illusion', in *Civilization, Society and Religion*, Harmondsworth: Penguin, 1985, p. 212.

61 Ibid., p. 213.
62 Sigmund Freud, 'Totem and Taboo', in *The Origins of Religion*, Harmondsworth: Penguin, 1985.
63 Ibid., p. 209.
64 Sigmund Freud, 'Obsessive Actions and Religious Practices', in *The Origins of Religion*, p. 33.
65 Freud, 'The Future of an Illusion', p. 226.
66 See E. E. Evans-Pritchard, *Theories of Primitive Religion*, Oxford: OUP, 1965, p. 25.
67 David Hume, *Enquiry Concerning Human Understanding*, edited by L. A. Selby-Bigge, Oxford: Clarendon Press, 1975, p. 165.
68 See Maimonides, *Guide for the Perplexed*, tr. S. Pines, Chicago: University of Chicago Press, 1963, ch. 58.
69 Aquinas, *Summa Theologiae*, 1.1,10.
70 See Dan R. Stiver, *The Philosophy of Religious Language*, Oxford: Blackwell, 1996, pp. 14–36.
71 Ludwig Wittgenstein, *Tractatus Logico-Philosophicus*, London: RKP, 1922, 4.016.
72 Ibid., 4.11.
73 Ibid., 6.53.
74 Ibid., 7.
75 Quoted in Friedrich Waismann, *Wittgenstein and the Vienna Circle*, Oxford: Blackwell, 1979, p. 47.
76 A. J. Ayer, *Language, Truth and Logic*, Harmondsworth: Penguin, 1971, p. 50.
77 Ibid., p. 52.
78 Antony Flew, 'Theology and Falsification', in Basil Mitchell (ed.), *The Philosophy of Religion*, Oxford: OUP, 1971, p. 13.
79 Ibid., p. 14.
80 See ibid., pp. 14–15.
81 R. M. Hare 'Theology and Falsification', in Mitchell (ed.), *The Philosophy of Religion*, pp. 15–16.
82 For a fuller statement of the emotive theory of ethics, see Ayer, *Language, Truth and Logic*, ch. 6; and C. L. Stevenson, *Ethics and Language*, New Haven: Yale University Press, 1944.
83 R. B. Braithwaite, 'An Empiricist's View of the Nature of Religious Belief', in Mitchell (ed.), *The Philosophy of Religion*, p. 89.
84 Basil Mitchell, 'Theology and Falsification', in Mitchell (ed.), *The Philosophy of Religion*, pp. 18–19.
85 See John Hick, 'Theology and Verification', in Mitchell (ed.), *The Philosophy of Religion*, pp. 53–71.

86   See A. Plantinga and N. Wolterstorff, *Faith and Rationality*, Indiana: University of Notre Dame Press, 1983.
87   George Lindbeck, *The Nature of Doctrine*, London: SPCK, 1984.
88   Ibid., p. 33.

Chapter 4   Alternative Approaches to the Philosophy of Religion

1   Meister Eckhart, quoted on the title page of D. Cupitt, *Taking Leave of God*, London: SCM, 1980.
2   'The Sea of Faith' movement within the Anglican Church is clearly indebted to Cupitt's radical reinterpretation of the central tenets of the Christian faith. Anthony Freeman's controversial *God in Us*, London: SCM, 1993, is to a large extent a simplified account of Cupitt's early theology.
3   For consideration of the debate between realists and non-realists (or anti-realists) see Peter Vardy, *The Puzzle of God*, London: Collins Flame, 1990.
4   Cupitt, *Taking Leave of God*, p. 19.
5   Ibid., p. 7.
6   Ibid.
7   Ibid., p. 5. In a later work, *Solar Ethics*, London: SCM 1995, Cupitt offers a modification of this view, suggesting a departure from this emphasis on the internal. For consideration of this aspect of his thought, see chapter 6.
8   Cupitt, *Taking Leave of God*, p. 19.
9   Jeremiah 31:33.
10   See Matthew 24:4–46; Mark 13.
11   See Luke 17:21.
12   Cupitt, *Taking Leave of God*, p. 14.
13   See D. Z. Phillips, 'Philosophy, Theology and the Reality of God', in D. Z. Phillips, *Wittgenstein and Religion*, Basingstoke: Macmillan, 1993, pp. 1ff.
14   Cupitt, *Taking Leave of God*, p. 103.
15   Ibid.
16   See Keith Ward, *Holding Fast to God*, London: SPCK, 1982.
17   See John Hick, *An Interpretation of Religion*, Basingstoke: Macmillan, 1989, p. 207.
18   See Freeman, *God in Us*, for a 'lay' reading of Cupitt's theology.
19   See chapter 6 for further development of this point.
20   See Vardy, *The Puzzle of God*, for this interpretation of Sutherland's work.

21 Stewart Sutherland, *God, Jesus and Belief*, Oxford: Blackwell, 1984, p. 16.

22 An example: having surveyed the dubious moral status of aspects of Richard Swinburne's theodicy, Sutherland's response is an exasperated 'Well!' (*God, Jesus and Belief*, p. 25).

23 Ibid.

24 Ibid., p. 77.

25 Ibid., p. 78.

26 See ibid., pp. 83ff.

27 Ibid., p. 85.

28 Ibid., p. 88.

29 Ibid.

30 Ibid., p. 89.

31 Ibid.

32 See chapter 3.

33 Ludwig Wittgenstein, *Notebooks 1914–1916*, Oxford: Blackwell, 1961, p. 74.

34 Paul Engelmann, *Letters from Ludwig Wittgenstein with a Memoir*, Oxford: Blackwell, 1967, p. 97 (italics in original).

35 Ludwig Wittgenstein, 'Lecture on Ethics', *Philosophical Review*, vol. 74, no. 1, 1965, p. 11.

36 Ludwig Wittgenstein, *Tractatus Logico-Philosophicus*, London: RKP, 1922.

37 Wittgenstein, 'Lecture on Ethics', p. 40.

38 Ibid., pp. 11–12.

39 Wittgenstein, *Tractatus*, 6.522.

40 Engelmann, *Letters from Ludwig Wittgenstein*, p. 7.

41 Ludwig Wittgenstein, *Philosophical Investigations*, Oxford: Blackwell, 1953, §65.

42 Wittgenstein, *Philosophical Investigations*, §43.

43 See chapter 3.

44 Ludwig Wittgenstein, *Remarks on Frazer's Golden Bough*, Doncaster: Brynmill Press, 1979, p. 1.

45 Ibid., p. 4.

46 Ibid.

47 Ludwig Wittgenstein, 'Remarks on Frazer's Golden Bough', in C. G. Luckhardt, *Wittgenstein: Sources and Perspectives*, Hassocks: Harvester, 1979, p. 72.

48 Ludwig Wittgenstein, *Lectures and Conversations*, Oxford: Blackwell, 1966, p. 56.

49 See chapter 3, pp. 87–8.

50 Ludwig Wittgenstein, *Lectures and Conversations*, p. 71.

51 Ludwig Wittgenstein, *Culture and Value*, Oxford: Blackwell, 1980, p. 64.
52 See Kai Nielsen, 'Wittgensteinian Fideism', *Philosophy*, July 1967, pp. 207ff.
53 See chapter 5.
54 For example, Grace Jantzen, John Rylands Professorial Research Fellow at the University of Manchester, uses the work of Luce Irigaray in her inaugural lecture 'Reflections in the Looking Glass: Religion, Culture and Gender in the Academy' (Wednesday, 30 October 1996).
55 See Mary Daly, *Beyond God the Father*, London: Women's Press, 1986.
56 Mary Daly, 'The Qualitative Leap Beyond Patriarchal Religion' (1975), in Marilyn Pearsall (ed.), *Women and Values*, Belmount: Wadsworth, 1993, p. 227.
57 Ibid.
58 See Sharon Welch, *A Feminist Ethic of Risk*, Minneapolis: Fortress Press, 1989.
59 Ibid., p. 111.
60 Ibid.
61 Ibid., p. 117.
62 James Nelson, 'Embracing Masculinity', in James B. Nelson and Sandra P. Longfellow (eds), *Sexuality and the Sacred*, Westminster: Mowbray, 1994, pp. 195–215.
63 Ibid., p. 197.
64 Ibid., p. 205.
65 Ibid.
66 Ibid.
67 Ibid., p. 212.
68 Ibid.
69 Luce Irigaray, quoted by Grace Jantzen in ' "New Morning of the World?" Luce Irigaray's Philosophy of Religion', given at King's College, London, February 1994.
70 Rosemary Radford Ruether, *Sexism and God-Talk*, London: SCM, 1983, p. 19.
71 See ibid., ch. 1.
72 Welch, *A Feminist Ethic of Risk*, p. 178.
73 See chapter 5 for a full discussion of the possible effect of feminist thinking upon the notion of immortality.
74 Luce Irigaray, *This Sex which is not One*, Cornell: Cornell University Press, 1985, p. 165.
75 See Daly, *Beyond God the Father*, pp. 33ff.

76 See Sallie McFague, *Metaphorical Theology*, London: SCM, 1983.
77 Starhawk, *Dreaming the Dark*, London: Unwin Hyman, 1990, p. 11.
78 Jane Caputi, *Gossips, Gorgons and Crones*, Santa Fe: Bear and Co, 1993, p. 237.
79 Christine Downing, *The Goddess*, New York: Crossroad, 1984.
80 Carol Christ and Judith Plaskow (eds), *Womanspirit Rising*, London: Harper and Row, 1979, p. 281.
81 Ibid.
82 Melissa Raphael, *Thealogy and Embodiment*, Sheffield: Sheffield Academic Press, 1996.
83 Raphael, *Thealogy and Embodiment*, p. 285.
84 Naomi Goldenberg, 'The Return of the Goddess', in Ann Loades and Loyal D. Rue (eds), *Contemporary Classics in the Philosophy of Religion*, Illinois: Open Court, 1991, p. 428.
85 Quoted by Jane Caputi in C. Larrington (ed.), *The Feminist Companion to Mythology*, London: Pandora, 1992, p. 430.

Chapter 5   Divine Action and the Beyond

1 Richard Swinburne, *The Concept of Miracle*, Basingstoke: Macmillan, 1970, p. 1.
2 David Hume, *Enquiry Concerning Human Understanding*, Oxford: Clarendon Press, 1975, p. 115.
3 Ibid., p. 110.
4 Ibid., p. 115.
5 Ibid., pp. 115–16.
6 Ibid., pp. 119–20.
7 Ibid., pp. 117–18.
8 See H. S. Reimarus, *Fragments*, London: SCM, 1971.
9 See J. L. Mackie, *The Miracle of Theism*, Oxford: Clarendon Press, 1982, ch. 1; and Patrick Nowell-Smith, 'Miracles', in Brody (ed.), *Readings in the Philosophy of Religion*, pp. 443–50 for examples of philosophers who follow Hume on this issue.
10 R. F. Holland, 'The Miraculous', in Brody (ed.), *Readings in the Philosophy of Religion*, p. 455.
11 Hume, *Enquiry*, p. 110.
12 Ibid., p. 128.
13 See Swinburne, *The Concept of Miracle*, p. 19.
14 B. R. Tilghman, *An Introduction to the Philosophy of Religion*, Oxford: Blackwell, 1994, p. 152.

15 Paul Tillich, *Systematic Theology*, vol. 1, London: SCM, 1978, p. 117.
16 Holland, in Brody (ed.), p. 451.
17 Ibid.
18 Ibid., p. 452.
19 D. H. Lawrence, 'Hymns in a man's life', in *Selected Literary Criticism*, London: Heinemann, 1956, p. 8.
20 William James, *The Varieties of Religious Experience*, London: Fontana, 1960, p. 444.
21 Peter Winch, *Trying to Make Sense*, Oxford: Blackwell, 1987, p. 119.
22 D. Z. Phillips, *The Concept of Prayer*, London: RKP, 1965, p. 121.
23 See John Bowker, *Meanings of Death*, London: Canto, 1993, for examples of attitudes towards death in the world's religions.
24 For discussion of this point, see D. Z. Phillips, *Death and Immortality*, Basingstoke: Macmillan, 1970, ch. 1.
25 See John Hick, *Death and Eternal Life*, Basingstoke: Macmillan, 1985, part V.
26 See John Hick, 'Theology and Verification', in Basil Mitchell (ed.), *The Philosophy of Religion*, Oxford: OUP, 1971, pp. 53–71.
27 See Hick, *Death and Eternal Life*, p. 276.
28 See Gilbert Ryle, *The Concept of Mind*, Harmondsworth: Penguin, 1963, p. 310.
29 See Antony Flew, *An Introduction to Western Philosophy*, London: Thames and Hudson, 1989.
30 See, for example, Plato's discussion of this in *Phaedo*.
31 H. H. Price, 'Two Conceptions of the Next World', *Essays in the Philosophy of Religion*, Oxford: OUP, 1972, pp. 98–117.
32 Ibid., p. 109.
33 Hick, *Death and Eternal Life*, p. 294.
34 See Phillips, *Death and Immortality*.
35 Ibid., p. 49.
36 Ibid., p. 60.
37 See Stewart Sutherland, 'What Happens After Death?', *Scottish Journal of Theology*, vol. 22, 1969, pp. 404–18.
38 Ibid., p. 407.
39 Ibid., p. 411, citing Kierkegaard's *Concluding Unscientific Postscript*.
40 Ibid., p. 412.
41 We might want to consider the way in which ex-Prime Ministers find it hard to let go of the reins of power, and, when they have,

often reappear to plague their successor with good advice!

42　A good example of this appears to have been Stalin, whose life was dominated by the fear of death and betrayal (see Erich Fromm, *The Anatomy of Human Destructiveness*, London: Jonathan Cape, 1974).

43　See Hick, *Death and Eternal Life* for the background to this idea.

44　See Simone Weil, *Waiting on God*, London: Fontana, 1959, pp. 114–15.

45　See *Daily Mail*, 3 August 1996, Weekend Supplement, pp. 10–11.

46　Ibid., p. 11.

47　P. D. James, *The Children of Men*, Harmondsworth: Penguin, 1992.

48　Leo Tolstoy, *The Death of Ivan Ilyich*, London: Bantam Books, 1981, p. 133.

49　See John Hick, *An Interpretation of Religion*, Basingstoke: Macmillan, 1989, p. 206.

50　For a Buddhist account of death, see Peter Harvey, 'A Buddhist Perspective on Death', in Julia Neuberger and John A. White (eds), *A Necessary End*, Basingstoke: Macmillan, 1991, pp. 105–21. In particular: 'Regarding whether "I" will continue after death, I go along with the Buddhist perspective concerning all phenomena as being devoid of a permanent substantial self' (p. 120).

51　See Ynestra King, 'The Ecology of Feminism and the Feminism of Ecology', in M. H. MacKinnon and M. McIntyre (eds), *Readings in Ecology and Feminist Theology*, London: Sheed and Ward, 1995, pp. 150–60.

52　Sherry Ortner, 'Is Female to Male as Nature is to Culture?', in MacKinnon and McIntyre, *Readings in Ecology and Feminist Theology*, pp. 36–55.

53　Otto Weininger, *Sex and Character*, London: Heineman, 1910.

54　See Aristotle, *On the Generation of Animals*.

55　See Kant, *On the Beautiful and Sublime*, Berkeley and Los Angeles: University of California Press, 1960.

56　Weininger, *Sex and Character*, p. 284.

57　Ibid.

58　'Growing Old Disgracefully', BBC2, 7 August 1996.

59　Rosemary Radford Ruether, *Gaia and God*, London: SCM, 1992, p. 252.

60　Ibid.

61　Don Cupitt, *Solar Ethics*, London: SCM, 1995, p. 2.

62　Ibid., p. 4.

63　Dennis Potter, *Seeing the Blossom*, London: Faber and Faber, 1994, p. 5.

Chapter 6 The Future of Religion

1 See Dietrich Bonhoeffer, *Letters and Papers from Prison*, trs. R. Fuller, F. Clarke and J. Bowden, London: SCM, 1971, p. 326.
2 For introduction to contemporary pagan movements, see Graham Harvey and Charlotte Hardman (eds), *Paganism Today*, London: Thorsons, 1996.
3 See Ronald Hutton, 'The Roots of Modern Paganism', in Harvey and Hardman (eds), *Paganism Today*, pp. 3–15.
4 See Peter Berger, *The Sacred Canopy*, Garden City, New York: Doubleday, 1967; Donald Wiebe, *The Irony of Theology and the Nature of Religious Thought*, Montreal: McGill-Queen's Press, 1991.
5 J. G. Frazer, *The Golden Bough*, London: Macmillan, 1922, p. 712.
6 Gordon Graham, 'Religion, Secularization and Modernity', *Philosophy*, vol. 67, no. 260.
7 See G. W. F. Hegel, *Lectures on the Philosophy of History*, New York: Dover, 1956.
8 See Richard Swinburne, *The Existence of God*, Oxford: Clarendon Press, 1979, ch. 14.
9 Tanya Luhrmann, *Persuasions of the Witch's Craft*, Oxford: Blackwell, 1989.
10 See p. 30.
11 This is perhaps the danger posed by fundamentalism. See Don Cupitt, 'Free Christianity', in Colin Crowder (ed.), *God and Reality*, London: Mowbray, 1997, p. 19, for discussion of this point.
12 See pp. 73–5.
13 Ludwig Feuerbach, *The Essence of Christianity*, tr. G. Eliot, New York: Harper and Row, 1957, p. 56.
14 Ibid., pp. 55, 145.
15 Voltaire, *Candide*, tr. J. Butt, Harmondsworth: Penguin, 1947, p. 144.
16 Feuerbach, *The Essence of Christianity*, p. 275.
17 See ibid., p. 277.
18 See Carol Christ, *The Laughter of Aphrodite*, San Francisco: Harper and Row, 1987; Beverley Clack, 'The Many Named Queen of All', in Deborah Sawyer and Diane Collier (eds), *Gender Issues and Contemporary Religion*, Sheffield: Sheffield Academic Press (forthcoming, 1998); Christine Downing, *The Goddess*, New York: Crossroad, 1984; Asphodel Long, *In a Chariot Drawn by Lions*, London: Women's Press, 1992.

19   Cupitt, 'Free Christianity', p. 15.
20   See Friedrich Nietzsche, *The Gay Science* (1887), tr. Walter Kaufmann, New York: Random House, 1974, §125.
21   Don Cupitt, *Solar Ethics*, London: SCM, 1995, p. 2.
22   Ibid., p. 4.
23   Similar ideas are expounded by Martin Heidegger in his *Being and Time*, Oxford: Blackwell, 1962, where he argues that human being is defined as 'being-towards-death'.
24   See chapter 4 for discussion of this stage in his thinking.
25   Cupitt, *Solar Ethics*, p. 9.
26   Ibid.
27   Hence Cupitt's damning comment on realism: 'The more firmly such a [realist] God is believed in ('fundamentalism' being the extreme case) the more demonic and disastrously *ir*religious religion becomes; whereas in true religion people feel divine world-forming, value conferring life welling up in themselves and flowing out through their own eyes and their fingertips' (Cupitt, *Solar Ethics*, p. 50).
28   Friedrich Schleiermacher, *On Religion* (1799), tr. J. Oman, New York: Harper and Row, 1958
29   Ibid., p. 87.
30   Paul Tillich, *The Shaking of the Foundations*, Harmondsworth: Penguin, 1962, pp. 63–4.
31   Of course, we might want to reverse this point: to what extent can we embrace secularism in an age that has witnessed genocide not only under the Nazis, but in the Soviet Union, Cambodia, Bosnia and Rwanda?
32   See Iris Murdoch, *The Sovereignty of Good*, London: Ark, 1985; *Acastos*, London: Chatto and Windus, 1986; *Metaphysics as a Guide to Morals*, London: Chatto and Windus, 1992.
33   See Richard Todd, *Iris Murdoch*, London: Methuen, 1984, p. 23.
34   Iris Murdoch, *The Time of the Angels*, Harmondsworth: Penguin, 1968, p. 31.
35   Ibid., p. 174.
36   Ibid., p. 195.
37   Ibid., p. 19.
38   Ibid., p. 94.
39   Todd, *Iris Murdoch*, p. 59.
40   Murdoch, *The Time of the Angels*, p. 35.
41   Ibid., p. 97.
42   See Iris Murdoch, *The Good Apprentice*, Harmondsworth: Penguin, 1985, p. 16.
43   Ibid., p. 31.

44 Ibid., p. 52.
45 Ibid., pp. 77, 91.
46 D. Z. Phillips, *From Fantasy to Faith*, Basingstoke: Macmillan, 1991, p. 30.
47 Quoted in ibid., p. 45.
48 Ibid.
49 Søren Kierkegaard, quoted in the introduction to *Brimstone and Treacle*, cited in Graham Fuller (ed.), *Potter on Potter*, London: Faber and Faber, 1993, p. 41.
50 Quoted in Fuller (ed.), *Potter on Potter*, p. 41.
51 Quoted in ibid., pp. 41–2.
52 Dennis Potter, *Brimstone and Treacle*, London: Samuel French, 1978, pp. 44–5.
53 Quoted in Phillips, *From Fantasy to Faith*, p. 33.
54 Potter, *Brimstone and Treacle*, p. 32.
55 Dennis Potter, *Seeing the Blossom*, London: Faber and Faber, 1994, p. 5.
56 Ibid.
57 Ibid.
58 Edward Thomas, 'Roads', in *The Work of Edward Thomas*, Ware: Wordsworth, 1994, p. 163.
59 Potter, *Seeing the Blossom*, p. 6.

Index